# Preparation for Life?

## The Paradox of Education in the Late Twentieth Century

WITHDRAWN

# Preparation for Life?

## The Paradox of Education in the Late Twentieth Century

*Edited by*
**Joan N. Burstyn**
Dean, School of Education
Syracuse University

 The Falmer Press

(A member of the Taylor & Francis Group)
Philadelphia and London

**UK**        The Falmer Press, Falmer House, Barcombe, Lewes, East Sussex, BN8 5DL

**USA**     The Falmer Press, Taylor & Francis Inc., 242 Cherry Street, Philadelphia, PA 19106-1906

---

First published 1986

**Library of Congress Cataloging in Publication Data**

Preparation for life?

    Includes bibliographical references and index.
    1. Vocational education—United States—History—20th century.  2. Vocational education—Great Britain—History—20th century.  3. Education, Humanistic—United States—History—20th century.  4. Education, Humanistic—Great Britain—History—20th century.
    5.   Professional education—United States—History—20th century.  6. Professional education—Great Britain—History—20th century.  I. Burstyn, Joan N.
    LC1045.P655   1986   370.11'3'0973   86-4561
    ISBN 1-85000-102-2
    ISBN 1-85000-103-0 (pbk.)

Typeset in 10/12 Bembo by
Imago Publishing Ltd, Thame, Oxon

*Printed in Great Britain by Taylor & Francis (Printers) Ltd, Basingstoke*

# Contents

# Contents

# Introduction

*Joan N. Burstyn*

The authors of this book come from a variety of backgrounds. Such diverse perceptions as theirs are rarely juxtaposed in one volume. What creates unity is that they have all addressed a paradox: educators who are bound by definitions and structures created in response to a technological revolution begun two hundred years ago, have now to reconceptualize their work to meet the intellectual, moral, and social implications of a new technology. Some of the book's authors are from the United States, and some from England. Some are administrators and managers, others teachers and researchers. Some work in universities, colleges or schools, others work in industry. Some are concerned with the education of adults, others with the education of adolescents and youth. All have worn several hats during their career, moving with ease from action to contemplation and back again to action. They been gathered together here to provide a broad spectrum of thought about liberal arts, professional, and vocational education.

Examining education in England during the sixteenth century, Kenneth Charlton describes the changes taking place in society at that time. What we refer to as liberal education was, in the sixteenth century, vocational education for those members of society who expected to govern the country. Others, wanting to train as navigators and land surveyors, who previously would have relied on experience as the most significant part of their training, with the advent of new technology began to need theoretical knowledge 'which traditionally would have been labelled "liberal".' Hence, the notion prevalent today that liberal education is that which teaches one to *know about something*, rather than *how to do something*, was not one that would have been understood by people in sixteenth century England.

Gordon Law examines the varied pattern of vocational schooling in nineteenth century America. He describes the claims of the academies to provide both a liberal and a vocational education. Many, he suggests, provided merely a smattering of vocational knowledge, although some no doubt employed experts and provided sequenced courses. For decades their clientele was satisfied with such schools. But after the Civil War people turned to public high schools and private schools specializing in training for one or two occupations only. The academies that survived changed into college preparatory schools. Law suggests there is a lesson in this decline for the comprehensive public high schools of our own day (and perhaps for the comprehensive university as well): the danger that institutions offering all things to all people will fail to please anyone. Law believes that significant changes in the institutions we have today can be made only when we face up to the conflicts that exist between management and labor, and when we develop a stable national policy on the relation of work to schooling.

Several authors conclude that the distinction we make between liberal arts and professional and vocational education is no longer valuable. David Riesman, comparing the professional education offered undergraduates at Carnegie-Mellon University with the liberal arts education offered undergraduates at Harvard University, suggests that the real distinction between the two groups lies in the length of trajectory each has accepted for their professional development. Harvard undergraduates, he suggests, tend to pursue their pre-professional liberal education with all the competitiveness of students in full-fledged professional programs. Riesman sees no inherent distinction between a liberating education in the sciences and in the vocations. Rather than content, what makes an education liberating, or liberal, he contends, is its depth of inquiry, the opportunity it provides for mentorship, and its 'usefulness in maintaining the peculiarly American tradition of resiliency.'

From a different perspective, Henry Winkler addresses some of the same issues. Reviewing the recent history of urban universities in the United States, Winkler concludes that the city draws all faculty, whether from the liberal arts or professional education, into interacting with it, to observe and analyze or to intervene in its activities. He quotes John Dewey to claim that education and society are integrated. Winkler draws a fine distinction between the right of individual faculty members to become advocates for community programs, and the need for them always to distinguish between their own voice and that of the University where they work. He makes a plea for more *irrelevance* in education, suggesting that a broad perspective on issues may be gained by studying subjects tangential to one's immediate concerns. He remarks that chief executive officers say they want well rounded people in industry, although recruiters who visit campuses on behalf of such corporations search for narrowly specialized, not liberal arts educated graduates. That contradiction, which aggravates college and university teachers, may be explained, one might add, by the fact that chief executive officers are referring to those who one day will replace themselves, a small group indeed, while the recruiters are seeking candidates for large numbers of entry level positions needing specific skills, and have no concern for other qualities that may be useful in higher level jobs.

Harold Silver, discussing recent changes in English higher education, claims that discussion about the content of education has been subordinated to discussion of access and structure. In examining what the content of higher education should be, he claims that employers in England stress the importance of personality characteristics rather than technical skills in new employees. As in the United States, top executives call for broad perspectives and analytical skills. As well as attending to the desires of employers, Silver contends that colleges and universities need to respond to the aspirations of students and their parents. In England, studies have shown parents' highest priorities are to have universities encourage their children to work hard, provide them with career guidance, and help them to develop skills in dealing with other people. Parents are not satisfied that these priorities are being met. Students, even in the liberal arts, have strong career objectives, which are often ignored by their university teachers. Silver concludes that universities will inevitably be drawn into debates over their relation to the labor market. Students bring with them into the university a set of employment aspirations that cannot be ignored. He pleads for universities to make students central to their concerns. 'You cannot talk about the purposes of universities in modern society, in my view, without asking what students want of them, and without discussing the implications for the institutions.' Lastly, Silver addresses the divisions that exist in England because of the binary system of education, raising issues relating to government influence in higher education that have significance for higher education in the United States as well.

In 'For Whose Benefit? The Objectives of English Studies Today' Mary Waldron discusses the pressures she has observed in England on teachers of English from students, parents, employers, and those she calls 'the experts'. Readers will find in her chapter many points that apply directly to the teaching of English in the United States today, where there are similar complaints from employers that new employees cannot communicate effectively, and from college teachers that freshmen at college are underprepared. Waldron cites complaints from British employers as far back as the 1920s; she could as well have quoted from an editorial in the *New York Times* of 25 November 1915 on the shortcomings of the common schools.[1]

Although there is a difference in how the division between primary and secondary education occurs in the two countries, a change in curriculum, similar to that in England, takes place in the United States: until about 11 years of age English is *language arts* and covers a variety of activities. Not until middle school (grades 5–6–7–8) or junior high school (grades 7–8–9) is English identified as a separate topic. There is similar confusion about the content of an English class. 'Some emphasize grammar, some emphasize literature, and, we hope, a growing number emphasize writing.'[2]

Parental concern for teaching to 'satisfy the examiners' is expressed in the United States as parents' concern for teaching to do well on the SATs and achievement tests. As in England, every critic of English education has a different complaint about what is wrong, and educational theory on the subject is in constant flux. For more than a decade American educators have been following closely the debate in England over the teaching of English. Part of the Bullock report, referred to in Waldron's chapter, was reprinted in the *English Journal*, a publication of the United States' National Council of Teachers of English; as a result the Bullock report has had a direct effect on American educators.

Waldron claims that in England by the late fifties and early sixties: 'English teaching had reached a cloud-cuckoo-land form from which practicalities were all but excluded.' In the United States, this form seems to have been reached in the late sixties and early seventies, at which time formal grammar almost disappeared from the curriculum as it did in England. During the 1960s, in the United States as well as in England, dialect became a social and educational issue, with reformers strenuously defending the student's right to his or her own language. Now, many American schools are embracing 'Language Across the Curriculum,' an idea that originated among educators in England, as Waldron describes. Her caveats and suggestions are, therefore, ones that apply to educators in both England and the United States.

Waldron's chapter suggests the close link between students' career expectations and their facility with language. In the following chapter, Sheila Pfafflin explores the links between science, technology, and the liberal arts. She claims that though mathematics and science were traditionally considered among the liberal arts, most people no longer fit them in that category. The sciences and the humanities no longer share a similar vocabulary or similar interests. Both have become more specialized. While both areas share the same purpose, to acquire knowledge, science has become big business in the twentieth century. Thus most people who study science intend to make a career in the area.

Pfafflin, a scientist working in industry, believes that the division between liberal arts and the sciences serves no-one well: an educated person needs both. On the one hand, liberal arts graduates who are scientifically and technically illiterate may have no opportunity in the future to serve society, however much they may wish to do so. She sees this as a danger that will particularly affect women and minorities who traditionally have been underrepresented in the sciences. The specter of liberal arts graduates employed, if at all, in low level jobs, is made more likely by the hierarchical structure of the sciences and mathematics which makes it difficult for liberal arts students to acquire scientific literacy. On the other hand, the current trend towards early specialization in the sciences, with few opportunities to take courses outside the narrow constellation required for one's major, makes it equally difficult for science majors to acquire a broad education in the humanities.

A problem in teaching science to non-scientists is that scientific facts become outdated rapidly. Should non-scientists be taught the process of scientific discovery instead? Should they be taught how to make informed judgments on scientific issues? According to Pfafflin, these questions have not been addressed by educators. She hopes that current research in the cognitive sciences may lead to a reassessment of the science curriculum so that much now taught by colleges and universities could be taught to younger students in high schools. She is concerned, however, that current changes in education may exacerbate a major problem she has addressed: that women and minorities will be shut out once again from the scientific and technological enterprise just as they were about to enter it in larger numbers.

The use of the professions as a model for the liberal arts is discussed by H. Bradley Sagen. Like Silver, he suggests that liberal arts programs have neglected the career aspirations of their students. By doing so they have lost potential students, especially those at the margin who have to ensure that they leave college with marketable skills. Sagen suggests that liberal arts programs take the professions as a model. Autonomy is granted by society to the professions in return for their members' service to society at large. That, at least, is the ideal on which professional autonomy is based. Unlike graduates from professional schools, liberal arts graduates do not have any sense of obligation to serve society; according to Sagen, they are concerned primarily with self-actualization. Professional schools develop in their students an attitude of professionalism. Students acquire this easily because they are taught by practitioners in the field. However, only those liberal arts students who will continue on to graduate work in their majors have such role models; others who wish to use their liberal arts backgrounds in practical fields find no role models in the university. Hence, argues Sagen, internship opportunities are essential for liberal arts students. Sagen argues that liberal arts programs need to establish a set of expectations regarding the use of liberal arts education, they need to identify the skills that graduates of their programs will have by the time they graduate, and, like the professional schools, these programs need to make, as one measure of their success, the placement of graduates in jobs.

The ways that liberal arts programs need to respond to current pressures are described differently by Alfred Kolb. In 'Community Colleges and the Liberal Arts: Tried Concepts, New Contexts,' Kolb argues that liberal arts faculty in community colleges are subject to different pressures from similar faculty at four year colleges and universities. He urges the development of faculty teams, linking those in liberal arts and vocational areas, to teach broad educational issues. He claims that community college students (and, one might add, many four year college students as well,) would be better served by programs that expect less breadth and more depth of reading. He supports the accreditation of non-traditional learning experiences on a much broader scale than currently.

A similar theme is developed by industry consultant Harold Goldstein, who suggests the extension of work-study programs from adolescence through adulthood. In order for this to occur, business leaders will have to be persuaded it is in their interest to make time for workers to undertake formal education. Having worked for many years developing educational programs in industry, Goldstein claims that two issues are crucial for education: timing and responsibility for one's own learning. Goldstein thinks that the separation of liberal arts and vocational education has arisen because people have tried to squeeze all education into a brief timespan of their lives. Like Pfafflin, he believes an educated person needs both kinds of learning, and he advocates the continuation of learning into adulthood by combining work and study from one's early teens.

Goldstein's chapter concludes with a call for further research into these ideas. Arthur Chickering provides samples of such research. Can liberal education and preparation for work be separated? Chickering says they cannot. He begins by demonstrating that the skills needed by an educated person today are the very ones Cardinal Newman described in the nineteenth century as being provided by a liberal education. Chickering then outlines some current research on human learning and development. He claims that development may be fostered through a variety of content areas. He links one's stage of development to one's comfort with a particular teaching-learning style. However, as Chickering makes clear, age and stage of development are not highly correlated. Hence, Chickering's analysis leads him to support the extension of individualized instruction. A logical extension of his analysis is the need for teachers at any level to be conversant with the latest research in human learning and development and with the practical skills most effective for teaching people at each stage of development.

In the concluding chapter, Joan Burstyn discusses the issues raised in this book in light of the changes that have taken place in the twentieth century with regard to people's definition of adulthood, and their experiences of reality. She claims that educators have been slow to comprehend the significance of these changes both for the content of education, and the structure of educational institutions. The future presents a challenge for us to reconstruct both.

### Notes

1  See *New York Times*, 25 November 1915, p. 12, Cols. 3 and 4.
2  Dr. Barbara King, Rutgers University, personal communication to the author, 17 April 1984. I am indebted to Dr. King for her comments on the teaching of English in American schools and colleges, and on the comparisons to be made with activities in England as described in this book by Mary Waldron.

# The Liberal–Vocational Debate in Early Modern England

*Kenneth Charlton*

Current discussions about the liberal-vocational curriculum usually arise out of some felt dissatisfaction with a curriculum that is too narrow (or too broad), too out-of-date (or too new-fangled), too irrelevant to present-day needs (or too short-sighted in its focus). It matters little to remind the various protagonists of A.N. Whitehead's insistence that 'the antithesis between technical and liberal education is fallacious', or of John Dewey's assertion that 'only superstition makes us believe that the two are necessarily hostile'.[1] The plain fact is that both the fallacy and the superstition (if such they be) persist not only in the minds of people, but in the arguments they marshall to influence the decision-making process in education. Nor will it help to follow the example of James B. Conant and his Harvard Committee, who eschewed the term 'liberal and entitled their Report *General Education in a Free Society*. Wishing to avoid using what they considered a value-laden usage ('which identified liberal education with the aristocratic ideal'[2]) the Committee replaced one adjective by another which indicated that education (by which was meant a 'good' education) should be 'general' — and not . . . a whole range of other value-laden characteristics.

The linguistic difficulties of engaging in curricular discussion should not, however, be allowed to camouflage the discussion's importance. In discussing liberal and vocational education we consider a range of matters of educational import: what constitutes a 'balanced' curriculum and who decides what is 'balanced'? Should not schools leave 'vocational' education to the employers, and if so, how is 'school' education to be characterized? In an age of rapid technological change how far and in what ways should 'education' change? In such an age what should be the place of 'the humanities' and 'the Arts'? And so on . . . .

Such questions, however, are not unique to our own time, and the purpose of this chapter is to provide a case-study of educational thought and practice in sixteenth and seventeenth century England. Crucial to the working out and implementation of the liberal–vocational distinction in this period were two traditions, inherited from the Ancient World and from medieval

Christendom and each modified by the Protestant reformers. Responses to changing circumstances produced varying degrees of emphasis on this or that aspect of the traditions. Not surprisingly different groups selected from the traditions those aspects which best suited their own purposes.

The classical tradition had as its original context the Greek city-state, with its two main social categories, citizens and non-citizens (slaves and resident aliens, mostly foreign merchants). Such a context provided the framework of Aristotle's *Politics* in which manual work was perceived as an activity inappropriate for a citizen, the performance of whose civic duties required both education and leisure. Such a citizen 'must not lead the life of mechanics and tradesmen, for such a life is ignoble and inimical to virtue and the performance of civic duties.' As Aristotle acknowledged when it came to implanting such a view in education, 'mankind are by no means agreed about the things to be taught.' But for the education of his future citizens, charged as they would be with the decision-making of the city-state, Aristotle entertained no doubts:

> ... children should be taught useful things which are really necessary, but not all things; for occupations are divided into liberal and illiberal, and to young children should be imparted only such kinds of knowledge as will be useful to them without vulgarizing them ... wherefore we call those arts vulgar which tend to deform the body, and likewise all paid employments, for they absorb and degrade the mind ... if they habitually practice them there will cease to be a distinction between master and slave.[3]

In practice, and more especially in the Roman world, the widening of citizenship to include freed slaves, foreigners, and merchants, gradually eroded this stance, giving rise to a more complicated prescription, as devised for example in Cicero's *De Officiis*.[4]

The theologians of the medieval church inherited this classical tradition, but had to reconcile it with the Christian doctrine that *all* its members were children of God. At the same time the church faced the need to maintain a diverse membership, living in a much more complex economic and political context, within the confines of a Church Universal. In a society whose complexity emphasized economic inter-dependence, Christian doctrine insisted that all useful activities were ordained by God, and were therefore equally acceptable to Him.[5] Whilst not confirming the (theoretical) degradation of work of classical times the medieval Christian church nevertheless maintained a hierarchy of work by insisting on the superiority of spiritual work, and placing above the particular kind of work of the regular clergy, the spiritual work of those taking the monastic vows of poverty, chastity and obedience and abiding by the rule of their Order, which, it was claimed, resulted in a level of excellence judged to be impossible outside such a community. It was, of course, no part of Christian doctrine to claim a social, political or economic equality among Christians.

Nor, it must be said, was it part of Martin Luther's teaching which challenged the belief that spiritual work was superior to secular work in the eyes of God, but did not assert that the social distinctions people made among themselves were invalid. In claiming a 'priesthood of all believers' he was criticizing the state of the clergy of his times, and recalling the Christian church to its early days. At the same time he was denying the clergy's (and particularly the regular clergy's) claim that theirs was the purest, the highest form of vocation. Plainly in Luther's day the regular clergy were not the most righteous group in the Christian church, but he was going beyond the contingent fact to re-assert as a matter of principle that *no* calling was superior or, to put it more positively, that every calling, every form of work, was of equal worth in the eyes of God and should therefore be so regarded by all Christians. In explicit terms he denied the Church's hierarchical distinction between 'spiritual' and 'secular' callings:

> The first thing to know is that there are no good works except those works which God has commanded (in the Decalogue) .... The first, highest and most precious of all good works is faith in Christ ... in this faith all works became equal and one work is like another .... The man who stays at home to support his family and care for wife and children rather than make a pilgrimage does a truly good work and one which is commanded by God.[6]

In this Luther was going beyond the 'good works' enjoined in the Ten Commandments to the secular tasks necessary to the economic prosperity of the Commonwealth. Calvin made the same point in his *Institutes of Christian Religion:*

> The Lord bids each one of us in all life's actions to look to his calling ... he has appointed duties for every man in his particular way of life ... a man of obscure station will lead a private life ungrudgingly ... it will be a slight relief from cares, labours, troubles and other burdens for a man to know that God is his guide in all these things. The magistrate ... the head of the household ... each man will bear and swallow the discomforts, vexations, weariness and anxieties in his way of life when he has been persuaded that the burden was laid upon him by God ... no task will be so sordid and base providing you obey your calling in it.[7]

For the puritans of late sixteenth and early seventeenth century England the matter was given classic expression in William Perkins' *Treatise of the Vocations or Callings of Men.* Here Perkins distinguished between a 'general' calling — the calling of Christianity, common to all who live in the Church of God, and a 'personal' calling, i.e., a particular office or vocation, which was honest and lawful, profitable to both the doer and the Commonwealth as a

whole (which enables him to exclude 'rogues, beggars and vagabonds' as well
as those who 'being enriched with great livings and revenues do spend their
days in eating and drinking, in sports and pastimes, not employing themselves
in service for church or Commonwealth').[8]

This distinction was not unique to the radical wing of the Church of
England. The 'Sundry Godly Prayers for Divers Purposes' of the *Edwardian
Primer* (1553) reminded 'labourers and men of occupations:' '. . . As the bird is
born to fly so man is born to labour . . . so thy godly pleasure is that no man be
idle, but every man labour according to his vocation or calling'. Wives, too,
were enjoined to pray 'Give me grace, I most entirely beseech thee to walk
worthy of my vocation;' (which, of course, was to reverence, obey and please
her husband and to be ruled by him). Again, in the Catechism, the gloss of the
Tenth Commandment required a child 'not to covet or desire another man's
goods . . . . But to learn to labour truly to get my own living and to do my
duty in that state of life into which it shall please God to call me' — the latter
phrase being stamped on the memories, if not the minds and hearts, of many
generations of children (and adults) to come.[9]

Such a strongly affirmed perspective had implications for a whole range
of educational questions: Who shall be educated? In what ways? Through what
subject matter? For what purposes? The medieval church had constantly
aspired to an educated clergy, whether through its monasteries, cathedral
schools or universities.[10] A major complaint of the Christian Humanists and
the Protestant Reformers of the early sixteenth century was the failure of the
church to achieve this aspiration. Calls for a better educated clergy were a
commonplace throughout the century.[11] It did not take the Reformers (of all
denominations) and their princes long to realize the dilemma implicit in
making an educated clergy a reality. In a Christian church essentially authoritarian, in that it based its teaching on admonition, injunction and commandment, the question was not whether the clergy should be educated in its
vocation, but how far it should be educated to go beyond administering the
sacraments using a prescribed liturgy, to an interpretative function based on
theoretical knowledge, with the attendant risk of heterodoxy and heresy in
such interpretations of God's word and the doctrine based on it.[12] Within the
Protestant churches what started as a freedom movement — freedom from the
Pope, and from the ordained priest as a necessary medium between a Christian
and his God — had its own intrinsic dangers. The safe-guarding and
maintenance of the newly-founded churches required the transformation of
voluntary action by freely-choosing Christians into compulsory participation
in a prescribed theory and practice. Religious education, the liberator, soon
became religious education, the prophylactic.

The problem of control, of both clergy and laity, produced its own
paradox, expressed in the label 'mechanick preacher', pejorative in its original
intention and use, yet willingly embraced by those to whom it was applied.
The term was applied to those radicals in the Puritan wing of the English
church who, their opponents claimed, were daring to take on a clergyman's

functions without training in the liberal arts and theology which were deemed essential to the carrying out of that function. Those to whom it was applied counter-claimed in two ways. Such training, necessarily taking place in grammar school and university, was socially divisive, separating the clergy from their flock. Secondly, and more important, it was theologically unnecessary, since all that was required for the performance of the function was that 'spirit', 'grace' or 'inner light' which characterized their life and their facility for expounding the Gospel. The education, at once liberal and vocational, in which they were deficient was not only unimportant but inessential. In the 'priesthood of all believers' there were plainly some who were *better* at expounding the Gospel than others; the difference did not lie in their book-learning, however, any more than level of moral behavior was determined by level of scholarship. According to some radical Puritans the only book to be learned was the Bible, whose truth made it self-sufficient, untouched by gloss and commentary from the superficially pious. If such claims made them 'mechanick preachers', so be it. The need for a learned ministry, one of the fundamental tenets of the Protestant Reformation, was thus turned on its head by a highly articulate minority, causing those in authority in church and state to safeguard orthodoxy by insisting, in the long term successfully, on the need for a learned ministry trained in the controlled environment of the university.[13]

A paradox of a different kind is use of the term 'star-shooter'. Similarly pejorative in origin, ship-masters used the term in the sixteenth century to deride those who insisted on using new methods and instruments to aid them in their navigation.

Like the 'mechanick preachers', the 'star-shooters' were happy to accept the label, but for the opposite reason. For them 'rule of thumb' and education by precept was no longer satisfactory. They needed new instruments for their long voyages out of sight of land, and to achieve greater precision (and therefore safety and commercial profit) in their coastal navigation.[14] By learning mathematical 'sciences' and their application to practical navigation, 'star-shooters' became more efficient navigators, and, at the same time, gained a status similar to that accorded to the traditional learned professions, the church, the law and medicine, each of which based their expertise on theoretical knowledge acquired through a bookish education. It was the 'star-shooters' then who distanced themselves from their more traditional colleagues by labelling them 'ignorant mechanicks.'

Similar responses are to be found in a whole range of 'new professions', labelled, in Aristotelian terms, as practising the 'mechanic arts' — which were by definition, therefore, illiberal. Land surveyors, for example, in an age when soaring land-values made the traditional ways of measuring land *per estimacionem* no longer acceptable, used theoretical mathematics to perfect a method of triangulation, again using new instruments and producing texts for the theoretically-based 'vocational' education deemed necessary for their status-claims. Edward Worsop in his *Discoverie of Sundrie Errors Committed by*

*Landmeaters Ignorant of Arithmetick and Geometrie* (1582) expressed the aspirations of his kind in a way that may stand exemplar for them all:

> Such sufficient skill as a surveyor should have before he ought to execute that office cannot be attained but by a longer study and a greater practice than is commonly thought to be had thereto. It is also one of the chargeablest studies that one can enter into. There are few that will take the pains to give perfect instructions to young beginners and to set them in the right course of study and practice, which is a great cause of much vain expenses. The mathematical part seemeth so dry and hard at the first entrance that some (as wearied) give over before they have passed half-way. Also measurers ignorant of geometry can make quicker despatches than the learned and skilful can, which so pleaseth the ignorant because it diminishes the present charge, that they little regard him that make true measure, which in truth is penny wisdom and pound foolishness .... If the learned and skilful did use conferences and decide ways how these inconveniences might be redressed, true knowledge advanced, and ignorance depressed, as the learned in other professions do, great utility would ensue .... If surveyors were in such order, as by good reason they should ... then as the learned in other professions are known from the unlearned so might they be.[15]

The same point is made by Richard More in his *Carpenter's Rule* ... (1602), which he dedicated to Henry Billingsley, whose translation of Euclid's *Elementes of Geometrie* (1570) he recommended to his readers and from which he acknowledged he had 'received all that little insight in Geometrie which I have attained unto.'[16]

In the several branches of the medical profession the physicians alone had acquired the status accorded to those with a 'liberal' education, in their case a bookish knowledge of Hippocrates and Galen acquired through a university course of study. The surgeons and apothecaries on the other hand practised 'mechanick arts', acquired by the traditional method of apprenticeship. In the early modern period, however, each of these groups determined to rid themselves, their studies and their work of this 'mechanick' status, by insisting on raising the theoretical level of their study and by developing the literature and the institutions to facilitate their members' achievement. Hitherto restricted to the treatment of 'surface' ailments the (barber) surgeons all too often found themselves called on to deal with internal complaints, especially with the increased incidence of gun-shot wounds. Similarly, apothecaries, traditionally merely the dispensers of 'recipes' prescribed by physicians, increasingly took on the role of diagnostician as well as druggist where no physician existed or one was likely to charge exorbitant fees. The surgeons, armed with the new anatomy of Vesalius, and the apothecaries, using the new Paracelsian inorganic remedies, thus not only acquired a theoretical base to their practice, but were able to deride the physicians for their continued reliance on out-of-date Galenic medicine. At the same time each group instituted lectures on their art in their Company's Hall, and, more importantly, text-books for the transmission not only of the new medicine but also of their new professional claims.[17]

One social group has yet to be mentioned, that of 'gentleman', and once again changing circumstances produced changing responses to educational problems. Deprived in the early modern period of their traditional military function (and justification) by mercenary armies and the use of gunpowder, and challenged by non-landowning but nevertheless wealthy citizens for the right to participate in government, the feudal aristocracy was urged to sustain its claim to a role in government by becoming 'educated', not in the traditional chivalric way, but in the bookish way of the Italian humanists, who typically went back to Greece and Rome for their model ruler and councillor.[18] One manifestation of these changes was the debate in the fifteenth and sixteenth centuries about the nature of gentility, which by the mid-sixteenth century had concluded that virtue not birth should be the distinguishing criterion of eligibility. Service at the Council table (whether directly or indirectly) was to be the 'calling', the 'vocation', the 'profession' of the new aristocracy.[19]

Once the new criterion was accepted its implementation would be relatively simple; the sons of those claiming 'gentility' and its attendant right to serve the commonwealth would prepare for their calling by first acquiring a schooling in Latin language and literature (whether in a grammar school or at home through a private tutor), and then by going on to university (as first generation undergraduates) to drink at the fountain of those *studia humanitatis* which fifteenth century Italian humanists had prescribed as essential for all who aspired to the secular arm of government. Whether, once admitted to university, the new generation of 'gentle' undergraduates were offered the new education or even studied it conscientiously is a moot point.[20] But the phenomenon is clearly relevant to any discussion of what constituted — or was considered to constitute — a 'liberal' or 'vocational' education. For despite the influx of new undergraduates, with quite different aims from those of their clerical contemporaries, the purpose of the universities did not change. They remained institutions for producing those who would serve the Commonwealth and its church, as the Tudor and Stuart sovereigns and their ministers made very plain by their close oversight of University officers.[21]

The debate about what was appropriate for a gentleman's education was still further complicated by the fact that the non-bookish, wholly practical and therefore 'illiberal' education of those of 'gentle' family continued to include, long after it had become dysfunctional, a large slice of their old chivalric education — fitness of body, skill of hand and eye in the use of sword and management of horses. This was not mere athleticism. Such bodily exercise would contribute — *mens sana in corpore sano* — to the well-being and therefore efficiency of the governor.[22] It would thus contribute in a direct way to the gentleman's function in society, and at the same time save the Aristotelian principle that a citizen-gentleman could engage in bodily 'labor' provided that it was not habitualized labor nor engaged in for monetary reward.[23]

Thus far we have considered the education — however labelled — of the upper and middle classes for their various roles in society. Not surprisingly the historian has plenty of evidence for this literate, articulate minority, especially since the period was one of change, of claim and counter-claim.

Much less evidence is available for the majority in society, who did not require the literate skills of their 'betters' to fulfill their functions in society. Their working skills were traditional, and were acquired by the equally traditional methods of precept and example. Since for the most part both the skills and the method continued to be functional they were not subject to debate; because they were considered satisfactory they did not produce the welter of documentation to which the historian can refer when considering the literate minority. The work practices of the unskilled laborer, in this period almost wholly agricultural, required no textbook, no innovative treatise. Such a worker belonged to no institution which might attempt to control his work practices, or haul him before its 'court' for some default.

The vocational education of the majority, in the limited sense of preparation for work skills, has to be described as informal, unsystematic and carried out orally by precept and example, and as often as not by the unspoken indication of attitudes, assumptions and prejudices. Moreover, this was likely to be true of many apprentices, as for example John Goffe of Penzance, apprenticed in 1459 to John Gibbs, with provision in the indenture that 'the aforesaid John Gibbs and Agnes, his wife, shall teach, train and inform and cause the aforesaid John Goffe their apprentice to be informed in the craft of fishing in the best way they know . . . .'[24]

As we have seen , there is plenty of prescriptive evidence that it was every man's God-given duty to work, and that to the best of his ability, as much for the good of the community as for his own soul. If he did not work he would be subjected to the harsh provision of legislation and proclamation against beggars, vagabonds and other 'idle rogues.' The religious and political education of the illiterate majority was therefore a crucial part of their vocational education, both 'general' and 'particular.'

The distinction between the literate few and the illiterate many has also to be made about the education of girls and women. The bulk of evidence about the status, role and education of women was, of course, written by men. Because it was infinitely smaller in quantity the evidence from women's writing has to be used with caution, since it was less likely to be representative even of women's aspirations. But whatever the source, the almost universal assumption was that a female's Christian vocation was to be subservient to man and in particular to the man she married. In this respect, females of the upper and middle classes were in no sense different from the rest of their gender. Their status in society was to be measured only in relation to the superior status of men. What predominated here was the (allegedly) 'Pauline' view which restricted females to the relatively circumscribed role of familial helpmeet — however much contributions to the economic sphere were permitted to or expected of them.

When it came to the content of the education there were, of course, decided differences between the upper and the middle classes, though even within the smaller group wide variation of emphasis would be found. For some, such as the daughters of Sir Thomas More, a complete education would require three kinds of content. The first, following the innovative prescriptions of fifteenth century Italian humanists,[25] would include a study, under a tutor at home, of carefully selected passages of Latin literature, aimed always, however, at the moral instruction of the girl in her duties in the family structure and ultimately in her role as wife and mother. In addition to this literary education, only superficially 'liberal', girls of the upper and middle classes would be taught the 'accomplishments' appropriate to their class — music, both singing and learning to play an instrument, dancing, needlework of a decorative kind, and writing of 'polite' letters and the learning of another language, usually French. In this genteel context such skills were considered essential as preparation for a satisfactory marriage. Indeed as the sixteenth century progressed into the seventeenth this second kind of content, considered to be more directly 'vocational', came to be accorded greater importance than a knowledge of Latin language and literature which was becoming increasingly counter-productive in the eyes of both male and female elders who advised young women that prospective husbands would feel inferior in the face of such erudition in a woman.[26] Moreover, there were still plenty of parents ready to use the 'pagan' argument against a study of the classics. Such works, despite the imprimatur of Christian humanists such as Erasmus and Vives, were still considered by some to be immoral and irreligious, and therefore to be shunned. In any case by the end of the sixteenth century even those who shared the humanist view would be able to recommend selected classics in English translation and thus allow women to avoid the tedium of learning Latin grammar. Even so, there were still parents and advisers who, thinking primarily of a girl's domestic duties, argued for a limited diet. Ralph Verney may have been a devoted Anglican but many a Puritan would have agreed with him when, on learning of his god-daughter's wish to learn Latin, Greek and Hebrew, he advised her 'Good sweet heart be not so covetous . . . believe me, a Bible . . . and a good plaine catechisme in your mother tongue, being well-read and practised is well worth all the rest and much more suitable to your sex . . .'[27] a view shared by Elizabeth Joceline who, expecting a child, urged her husband that, if the baby were a girl, 'I desire that her bringing up may be learning the Bible, as my sisters doe, good housewifery, writing and good works; other learning a woman needs not.'[28] In this, of course, they were emphasizing the third and most important element of a young gentlewoman's upbringing, her religious education. Lady Ann Halkett's autobiographical description may stand exemplar in its emphasis for most of her class, who received their education either at home or in the household of another:

> My mother . . . paid masters for teaching my sister and mee to write,
> speak Frenche, play on the lute and virginalls and dance, and kept a
> gentlewoman to teach us all kind of needlework .... But my
> mother's greatest care ... (was to ensure that we were) instructed
> never to neglect to begin and end the day with prayer, and orderly
> each morning to read the Bible, and ever to keepe the church as offten
> as there was occasion to meet there either for prayers or preaching.[29]

However, John Dury was not alone in believing that the emphasis was not
always as it had been in Lady Ann's case, when he complained of 'the
education of young gentlewomen which in most places tends only to teach
them how they become objects of lusts and snares unto young gentlemen ...
(when instead) they should become modest discreet and industrious
housewives.'[30]

Increasingly the daughters of middle-class parents were sent away to
small private boarding schools which emphasized accomplishments and
religious education as their main objectives. John Evelyn noted in his diary for
17 May 1647 that he went 'to Putney ... to see the Schools or Colledges of the
Young Gentlewomen' and it was to Mrs. Salmon's school at Hackney that as
Kathleen Fowler 'the matchless Orinda' went, aged eight, to begin her formal
education. Mrs. Playford's school opposite the church at Islington offered (in
the 1670s) tuition in 'all manner of curious (needle) works ... reading,
writing, dancing and the French language', and it was for the pupils of Josias
Priest's 'school for young gentlewomen' in Chelsea that Henry Purcell wrote
his *Dido and Aeneas* (c. 1688–89).[31]

Nor were such schools confined to the metropolis and its environs. In
1656 the cleric-farmer Ralph Josselin sent his daughter Jane, aged 10, to Mrs.
Piggott's school in Colchester. His other daughters, Mary and Elizabeth, were
sent to similar establishments at White Colne and Bury St. Edmunds,
respectively.[32] Henry Oxinden's second wife, Katherine, had been sent by her
yeoman father, for four years, to be 'at school amongst other gentlemen's
daughters', and he sent his own daughters, Margaret and Elizabeth, to a school
in Mersham, Kent, run by Mr. Beavan, who assured him that

> Besides the qualities of music, both for the virginals and singing (if
> they have the voices) and writing (and to cast accounts which will be
> useful to them hereafter) he would be careful so that their behaviour
> be modest and as becomes their quality and that they grow in
> knowledge and understanding of God and their duty to Him which is
> above all ... I presume (he concluded) you will think £30 a year for
> both reasonable, when you consider the hardness of the times (1647)
> and that there is more trouble with girls than boys.[33]

Adam Martindale's oldest daughter, Elizabeth, was 'bred up at home to her
books and her pen, and in Warrington and Manchester to her needle and
musick, though the latter she loved not and after forgot it'. Celia Fiennes on

the other hand, visiting Shrewsbury in 1698, noted 'a very good school for gentlewomen for learning (needle)work and behaviour and music'.[34]

Yet the women of the upper and middle classes found themselves ground between the upper and nether millstones. John Collett recounted in his common place book (1633) how 'when a learned maid was presented to King James for an English rarity because she could speake and rite pure Latine, Greeke and Hebrew, the King ask'd "But can shee spin?"' Sir Miles Sandys was merely repeating a general view when in his conduct book *Prima Pars Parvi Opusculi* (1634) he insisted that 'to make them scholars were frivolous . . . learning in a woman is like a sundial in a grave.' It is not surprising that at the end of the century Defoe still felt it necessary to proclaim that he 'would have them take women for companions and educate them to be fit for it'. Yet in this he was going no further than Richard Mulcaster had in his *Positions* (1581) in his chapter on 'young maidens', where he justifies his positive stance by referring to their 'naturall towardnesse', and calling for 'that treasure bestowed upon them by nature to be bettered in them by nurture'.[35]

Part of the duties of Dury's 'industrious housewives' involved, of course, the domestic skills of child-rearing, food-preparing and cooking, spinning, weaving, garment-making and so on. For the vast majority these would be passed on by word of mouth and by example, acquired by first-hand experience. For those who could read the printing press provided a vast range of practical aids to assist them in fulfilling their vocation of housewife. These included general works of reference and advice such as Gervase Markham's *The English Housewife* (1615), and specialist books such as the anonymous *Booke of Curious and Strange Inventions Called the Firste Parte of Needleworkes . . .* (1596) and *The Needles Excellency . . .* (1640); Leonard Mascall's *The Husbandlye Ordring and Gouvernmente of Poultrie . . .* (1581) which was directly addressed to the 'goodwife' and included sections on how to choose a good cock or hen, how to nurture newly-hatched chickens, how to 'keep eggs long' and tips on fattening, killing and plucking; and above all medical books of all kinds, such as the anonymous *Widdowes Treasure, plentifully furnished with sundry precious and approved secrets in physicke and chirugery . . . hereunto adioyned sundrie prittie practises and conclusions of cookerie . . .* (1595) and *The Ladies Cabinet Opened wherein is found hidden several experiments in preserving and conserving, physicke and surgery, cookery and housewifery* (1639).

Even those daughters of gentlemen who were destined for a life surrounded by servants were expected to have some knowledge of these practical matters, though even here dangers were perceived and had to be guarded against. James Sandford, for example, complained that many medical books specifically written for women were filled with 'recipes to increase carnall desire . . . to restore virginitie at time of marriage . . . to keep the bellye in one state', to say nothing of all the beautifying recipes which could do nothing but foster vanity and worldly sexuality.[36] Thomas Raynolde, in his midwifery book *The Byrth of Mankynde otherwyse named the Woman's Booke* (1545, and many times reprinted), felt obliged to anticipate the 'abusion of this booke . . .

by ligght and lewd persons ... (since) every boy and knave had of these bookes, readying them as openly as the tales of Robin Hood'. Even so, he argued,

> it shal be no displeasure to any honest and lovying woman that her husband shall reade suche thynges ... (which would supply the roome and place of a goud mydwyfe) ... (Moreover) many honour-able ladies and other worshypfull gentyl women ... frequent and haunte women in theyr labours carienge with them this booke in theyr handes and causynge suche part of it as doth chiefly concern them the same purpose to be red before the mydwyfe and the reste of the women then beyng present.[37]

None of the debates so far referred to took place in a vacuum. Part of the context in which changing attitudes to education can be discerned was the development of a necessary technology to enable the aspirations and the knowledge on which they were based to be implemented in a practical way. In fields of human endeavour where rule of thumb and tradition had held sway for so long 'scientific' technology was making its presence felt.

This was most readily apparent in the more overtly 'vocational' fields of navigation, cartography and surveying. Here the development of new instru-ments, resting on a theoretical base of mathematics, permitted much more precise measurements.[38] Even in that most conservative field, agriculture, the early modern period witnessed more urgent attempts to improve people's control over their physical environment by more efficient farming methods through land draining, the introduction of new root crops and their rotation with the traditional cereal crops.[39] In each of these cases calls for a 'vocational' education in the new methods at the same time insisted on the need for theoretically-based knowledge which traditionally would have been labelled 'liberal'. And once again the landowning gentleman was urged to keep abreast of such developments. Henry Percy, the Ninth Earl of Northumberland, for example, enjoining his son to

> understand your estate generally better than any one of your officers ... for ordinarily I have marked all men that consume their estates are for the most part ignorant of what they have, what the worth is, what particular commodities thereof may be ....[40]

The application of theory to practice was not, however, relevant to the greatest technological change of the period, the invention and development of the moveable type printing press. Here a relatively simple improvement in efficiency produced results of enormous consequence for education.

As always it was not merely the fact of mechanical invention which was significant, but the uses to which the invention was put.[41] In our case what was of greatest importance was the production of books not only for the scholar but also for the more humble reader. The great folio volumes of scholarship continued to be produced for both academic and professional purposes. But what enabled the seeds of the new attitudes to 'vocation' and 'vocational' education to bear fruit was the production, in very large number, of quarto, octavo and duodecimo volumes, handy in size, cheap in price and as often as not appropriately illustrated to facilitate understanding.

Latin was, of course, the traditional medium of a bookish education. For the surgeons and apothecaries, the shipmasters and 'land-meaters' this posed a dilemma which they clearly recognized. They acknowledged that one reason for their low status was the fact that large numbers of uneducated people practiced their profession. At the same time the literature required for professional study by their members had of necessity to be in English and not as with the 'learned' professions in Latin. The writers of professional texts had, therefore, to justify their use of the vernacular whilst at the same time defending themselves against the charge of 'flooding' the profession. In his 1586 translation of Galen's *Methodus Medendi*, Thomas Gale insisted that he did not aim

> to make everie bodie cunning in the arte of medicine.... I doe not meane (he went on) that honest artists, as tailors, shoemakers, weavers or any other handie occupations that they should leave their artes wherein they are perfecte and fal to this arte of medicine, for I doe wishe with all my hearte that politicke laws might be made to constrain everie man to followe that arte in which he hath bene well instructed and brought up in.[42]

Not surprisingly those practicing the 'mechanick' branches of medicine were not unanimous in wishing to maintain a professional limitation on their numbers. Thomas Tymme, for example, in offering an English translation of the works of Josephus De Chesne (a Paracelsian whose work had been first translated by John Hester), insisted that medical knowledge, like a knowledge of the Scriptures, should be diffused as widely as possible, even amongst laymen.[43]

The transmission of ideas and information was thus enormously enhanced by the production of books in the vernacular language. At the beginning of the period writers felt it necessary to apologize for the use of a non-scholarly language. By the end of the century no such apology was offered, for by that time there was not only a lucrative market to be tapped, but the vernacular had established itself as a perfectly satisfactory literary medium, whether used by a translator or by an original writer.

By the early seventeenth century almost the whole corpus of Greek and Latin writing from the Ancient World was made available by translators,[44] who could now claim with justice that theirs was a literary art, using a developed language which had not been available to William Caxton and his fellow translators into the vernacular in the late fifteenth century. As Sir Thomas North, an early translator of Plutarch's *Lives* (1579), put it: 'The office of translator consisteth not only in the faithful expressing of his author's meaning, but also in a certain resembling and shadowing out of the form of his style and the manner of his speaking.'[45]

The wide range and quality of such translations of the classics thus enabled members of the upper and middle classes to absorb the ethics and politics of the Ancient World, those two aspects of classical literature which the earlier humanists had assumed would be read in the original. But even if the English gentleman had acquired a mastery of the Latin language sufficient to enable him to read (rather than 'plough through') Roman literature (and this is to be doubted), he certainly would not have been able to read his favorite Plutarch in the original Greek. Moreover, he was just as likely to have acquired his 'knowledge' of the classics through the sixteenth century equivalent of the medieval *florelegia*, selections of pithy sayings from a wide variety of authors such as Sir Thomas Elyot compiled in his *Banket of Sapience* (1539), or William Baldwin in his *Treatise of Morall Philosophie Contayning the Sayings of the Wise* (1547). Each was reprinted many times, and dozens of similar texts were produced during our period.

A further point needs to be made in conclusion. It is tempting to assume that the gentlemen of early modern England read such literature 'for its own sake' as part of a 'liberal' education. To be sure the prescribed education was intended for a 'leisured' class, but this was not to be equated with an *idle* class, for its members would be busy in the business of government whether at national or local level. Not only did they claim a share of government, they were expected to do so by their ruler, not least by Queen Elizabeth whose 'stacks of statutes' required a deal of administering. Their 'vocation' was government and their (vocational) education was intended to prepare them for the more efficient carrying out of that function. Their rewards would be tangible enough, gifts of land or the revenues from land, which would further supplement their income from land which made them 'gentlemen' in the first place. It would have been unthinkable for any educated person in the early modern period to have asserted, as historian J.B. Bury did in 1891, that 'any attempt to conciliate the enemy by alleging that Greek, after all, may have uses is disloyalty to the ideal of a liberal education'.[46] Indeed Bury was ignoring the Bidding Prayer of his own university: '. . . and that there may never be wanting a succession of persons duly qualified for the service of God in Church and State, we implore this blessing on all places of religious and useful learning.'[47] Vives, along with others, was unambiguous on the matter: 'This then is the fruit of all our studies; this is the goal. Having acquired our knowledge we must turn it to usefulness and employ it for the common good.'[48] John Knox would probably have not approved of the juxtaposition, but when he set out his plan for national education in his *Second Book of Discipline* he too insisted:

> If they be found apt to learning and letters, then may they not — we mean neither the sons of the rich nor yet of the poor — be permitted to reject learning, but must be charged to continue their study so that the commonwealth may have some comfort by them.[49]

Two generations later Comenius was urging the same point:

> ... let us teach them ... to learn not for the sake of knowing but for the sake of exercising themselves not only for the sake of exercise but in order to attain the goal of all activities which is rest and happiness.[50]

As usual Bacon put it more succinctly: 'Crafty men contemn studies; simple men admire them; wise men use them.'[51]

## Notes

1   A.N. WHITEHEAD, (1962 edn.) *The Aims of Education and Other Essays*, London, p. 74; J. DEWEY, (1916) *Democracy and Education*, New York, p. 258 and chs. 19, 20 and 23 *passim*.

2   THE HARVARD REPORT, (1945) *General Education in a Free Society*, Cambridge, Mass., pp. viii–ix and 55; See, also, A.N. WHITEHEAD, *Aims of Education*, p. 71.

3   ARISTOTLE, *Politics* VII. 8, 1328b; 1337b; III. 4, 1277b; PLATO, *Laws* XI, 919; XENOPHON, *Oeconomicus*, IV.2, 3.

4   CICERO, *De Oficiis* I. 42 and 44.

5   J. LE GOFF, (1980) *Time, Work and Culture* (translated by A. GOLDHAMMER), Chicago, pp. 107–21.

6   LUTHER, (1966) 'Treatise on good works' (1520), in *Luther's Works*, Philadelphia, 44, pp. 18, 23, 26 and *passim*; see, also, his 'On monastic vows' (1521), in *Ibid.*, pp. 243–400 and 'Sermon on the fifth chapter of St. Matthew' (1532), in *Ibid.*, 21, p. 34.

7   CALVIN, *Institutes of Christian Religion* Book III, chapter 10.

8   W. PERKINS, (1616) 'A treatise of the vocations or callings of men,' in *Works*, 3 vols., Cambridge, I, p. 747 ff.

9   J. KETLY (ed.), (1844) *The Two Liturgies AD 1549 and AD 1552 ...*, Cambridge, Parker Society, pp. 371, 459–60, and 465.

10  G.R. EVANS, *Old Arts and New Theology: the Beginnings of Theology as an Academic Discipline*, Oxford, Clarendon Press, 1980.

11  E.H. HARBISON, (1956) *The Christian Scholar in the Age of the Reformation* New York, Charles Scribner's Sons. G. STRAUSS, (1978) *Luther's House of Learning: Indoctrination of the Young in the German Reformation*, Baltimore, Johns Hopkins University Press.

12  R. O'DAY, (1979) *The English Clergy: the Emergence and Consolidation of a Profession 1558–1642*, Leicester, Leicester University Press.

13  C. HILL, (1969) *Society and Puritanism*, London, Pantner Books.

14  W. BOWNE, (1577) *A Regiment of the Sea* London, To the Reader. See, D.W. WATERS, (1958) *The Art of Navigation in England in Elizabethan and Early Stuart Times* London, Hollis and Carter. Shakespeare's Iago made the same kind of criticism of Cassio, his rival for military command, calling him 'a great arithmetician' who relied on 'the bookish theoric', *Othello* I.i, 19–24; See, L. DIGGES, (1579) *An Arithmeticall Militore Treatise Called Stratioticos* ....

15  E. WORSOP, *op. cit.* Dedicatorie Epistle and Sigs. I.i, K.i. verso. Thomas Paynell (1537) had earlier enjoined land surveyors to 'consider then this liberal science called geometrie', in his prefatory letter to Richard Benese, *The Maner of Mesurynge all maner of lande* ....

16  R. MORE, (1602) *The Carpenters Rule, or a booke showing many plaine waies truly to measure ordinarie timber or other extraordinarie sollids or timber, with a detection of sundrie great errors generally Committed by Carpenters and others measuring timber much to the buyers losse.*

17  V.L. BULLOUGH, (1966) *The Development of Medicine as a Profession* New York, Hafner Publishing Co.; R.S. ROBERTS, (1962) and (1964) 'The personel and practice of medicine in tudor England', *Medical History*, 6: 363–83 and 8: 217–34; M. PELLING and C. WEBSTER (eds.), (1979) *Health, Medicine and Mortality in the Sixteenth Century* Cambridge, Cambridge University Press, pp. 165–235; A.G. DEBUS, (1965) *The English Paracelsians* London, Oldbourne. For earlier debates, J. RIDDLE, (1974) 'Theory and practice in medieval medicine', *Viator*, 5: 157–84.

18  See, K. CHARLTON, (1965) *Education in Renaissance England* London, Routledge and Kegan Paul chs 2 and 3.

19  F. CASPARI, (1968 edn.) *Humanism and the Social Order in Tudor England* New York, Teachers College Press; P.N. EEIGEL, (1952) 'English humanism and the new Tudor aristocracy', *Journal of the History of Ideas*, 13: 450–68.

20  Compare J.H. HEXTER, (1950) 'The education of aristocracy in the renaissance', *Journal of Modern History*, 22: 1–20 (reprinted (1961) in his *Reappraisals in History*, London, Longmans pp. 45–70); M.H. CURTIS, (1965) *Oxford and Cambridge in Transition, 1558–1642* Oxford, Clarendon Press; H. KEARNEY, (1970) *Scholars and Gentlemen: Universities and Society in Pre-Industrial England 1500–1700* London, Faber and Faber, with W.T. COSTELLO, (1958) *The Scholastic Curriculum at Early Seventeenth Century Cambridge*, Cambridge, Mass. Harvard University Press; C. HILL, (1965) *The Intellectual Origins of the English Revolution* London, Oxford University Press, Appendix 'A note on the universities', 301–14; L. JARDINE, (1975) 'Humanism and the sixteenth century Cambridge arts curriculum', *History of Education* 4: 16–31.

21  See, CHARLTON, *Education in Renaissance England*, pp 151–2.

22  As in T. ELYOT, (1531) *The Boke Named the Governor*, Book I, chap. xvi; B. CASTIGLIONE, *The Book of the Courtyer*, translated by SIR T. HOBY (1561), Sigs. Ciiii verso, Diii recto; J. CLELAND, (1607) *The Institution of a Young Nobleman*, p. 127; H. PEACHAM, (1622) *The Compleat Gentleman*, p. 179; see also, the '1541 statutes of Canterbury School': 'and they shall not practise any games which are not of gentlemanly appearance and free of all lowness', in A.F. LEACH, (ed.) (1911), *Educational Charters and Documents*, Cambridge, Cambridge University Press, p. 469.

23  ARISTOTLE, *Politics* VII. 8, 1337b; see also, CICERO, *De Officiis* I. 42

24  A.E. BLAND, P.A. BROWN and R.H. TAWNEY, (eds.), (1914) *English Economic History: Select Documents*, London, G. Bell and Sens, p. 147.

25  See L. BRUNI's advice to Baptista Malatesta, in W.H. WOODWARD (ed.), (1963 edn.) *Vittorino da Feltre and Other Humanist Educators*, New York, Teachers College Press, pp. 119–33.

26  R. HERRICK, for example, was not unusual in praying for an 'unlearned' wife in 'His Wish', *Poems* C.L. MARTIN (ed.) (1965) Oxford, Clarendon Press, p. 294.

27  M.M. VERNEY, (1894) *Memoirs of the Verney Family*, 3 vols., London, Longmans, III, p. 73.

28  *The Mothers Legacie to Her Unborn Childe* (1624), Epistle Dedicatorie, Sig. B 5 verso.

29  J.G. NICHOLS (ed.), (1875) *Autobiography of Lady Anne Halkett*, Camden Society,

N.S XIII, pp. 2–3.

30  J. DURY, (1653) *Some Proposals Towards the Advancement of Learning*, in C. WEBSTER (ed.), (1970) *Samuel Hartlib and the Advancement of Learning*, Cambridge, Cambridge University Press, p. 190; see also, G.E. FUSSELL, (1953) *The English Countrywoman: a Farmhouse Social History 1500–1900*, London, Andrew Melrose.

31  E.S. DE BEER (ed.), (1955) *The Diary of John Evelyn*, 6 vols., Oxford, Oxford University Press, II, p. 555; P.W. SOMERS, (1931) *The Matchless Orinda* (Cambridge, Mass., Harvard University Press, 12; 'Middlesex,' *Victoria Country History*, London, Oxford University Press, I, p. 252; *Sammelband der Internationalen Musik Gesellschaft*, V (1903–4): 506ff.

32  A. MACFARLANE, (1970) *Family Life of Ralph Josselin*, Cambridge, Cambridge University Press, pp. 49 and 93.

33  D.M. GARDINER, (1933–7) *The Oxinden Letters*, 2 vols., London, Oxford University Press 1933–37, II, p. 128.

34  G.R. PARKINSON (ed.), (1845) *The Life of Adam Martendale*, Chetham Society, IV, pp. 206–9; C. MORRIS, (1949) *The Journeys of Celia Fiennes*, London, rev.ed., Crescet Press, p. 227.

35  W.J. THOMS (ed.), (1835) *Anecdotes and Traditions Illustrative of Early English History and Literature*, Camden Society V, p. 125; SANDYS, *op. cit.*, p. 128; D. DEFOE, (1697) *Essay Upon Projects*, London, pp. 302–3; MULCASTER, (1581) *Positions*, London, p. 171.

36  J. SANFORD, (1569) *Of the Vanitie and Uncertaintie of Artes and Sciences*, London, p. 115 (translation of C. AGRIPPA (1534) *De Incertitudine et Vanitate Omnium Scientiarum et Artium ...*).

37  RAYNOLD, *op.cit.*, 'Prologue to the Women Readers', sigs, Ciiii verso, vii recto, viii recto and verso.

38  See, for example, E.G.R. TAYLOR and M.W. RICHEY (1962) *The Geometrical Seaman: a Book of Early Nautical Instruments*, London, Hollis and Carter; A.W. RICHESON, (1960) *English Land Measuring to 1800: instruments and practice*, Cambridge, Mass., Harvard University Press S. TYACKE (ed.), (1983) *English Mapmaking 1500–1650: historical essays*, London, British Library.

39  See, for example, G.E. FUSSELL, (1947) *The Old English Farming Books from Fitzherbert to Tull 1532–1730*, London, Crosby, Lockwood.

40  H. PERCY, Ninth Earl of Northumberland, (1609) *Advice to His Son*, G.B. HARRISON, (ed.) (1930) London, Ernest Benn, p. 82; see also M.E. JAMES, (1955) *The Estate Accounts of the Earls of Northumberland 1562–1637*, Surtees Society CLXIII, xi ff., v *passim*; G.R. BATHO, (1957) 'The education of a stuart nobleman', *British Journal of Educational Studies*, V, May, pp. 131–43. SIR WALTER RALEIGH made the same point in his 'Instructions to his son and posterity', in *Works*, W. OLDYS and T. BIRCH (eds.) (1829) 8 vols., Oxford, VIII, pp. 565–6, as did the anonymous author (1555) of *Institucion of a Gentleman* London, pp. 5–6.

41  E. EISENSTEIN, (1979) *The Printing Press as an Agent of Change* 2 vols., Cambridge, Cambridge University Press.

42  T. GALE, (1586) *Certaine Workes of Galens called Methodus Medendi ...* London, Epistle Dedicatorie, Sig. Aiii verso; see also, N. CULPEPPER (1649) *A Physicall Directory*, — his translation of the *Pharmacopoeia Londiniensis* — Sig. B2 recto.

43  T. TYMME, (1605) *The Practice of Chymicall and Hermeticall Physicke*, London, Epistle Dedicatorie.

44  R.R. BOLGAR, (1964 edn.) *The Classical Heritage and its Beneficiaries from the*

*Carolingian Age to the End of the Renaissance*, New York, Harpor Torchbook, p. 328.

45  North, *op.cit.*, To the Reader.

46  J.B. Bury, (1891) 'Compulsory Greek: Reflections Suggested by the Greek Victory at Cambridge', *Fortnightly Review*, N.S. 50, July–December, 818; '. . . the true function of a University is the teaching of useless learning.' p. 813.

47  P. Deamer (ed.), (1904) *Five Forms of the Bidding Prayer*, Oxford, A.R. Mowbray, p. 2.

48  F.Watson, (1913) *Vives on Education*, Cambridge, Cambridge University Press, p. 283.

49  J. Knox, (1560) *First Book of Discipline*, in W. McGavin (ed.), (1831) *The History of the Reformation of Religion in Scotland by John Knox, to which is appended several other pieces of writing* . . . Glasgow, p. 499.

50  Comenius, *The Way of Light*, (translated by E.T. Campagnac (1938)) Liverpool, Liverpool University Press, pp. 132–3.

51  Bacon, 'Of Studies,' *Essays*.

# Practical Schooling of the Nineteenth Century: Prelude to the American Vocational Movement

*Gordon Law*

Historical studies of American vocationalism have focused mainly on the period between 1880 and 1920. Urbanization, progressivism, populism, capitalism, social welfare, child labor, immigration, organized labor, school attendance laws, and industrialization are among the perspectives treated. But as noted by Rodgers and Tyack, neither the 'house' historians nor more recent revisionists have examined the early stages of vocational schooling, 'before the expansion of secondary education and the emergence of an explicit vocational curriculum.'[1]

School professionals turned historians, described by Bailyn as 'educational missionaries,' have neglected to treat such paths to learning as home and family, apprentice training, specialized vocational schooling or private academies. The main weakness of these writers, according to Bailyn, has been their single-minded promotion of universal free public education and their resultant lack of interest in other historical perspectives.[2]

It is the purpose of this chapter to explore some of the major approaches to vocational schooling that gained popularity during the nineteenth century. Within this context attention has been given to the emergence of schools as a nineteenth century phenomenon; the principal populations served and institutional forms involved; the sharp difference in attitude toward vocationalism between Europe and America; the special role of the American academy in the advancement of popular, practical and secular education; and the failure of its successor, the public high school to fulfill its early mission as an extension of the common school.

## The Emergence of Schools

The nineteenth century, more than any prior period in history, was a time of revolutionary change. Fuelled by the driving force of commerce and industry on both sides of the Atlantic, the western culture which had developed through centuries of evolution was quite suddenly undergoing a remarkable transformation. The ways in which people would live and work, engage in government, settle national disputes, and transmit customs, skills, knowledge and beliefs, from one generation to another, were all undergoing an accelerating succession of changes. In the United States, where extensive industrial development had been delayed until after the War of 1812, the period between 1820 and 1860 was one of unprecedented growth: the population multiplied three times — from ten to thirty million; the ratio of people living in cities to those in rural areas changed from one in fifteen to one in three; and great strides were made in commerce, industry and transportation.[3]

These developments led to an urgent demand for people with advanced levels of education. With glittering prizes available for individuals who could calculate, design, survey, navigate, construct or oversee, there was a proliferation of new schools — designed to serve a much greater proportion of the general population. These included: proprietary or private venture schools; nonprofit schools of trades and industries run by social agencies, private benefactors and branches of government; agricultural schools, and state land grant colleges, typically sponsored by state or regional agricultural societies; technical institutes and colleges which pioneered in the new fields of engineering; specialized schools of business and commerce; normal schools for the preparation of common school teachers; multi-purpose academies and colleges; and commercial/technical/trade schools run by private industries.

In addition to this array of institutions designed to serve the social and educational needs of a broadening middle class were schools for the walking wounded of industrial society, primarily children of the urban poor. Here were found farm and industrial schools for ragged, orphan or delinquent children, typically placed in rural settings to give the children involved a more wholesome environment. This social rehabilitation branch of vocationalism, with isolated strands going back to the middle ages, became well established by the mid-1800s.

## Practical Schooling for Social Reform

A pressing contemporary issue for vocational education is one of purpose: should vocational schools and programs select only capable and motivated individuals for intensive instruction that prepares them for gainful employment in highly skilled or technical occupations; or is public vocational schooling more appropriately applied to a social engineering function — to rehabilitate persons whose cultural or individual handicaps limit their opportunities for job success? In a period when American industrial productivity is falling behind European and Oriental competitors, and when the rate of urban youth unemployment remains frighteningly high, it is clear that neither purpose can be ignored.

The social engineering mission for schools, and the associated premise that the development of 'useful skills' will rehabilitate the victims of poverty, has been popular for approximately two centuries. Late in the eighteenth century the rapidly growing cities of London and Paris, with their hordes of landless poor were the sites of ragged schools run by religious and charitable organizations. In rural Neuhof, Switzerland, John Pestalozzi opened his home to local war orphans and pauper children in 1774, thus beginning a lifetime of dedication to child-centered schooling. Shortly thereafter, in Boston, Philadelphia and New York, schools and asylums were established for pauper and delinquent children. The idea that corrective institutions should prepare inmates to be useful citizens and productive workers, in part derived from the influence of Pestalozzi, found expression in the German Roughen-Haus of Demetz, the Colonie Agricole of Mettray, France[4] and in American Reform schools.

By 1848 when the State of Massachusetts opened its Boys Reform School, the rehabilitative mission was inherent in its title. With the words school and reform deliberately chosen by its founders, the intention was to re-make urban delinquents. Employing a cottage system, later adopted by New York, in order to simulate a family environment, the Reform School applied Pestalozzi's teaching in what the founders called a child-centered prison — 'at once a home and school for learning correct attitudes and useful skills.'[5] The State Board of Charities, as the administrative unit responsible for the new institution considered it 'a lever for the elevation of the race, more potent than any human instrumentality, to wit, a lever of parental love.'[6] The irony in this florid optimism, as noted by Katz, was that it soon gave way to disenchantment. By 1865, some seventeen years after the school's founding, some of the social reformers who had cheered its establishment, were now calling the effort a failure. Instead of transforming urban delinquents into useful citizens, it was reported, the School had become a training grounding for adult criminals.[7]

Other American efforts at using vocational instruction for social rehabilitation were missionary schools for American Indian children, Girard College for Philadelphia orphan boys, and late in the nineteenth century, the large number of industrial schools established by private charities. The Hampton Normal and Agricultural Institute for Negroes, founded by Colonel Samuel Chapman Armstrong in 1868, may also be considered as a vehicle for social rehabilitation as it provided trade training and the Puritan work ethic for former slaves and their children.[8]

Girard College, which resulted from a two-million-dollar bequest by Stephen Girard to the City of Philadelphia in 1832, provided a 'sound education (not forbidding but not recommending the ancient languages)' for at least 300 orphan boys. Originally, the boys were given academic instruction in the college and then were bound out to city officers as apprentices. Later, the college added trade shops, for teaching printing, masonry, carpentry, and other skilled occupations.[9]

In the 1880s, by which time New York City had become the largest port of entry for European immigrants, the living conditions in crowded tenements were brought to the attention of the general public by Jacob Riis and other muckraking reporters. Stating that the industrial schools of the period were filling the gap between the tenement and the public school, Riis reported that the Children's Aid Society, with twenty-one such institutions, and the American Female Guardian Society operating twelve, were providing some degree of practical instruction to approximately 15,000 children. The Children's Aid Society stated the purpose of its schools as follows:

> It is to receive and educate children who cannot be accepted by the public schools, either by reason of their ragged and dirty condition, or owing to the fact that they can attend but part of the time, because they are obliged to sell papers or to stay at home to help their parents. [10]

When discussing the nature of instruction of the industrial schools, Riis reported that:

> The curriculum of the Industrial Schools is comprehensive. The nationality of the pupils makes little or no difference in it. The start, as often as is necessary is made with an object lesson — soap and water being the elements and the child the object. As in the kindergarten, the alphabet comes second on the list. Then follow lessons in sewing, cooking, darning, mat weaving, pasting and dressmaking for the girls and in carpentry wood carving, drawing, printing, and like practical 'branches' for the boys, not a few of whom develop surprising cleverness at this or that kind of work. [11]

Riis also remarked that the hot lunch provided by the schools may have been their most important contribution to the welfare of these children.

Citing the problem of what to do with older boys, 'who have grown up without any training but that in street trades,' Riis mentioned the recently opened New York Trades Schools as a move in the right direction. Probably Riis did not yet realize that the rigorous and highly selective Trades Schools, established by Richard T. Auchtmuty to break the monopoly hold of building trade unions, would have little influence on the lives of pauper children. [12]

Soon after Jacob Riis and other muckrakers were publicizing the deplorable conditions in urban slums, a number of industrial states passed child labor and compulsory school attendance laws, thus forcing a much larger proportion of children of the ten to fourteen age group to remain in school. It was to the problem of coping with this age group that vocational/industrial education was in part directed.

In 1905, when the Douglas Commission to study the need for industrial education in Massachusetts was instituted, one of the central questions addressed was how to make public schooling more appealing to potential dropouts. Criticizing manual training as a poor substitute for 'real' vocational instruction, the Commission recommended the inauguration of grade school shopwork that would increase the 'industrial intelligence' of those children who would soon be entering the workforce.[13]

The Douglas Commission also recommended the establishment of public trade schools, in which young people who had made a definite vocational choice would receive intensive instruction leading to employment in one of the apprenticeable trades. This duality of purpose — to provide basic or rehabilitative schooling for future factory operatives and, on the German model, train skilled workers, which was explicit in the Douglas Commission recommendations, found its way into the language of the Smith-Hughes and subsequent federal acts.[14]

## Vocational Emphasis in Europe and America

Although the types of vocational schools and programs introduced in the United States were quite similar to those of Europe, fundamental differences existed in terms of emphasis and commitment, and in the characteristics of the students involved. In Europe, vocational training in skilled trades, domestic and needle occupations, and technical subjects was seen as a vital component in the fierce competition between emerging industrial states. From the time of Napoleon and continuing through the nineteenth century, the military/industrial benefits of a skilled workforce were generally recognized. Attempting to catch up to the British in technical knowledge and industrial productivity, the governments of France, Austria, Belgium, and the German States became directly involved in the subsidy of vocational instruction. They also marshalled the collaboration of skilled trade associations and industrial management in the development of school-to-work linkages that were never attained in the United States. In contrast, American vocationalism was typically local and private, and limited to either the landless poor or the emerging middle class.

During the mid-1800s when European states were establishing hundreds of trade and technical schools, Americans gave little attention to such instruction as they turned their energies to the proliferation of academies and colleges. In the forty year period between 1820 and the Civil War the number of academies in the United States grew from approximately 200 to more than 6000! The rise of institutions that called themselves colleges was also phenomenal. From the nine colleges that existed at the time of the Revolution, the tally a century later was over 700. This amazing growth of higher education institutions, which had no parallel in Britain or the Continent of Europe, was a striking testimony to the middle class orientation of American people. Americans built their educational systems on the principles of individual enterprise and upward mobility. Too active and restless to cultivate advanced craftsmanship, Americans found it more expedient to import skilled journeymen than train their own. The first legitimate trade school in America did not appear until 1881, a full century after such schools were established in Europe.

And this institution, the New York Trades Schools, was inaugurated to break the power of unions, not to work cooperatively with the skilled workforce.[15]

European ventures in vocational education, although given considerable attention in American education journals, were not seen as models for emulation until late in the nineteenth century. When Horace Mann, on returning from his tour of European schools, gave his famous 'Seventh Annual Report' to the Massachusetts State Board of Education in 1843, the only form of practical schooling he recommended for adoption in America was instruction in drawing.

The *American Annals of Education*, as early as the 1830s, was giving its readers detailed accounts of novel approaches to education. In the United States, such new ventures as manual labor schools and colleges, the Rensselear School at Troy, practical instruction for civilizing American Indians, and the Boston Farm School for rehabilitating youthful offenders were described in this periodical. The *American Annals* also functioned as an important vehicle for publicizing the schools of Europe, giving attention to Pestalozzi and his disciples, the kindergarten and normal school movements and the development of agricultural, trade, fashion, commercial and technical schools in Britain, Sweden, Switzerland, Vienna, and several of the German states.

Late in the century the *Education Magazine*, in a section entitled 'Foreign Notes', featured European systems of education with their heavy emphasis on vocational training. The April 1895 issue of *Education* reported that no less than 123 specialized schools for boys and thirty-six for girls were teaching vocational subjects in Belgium. Of the girls' schools, nineteen were involved in domestic industry — teaching lacework, embroidery, knitting and glove making; five schools combined domestic subjects with more highly technical work; and twelve others were listed as technical schools. For boys Belgium had forty-three trade schools, thirteen technical institutes and thirty-seven industrial schools. Costs for the operation of these institutions were shared by the State (37 per cent), Province (12 per cent), Commune (31 per cent) and private sources (20 per cent).[16]

The September 1896 issue of *Education* focused on the technical schools of Switzerland, reporting that the Polytechnical School in Berne was devoted to architecture, civil engineering, forestry, mechanisms, chemistry and teacher preparation. Sixteen lower technical schools provided instruction in agriculture and trades most needed in the local region and six commercial schools addressed white collar occupations. Switzerland also had eighteen schools of domestic economy and one for the preparation of servants.[17]

## Vocational Education in the Private Sector

At the time when European states were making serious commitments to the operation of trade, commercial, domestic, industrial and technical schools, the vocational training efforts in America were far less extensive. Aside from the

West Point Military Academy, fashion and polytechnical schools in Philadelphia, Farmers High School of central Pennsylvania, and the State Reform School of Massachusetts, the bulk of vocational schooling in nineteenth century America was taking place in private institutions. The sponsors of these programs ranged from wealthy patrons, such as Stephen Van Rensselear, to profit-seeking proprietors. Religious orders, charitable agencies, and commercial/industrial organizations were also involved in vocational instruction.

Opened in 1825 as a coeducational institution for working class youth, the Rensselear School of Troy, New York was originally designed, as stated by its founders,

> to qualify teachers for instructing youth in villages and in common school districts belonging to the class of farmers and mechanics by lectures or otherwise, in the application of the most important principles of chemistry, natural philosophy, natural history and practical mathematics, to agriculture, domestic economy, the arts and manufactures; thus giving instruction in the application of science to the common purposes of life.[18]

Although many of the School's early graduates went on to become teachers, it was the technical curriculum that prevailed. Responding to the growing demand for civil and mechanical engineers, and for professors of science and technology in developing institutions, RPI became the nation's first American college to specialize in this new profession.

The Rochester Institute of Practical Education, established in May 1831, by Christian revivalists of western New York, combined trade training with religious instruction and manual labor activities in the preparation of frontier ministers. The Institute, through its rigorous sixteen hour daily regimen of work and study, conditioned a student body of forty for the hardships of western settlements, where practical skills in carpentry and farming were valuable assets for rural preachers.[19]

American private venture schools, in which experienced practitioners would, for a fee, instruct students in a particular vocation, had served as important vehicles for practical instruction from the colonial period. Filling a void not satisfied by Latin grammar schools, or by traditional apprenticeships, these schools offered courses in both cultural and practical subjects. Among the most popular occupations treated were bookkeeping and shorthand, navigation, needle work, and surveying. Reading, writing, mathematics and natural sciences, as well as art, music, painting and elocution were also offered by private entrepreneurs, for both cultural and utilitarian purposes.[20]

By the 1840s, when thousands of new academies were in operation, many of the subjects previously handled by private venture schools were incorporated in their curricula. From the catalog descriptions of these courses, it would appear that their vocational value was somewhat uneven. Although some of the practical subjects continued to be taught by experts in the field, others were assigned to generalists with no practical experience in the particular occupation.

During the second half of the century, when the United States moved into contention as a major industrial nation, the shortage of skilled craftsmen and technicians led many larger industries to establish their own schools. Lacking toolmakers — those master mechanics who could make machines to make machines — and practitioners in other technologies, such companies as United States Steel, Westinghouse, General Electric, and the R. Hoe Printing Press Company formed corporate trade and technical schools.[21] In the growing chemical, communications, and pharmaceutical industries, where secret formulae and manufacturing techniques were closely guarded, it became customary for company schools to upgrade selected employees through stages of technical knowledge. Shrouded from public view, such corporate training continues today as an important component in several high technology industries.

## Adult Self-Improvement

The American thirst for self-improvement found expression in several adult institutions. Lyceums, which were closely attuned to literary and cultural advancement brought ordinary citizens in touch with such luminaries as Ralph Waldo Emerson, Daniel Webster, Nathaniel Hawthorne and Henry D. Thoreau in a setting similar to that of a town meeting. Founded in 1826 by Josiah Holbrook in Millbury, Massachusetts, the Lyceum Movement made significant contributions to the flowering of New England. A parallel activity devoted more to religious matters, was the Chautauqua Circuit, which flourished after the Civil War. In addition to lyceums and chautauquas were learning institutes directed toward the improvement of working farmers, mechanics and teachers.

The gathering together of farmers to socialize, buy and sell, and exchange practical knowledge, was a common practice long before Europeans settled in North America. But in the new world, where farmers were typically owners and proprietors who lived on their separate holdings, their isolation, ignorance, and loneliness could be devastating. One of the antidotes to this condition was the establishment of farmers' institutes.

Typically organized by county agricultural societies, farmers' institutes were three or four day sessions in which formal instruction and general discussion would address some local aspect of agriculture such as fruit growing, land drainage, fertilization, crop rotation, plant diseases or selective breeding of farm animals. Although some eastern colleges such as Yale, were beginning to study the scientific aspects of farming in the 1830s, the bulk of instruction was given by successful farmers rather than college professors.[22]

The American mechanics' institute movement which began in the 1820s and flourished for about thirty years, was derived in part from British models.

Founded in 1800 by Dr. George Birkbeck of the University of Edinburgh, British mechanics' institutes provided basic literacy and technical instruction to apprentices and journeymen many of whom were finding their traditional hand crafts threatened by industrialization. Originally sponsored by college professors and dissenting ministers, mechanics' institutes were formed in virtually every urban center of England, Scotland and Western Europe.[23]

American mechanics' institutes were influenced by Benjamin Franklin's Junto of the 1700s, with the participation of merchants, public officials and builders in contrast to the worker-oriented institutes of Britain. This alignment to the proprietor class is evident in the 1824 mission statement of the Franklin Institute of Philadelphia:

> RESOLVED, that it is expedient to form a Society for the promotion of the useful arts in Philadelphia by extending a knowledge of mechanical science to its members and others at a cheap rate. RESOLVED, that the best mode of attaining this object will be by the establishment of POPULAR LECTURES, by the formation of a cabinet of MODELS and MINERALS, and of a LIBRARY, and by offering PREMIUMS on all useful improvement in the Mechanical Arts. RESOLVED, that the Society shall consist of Mechanics, Manufacturers and others friendly to the useful arts.[24]

During the 1830s, when farmers and mechanics were organizing educational institutes, common school teachers were also banding together in self-improvement activities. With little support from state legislators, and lacking the position of respect enjoyed by their European counterparts, American teachers made serious efforts to improve their competencies and professional status.

Similar to those of farmers, teachers' institutes were typically held quarterly for three or four days. Usually sponsored by county teachers associations, these institutes combined lectures with sessions devoted to the debate and discussion of local issues. The lectures, given by learned contemporaries from colleges and academies, dealt with moral and inspirational topics and practical instructions relating to a specific subject. Discussion sessions treated methods of teaching the common branch subjects, and some of the burning issues of the day, such as the values of professional organization, benefits and dangers of coeducation, and in eastern Pennsylvania, the relative merits of bi-lingual education.[25]


### The Manual Labor Movement

The immense influence of Pestalozzi, that impractical visionary whose ideas transcended his success as a school master, and the model schools of de Fellenberg, his sometime associate and disciple, contributed an approach to practical education that became known as the manual labor movement.

Central to this movement were ideas that a school should function like a loving family, that learning is best when applied to real life situations, and that learning by doing is important for children of all social classes. The success of these ideas had been demonstrated in the exemplary schools of Hofwyl and Yverdun.[26]

The term manual labor came from the fact that both Pestalozzi and de Fellenberg believed that all students, whether pauper children or the sons and daughters of middle class families, would benefit from exposure to hard physical work. Through farm practice and shopwork in carpentry, cabinet making and bookbinding, students would contribute to the income of the school, and at the same time develop a healthy respect for physical labor and those engaged in it. This concept was applied to many forms of schooling in the United States — from colleges, such as Lafayette and Knox, to farm and industrial asylums for delinquent children. Robert Owen's experimental school of New Harmony Indiana employed manual labor precepts as did the Germantown Academy in Pennsylvania, Bronson Alcott's Temple School of Boston, the Gardiner Lyceum in Maine, and the Oneida Institute of Science and Industry at Whitesborough New York. Reaching a peak of popularity in the 1830s, manual labor schools continued to flourish for another twenty years, after which time many of the farm-shop activities were discontinued as time consuming and impractical.[27]

## The American Academy

Of all the school forms that became popular during the eighteen hundreds the American academy was one of special importance. Private, mainly non-sectarian and frequently coeducational, these creations of the burgeoning middle class played an important role in American movement toward a universal system of free secondary education.

Patterned on British dissenting academies and German *realschulen*, both products of the Protestant Reformation, a handful of academies were established in New England and the middle colonies during the colonial period. Following the American Revolution, as citizens of the new nation saw higher schooling as a vehicle for upward mobility, the academy became a principal instrument for the attainment of financial advancement and improved social status. By the 1850s, when the academy movement reached its zenith, more than 6000 such institutions, educating more than a quarter of a million American boys and girls, were reported to be in operation.

Three missions of academies, carried out through a multitude of courses, were training for 'life', preparation for college, and the development of vocational competencies. Many of the academies, female seminaries, literary institutes, or collegiate schools, as they were also called, stated their goals to be 'all things useful and all things ornamental', a term used by Benjamin Franklin in 1749. Translating the views of Milton and Locke to the American culture,

Franklin struck out against the Latin Grammar School in his 'Proposals Relating to the Education of Youth in Pennsylvania'. Calling for a realistic open-ended curriculum for students from a wide range of social backgrounds, Franklin endorsed the application of schooling to a rapidly changing culture. Specifically, he recommended the study of modern languages, history and geography, mathematics and science — and the practical application of learning to the improvement of agriculture, commerce, government, transportation and industry.[28]

Franklin's vision of an all-purpose school for a large slice of humanity was far ahead of its time; the Philadelphia College, Academy and Charitable School he helped establish in 1751 was quickly channelled by its board and administration toward a more traditional role, but Franklin's ideas concerning the education of youth, as well as his model for the self-advancement of working adults, began to yield significant benefits some hundred years later.[29]

### The Changing Mission of Private Academies

During the first half of the nineteenth century academies functioned as multi-purpose institutions, combining study of the Greek and Latin classics with general academic courses, and giving considerable attention to the development of vocational competencies — in such fields as bookkeeping, shorthand, agriculture, navigating, surveying and teacher preparation. Although preparation for college was one of the missions of these schools, it represented a relatively small proportion of the total program. In 1850, for example, when more than 15,000 students were enrolled in New York State academies, an extremely small proportion, approximately 135 a year, were reported to be entering the eight colleges of the state.[30]

In the twenty years between 1860 and 1880, a radical change took place in the avowed purpose of private academies. As the number of such schools dropped from more than 6000 to approximately 2000, the ambitious expansive and idealistic goal to be all things useful and all things ornamental was abandoned; by the 1880s the great majority of academies still in operation, together with recently established church-related and 'independent schools', focused their resources on college preparation.

An examination of data extracted from New York State Regents' Reports reveals that a sharp reduction in the number of courses offered by academies began during the Civil War years. By 1875 the number of course titles fell from more than one hundred to approximately thirty. With the exception of courses relating to commercial education, virtually all subjects with vocational characteristics were dropped at this time.[31]

Four factors contributed to this abandonment of practical subjects on the part of academies. These were the failure of academies to deliver quality programs in all subject areas; the rapid proliferation of new colleges which created a need for greatly expanded college preparatory programs; the emergence of specialized schools with professional or vocational goals; and the growing acceptance of the free public high school as the legitimate replacement for academies.

## Public High Schools in the Age of Academies

Although first established in New England in the 1820s, public high schools did not take a leading role in the delivery of secondary education until much later. In 1850 when the academy movement was at its peak high schools still constituted less than one-fifth of the secondary school enrollment; by 1875 the ascending curve of high school populations crossed the declining tally for academies. During the last twenty-five years of the century, as many of the older academies were replaced by high schools, a new group of college preparatory schools came into being, thus keeping the number of private schools at about the 1875 level of 2000. During this same period, as many states authorized tax money for secondary schooling, and the Kalamazoo Supreme Court Decision legitimized such action, the growth of public high schools was phenomenal.[32]

## How Public Schools Became College Preparatory Institutions

Although originally conceived as upward extensions of the common elementary schools, with instructional programs appropriate for all social groups, the public high schools of the late 1800s became identified with middle class respectability. The takeover of public high schools by elitist interests is seen by Robert Church as caused by the influence of middle class parents, who 'grasped the opportunity to differentiate their children from those of the poorer classes. While the common grammar school introduced the lowest classes to the dominant American values, the earliest high schools and other secondary training classes were filled by middle class children whose parents sought to advantage them in the pursuit of wealth.' Church stated further that 'through World War I high schools buttressed middle class children against lower class competition for clerical and white collar employment, and provided many with the skills and credentials to enter the expanding professions.'[33]

If ambitious parents were important contributors to the changing mission of high schools, so also were many of the leaders in the emerging American system of education. If not yet an 'establishment', the complex of college presidents, local school administrators, officers of the National Education Association, heads of state and regional teachers associations, representatives of new accreditation organizations, and administrative leaders of state and national offices were beginning to assert themselves as an interlocking web of special interests influencing formation of educational policy.

Within this new network of professional educators, the National Education Association played an especially important role in the development of a standard national high school curriculum. Beginning in the 1880s, the NEA sponsored a series of commissions, committees and study groups to analyze and make recommendations regarding the American system of education. Of many such activities, the work of the Committee of Ten was especially important. Established in 1892, the Committee was charged with the responsibility to investigate and recommend changes in both the college admissions structure, and the curriculum of the secondary school.[34] The appointment of the Committee of Ten came from a growing concern among college presidents as to what standards should apply to American colleges, and along with this question, what secondary school curriculum would be most appropriate for college preparation. As the rapid proliferation of American institutions offering the baccalaureate degree brought an extremely wide range of approaches to higher education, it is understandable that college presidents, then active members of the NEA, would attempt to establish uniform standards for students preparing for college admission.

Through a series of meetings with many sub-groups, the Committee of Ten, headed by Harvard University President Charles W. Eliot, arrived at a conclusion that a high school curriculum with four major areas of concentration — classics, Latin-scientific, modern languages, and English — would not only provide an adequate background for college admission, but would also best serve the non-college-bound high school student.[35]

The final report of the Committee of Ten had a great influence on the creation of a standard national curriculum for secondary education. Without question, it strengthened the ability of high schools to compete with academies in the preparation of students for college admission. Also, it identified college preparatory subjects as the legitimate foundation for all high school studies, thus relegating to a peripheral status such other courses as art, music, manual training, home economics and commercial subjects.

This action taken at a time when less than seven percent of American high school age youth were in high school, appears to be an example of benign arrogance, a tragic blunder that had a direct influence on the isolation, insulation and separation of non-college subjects. As noted by Grant Venn, 'the onrush of industrial and technological revolution in this country had, by the turn of the century, resolved the need for formal vocational training . . . . For many reasons, many institutions theoretically capable of providing this nation's youth with vocational training failed to do so.'[36] Venn went on to state that, since the educational community resisted the intrusion of vocational education, 'vocational education was pushed into the educational system; when it came in, it did so on its own terms.'[37]

## The American Vocational Movement

The American vocational movement has been described by Cremin as the confluence of several independent strands that ran parallel to one another for a number of years before they joined together at about 1910 in a concerted drive for federal legislation.[38] The major components of the vocational education movement, which had been slowly building since the 1870s, included:

- the longstanding concern of rural people for a greater degree of practical non-college schooling in agriculture and home economics;
- the manual training movement, which began as an enlightened approach to engineering technology, but by the early 1900s had been adopted by public schools as a form of pre-vocational shopwork;
- studies of industrial education needs, conducted in Massachusetts in 1905 and 1906, which led to the establishment of a state system of vocational education;
- formation in 1906 of the National Society for the Promotion of Industrial Education, a political action combination of commercial and industrial leaders, educators and social workers, and representatives of organized labor;
- following the lead of Massachusetts, the establishment of state systems of vocational education in Connecticut, New York, New Jersey, and other states;
- the appointment in 1914 of a National Commission on National Aid for Vocational Education, which led directly to the form and substance and final passage of the Smith–Hughes Act of 1917.

## Summary

This survey of practical education leads me to conclude that contemporary attitudes toward vocational education in the United States as reflected in popular literature, governmental policy and local delivery systems, are rather consistent with those of the past century, when the nation was emerging as a major industrial power. The comprehensive high schools and community colleges, those contemporary manifestations of multi-purpose education, have similarities to the private academy. Although academies never had the financial resources, large enrollments, or physical and faculty resources of today's high schools and two-year colleges, their efforts to provide a wide range of academic and applied courses, couched in a mission to prepare young people for 'life', cultural improvement and occupational competency are quite consistent with those of comprehensive high schools and community colleges. The failure of academies to be all things to all people deserves our attention today as we assess the present crisis in public schooling. Is it possible that schools for everyone, despite their admirable goals of providing optimum opportunities for the greatest number, are breaking down under the burden of diversity?

We also need to apply historical perspective to some of the pressing issues regarding vocational schooling — in particular its failure to reduce urban unemployment or produce a more productive workforce. To this end we need to compare the development of practical education in America with that of other industrial nations in terms of governmental commitment, social orientation of students, participation of industrial management and organized labor, and the role of the public school establishment in determining the purpose and posture of vocational classes. The American preoccupation with middle class schooling, together with the assignment of a social welfare mission to vocational classes, in settings typically removed from the workplace, may have compromised the true purpose of vocationalism. There may indeed be a need for significant changes in vocational schooling. But to change educational institutions without addressing the continuing conflict between management and labor, or the lack of a stable national policy on work and schooling, would yield little benefit, as the problems facing vocationalism transcend the province of public educators.

## Notes

1   D. RODGERS and D.B. TYACK, (1981) 'Research areas' in *Work, Youth and Schooling*, H. KANTOR and D.B. TYACK, (Eds)., Stanford, Stanford University Press, pp. 24–7. (1927) *American Journal of Education* 14, No. 2 May, pp. 42–74.
2   B. BAILYN, (1960) *Education in the Forming of American Society*, New York, Vision Books.
3   T.C. COCHRAN and W. MILLER, (1961) *The Age of Enterprise*, New York, Harper and Brothers.
4   C.A. BENNETT, (1926) *History of Manual and Industrial Education*, Peoria, Chas. A. Bennett Pub. Co., p. 276.
5   H. BARNARD, (1856) 'Family training and agricultural labor in reformation education', *American Journal of Education*, 1, 4, May, p. 609.
6   M.B. KATZ, (1968) *The Irony of Early School Reform*, Boston, Beacon Press, p. 186.
7   *Ibid.*, p. 204.
8   J.D. ANDERSON, (1981) 'The historical development of black vocational education' in KANTOR and TYACK, *Work, Youth and Schooling*, p. 185.
9   (1832) 'Munificent bequest for education', *American Annals of Education*, II, March, p. 129.
10  J.A. RIIS, (1892) *The Children of the Poor*, New York, Charles Scribner and Sons, p. 189.
11  *Ibid.*, p. 200.
12  *Ibid.*, p. 211.
13  L.S. HAWKINS, C.A. PROSSER, and J.C. WRIGHT, (1951) *Development of Vocational Education*, Chicago, American Technical Society, p. 33.
14  *Ibid.*, p. 34.
15  L.A. CREMIN, (1968) *The Transformation of the School*, New York, Vintage Books, p. 35.
16  (1895) *Education*, XV, April, p. 507.
17  (1896) *Education*, XVII, Sept, p. 58.
18  (1831) 'Rensselaer school at Troy,' *American Annals of Education*, I, July p. 308.
19  (1831) *American Annals of Education*, I, Oct. pp. 489.

20  R.F. Seybolt, (1935) *The Private Schools of Colonial Boston*, New York, 1969 reprint by Arno Press.

21  H. Kantor 'The economic and political context' in Kantor and Tyack, (Eds.), *Work, Youth, and Schooling*, p. 26.

22  L.A. Cremin, (1980) *American Education The National Experience 1783–1876*, New York, Random House, p. 338.

23  J.W. Hudson, (1851) *The History of Adult Education*, London, 1969 reprint by New York, A.M. Kelley.

24  C.A. Bennett, (1926) *History of Manual and Industrial Education*, Peoria, Charles A.Bennett Pub. Co., p. 319.

25  (1856) *Pennsylvania School Journal* V, July. As the house organ for the State Teachers' Association, the *Pennsylvania School Journal* gave considerable attention to county teachers' institutes.

26  (1837) *American Annals of Education* VII, May, p. 186.

27  C.A. Bennett, (1926) *History of Manual and Industrial Education*, Peoria, Charles A.Bennett Pub. Co., pp. 182–207.

28  T.R. Sizer (1964) *The Age of the Academies*, New York, Teachers' College, Columbia, pp. 1–48.

29.  *Ibid.*

30  G.F. Miller, (1922) *The Academy System of the State of New York*, Albany; 1969 reprint edition, by Arno Press and the New York Times. p. 59.

31  *Ibid.*, p. 109.

32  R.L. Church, (1976) *Education in the United States*, New York, The Free Press, p. 290.

33  *Ibid.*, p. 237.

34  National Education Association, (1893) *Report of the Committee on Secondary School Studies*, Washington, Government Printing Office.

35  *Ibid.*, p. 10.

36  G. Venn, (1964) *Man, Education and Work*, Washington: American Council on Education, p. 63.

37  *Ibid.*, p. 64.

38  Cremin, *Transformation of the School*, p. 50.

# Professional Education and Liberal Education: A False Dichotomy*

*David Riesman*

## I

In his guide to American colleges and universities, Edward Fiske, the Education editor of the *New York Times*, refers to Carnegie-Mellon University as 'the Switzerland of American universities.'[1] The analogy is apt if one thinks, not only of the several indigenous languages of Switzerland, but also of Switzerland as a small country which seems to do well those things in which it specializes. CMU, like Switzerland, also has managed to maintain financial soundness. I see the demand for excellence at CMU's professional schools as providing a kind of Alpine scenery in which performers must climb very high, CMU being one of the top schools of music, dramatic and fine arts to be found anywhere. Another Alpine range exists in the faculties of Engineering and Science, in Management and the Graduate School of Industrial Administration.

Perhaps a bit squeezed among the ranges is the College of Humanities and Social Sciences. At the graduate level, in addition to a distinguished program in cognitive psychology, there is an innovative one in applied history, which seeks to prepare individuals for non-academic careers, whether in the Foreign Service or other foreign programs, or in work for multinational corporations — indeed, wherever abilities for historical analysis and clarity in writing can be vocationally useful. The program in rhetoric gives a DA to people who are not going to become 'lit. crit.' faculty members, but who learn how to teach

* This chapter is an expanded version of an address given at Carnegie-Mellon University, 5 October 1981. For suggestions in preparing it, the author is indebted to Professors David and Lois Fowler, respectively of the departments of history and English in the College of Humanities and Social Science at Carnegie-Mellon University. For financial support, the author would like to acknowledge the assistance of the Institute for Educational Affairs, the Ford Foundation, and the Exxon Education Foundation.

sometimes semi-literate high school graduates to write lucidly and speak effectively. At the undergraduate level, the College of Humanities and Social Sciences provides a core program as well as elective courses for students in all the other schools (except in the case of the School of Fine Arts, where arrangements to mesh professional programs with the core program are still being worked out). As in any commandeered curriculum, courses in the core program have to be taught with exceptionally compelling power to turn the involuntary student into the highly motivated one, and this feat is accomplished with what to me is astonishing frequency. In the elective sections, where students in the professional schools have a choice among courses in the College of Humanities and Social Sciences, they bring to these courses the same motivation and elan they exhibit in their professional programs. The engineers, for example, act as if they are persuaded that they wish to become something more than technically proficient, and that an element of the 'something more' can be found in courses in history, sociology, or literature.

In terms of program, I can think of only one other American academic institution which is comparable and that is Cooper Union in New York City, focusing on engineering and science, architecture, and fine arts. Cooper Union is small and non-residential (having been set up as a tuition-free institution for the ambitious and hard-working poor). Here also many students commute, but CMU is much larger, internationally visible with a gratifying number of foreign students to help de-provincialize monolingual Americans, and with a residential student population large enough to sustain an active community, with a large number of cultural events, and an exciting intellectual life.

There are, of course, other institutions, in addition to Cooper Union, for example Pratt Institute, which concentrate on undergraduate professionalism both in science and engineering and in architecture and the arts, though in this and other instances at considerably lower levels of selectivity and distinction.

There is also one unique women's college that opened its doors a year earlier than did Carnegie Institute of Technology, as Carnegie-Mellon University was originally called. Simmons College in Boston, which departed from the locally prevailing conventions as to the proper education for young women and set itself up as a private urban institution to offer professional training to women, at the outset in the more traditional fields for working-class and lower-middle-class women, such as nursing, social work, other health related areas, and teaching. More recently, Simmons has developed undergraduate professional programs in banking, both for students right out of high school and for older women currently employed as tellers or bank clerks who wish to re-enter banking at management level, and also programs in corporate business.[2] Simmons College thus foreshadowed the later more massive shift of ambitious and educated young women who have been seeking, not *jobs,* which would sustain them until marriage or in case they had to become breadwinners, but more or less full-time *careers,* which might or might not be combined with marriage and having one or two children. Only in recent years has Chatham College, CMU's Pittsburgh neighbor which is also a women's college, moved away from its exclusively liberal arts orientation toward providing undergraduate professional training and internships for those undergraduate women who wish such opportunities, though as one might imagine it has not done so without resistance from traditional liberal arts devotees on the faculty and the Board of Trustees.

## II

In one respect CMU, despite its eminence in engineering, management, and applied science, shares problems with other less eminent institutions. *Science*, the journal of the American Association for the Advancement of Science (25 September 1981) has an article by John Walsh, 'Engineering education under stress,' indicating how in the engineering and computer science departments at Iowa State University there are not sufficient faculty members or laboratory facilities to respond to the enormously increased student demand.

Even at a relatively local school, such as Worcester Polytechnic Institute, students who graduate with a baccalaureate degree in one of the engineering or applied science specialties earn more their first year out than many of the junior faculty who have taught them, leading WPI to depend for graduate teaching assistants on foreign students from Turkey, Taiwan, and elsewhere, whose ability to communicate in English with the somewhat provincial WPI students is hardly spectacular. Inevitably, no university is going to be able to compete with industry. The very professionalism on which some CMU faculty justly pride themselves may lead them also to compare their situation, not with other academics who have chosen a vocation that was never intended to be highly lucrative, but with their peers in industry. Industry, as it is sometimes put, is eating its own seed corn when it recruits baccalaureate degree students rather than encouraging them to go on for the doctorate in order to be prepared to train a new generation of scientifically capable engineers.

## III

If CMU shares certain problems of all academic institutions which are concentrated in the expanding areas of student interest, its difference remains evident from what has become the characteristic private liberal arts college, either free-standing or the undergraduate segment of a great research university.

The student sub-cultures at CMU differ dramatically from those in the highly selective liberal arts colleges in that most CMU students see their baccalaureate degrees as terminal, while most students in the liberal arts colleges see the baccalaureate as simply a step toward further professional training, an ante-chamber to their own serious professional training. The divisions are not watertight; thus, a minority of undergraduates at colleges such as Harvard, Amherst, Swarthmore, Hopkins, or Chicago plan not only for a period of work after the baccalaureate prior to graduate school, but do not have graduate school plans at all. For example, some may enter journalism directly, without going to a graduate school of journalism; some may take their chances in the arts; some may try for jobs in business or put off their decision by joining the Peace Corps or working for some similar organization, or as a staff aide to a congressman or a congressional committee. Correspondingly, some CMU students will be going to medical school, PhD programs, or graduate programs in management or engineering. However, the general tone at CMU is set by the emphasis on professional training, which I define as work at the baccalaureate level which is sufficient to allow a graduating student in engineering, computer science, management, and related areas to go to work Monday,[3] and students in the College of Fine Arts to be ready for employment Monday, in fields often so chancy that 'Monday' may not come for a long time (despite the close connection between CMU's eminent program in dramatics with leading theater and repertory companies, and similar ties for its elegantly skilled musicians).

In contrast, the majority of students at Harvard College and similar colleges which have maintained their commitment to the liberal arts and sciences can be termed pre-professional, in the sense that college is the antechamber required by the prestige of medicine, law, and graduate programs in management and public policy, through which students must pass in order to become professionals at the post-baccalaureate level. They feel under pressure and are headed toward a narrow set of gates marked 'medical school,' 'law school,' 'school of business,' or 'public management.' Their eye is principally on grades, not on what they are supposed to be learning, some of which will be repeated later on in the professional schools.

To be sure, Harvard and other liberal arts colleges within major research universities continue to send a declining number of students into PhD programs, though in proportion to numbers, more students seek academic careers who graduate from independent liberal arts colleges where there are close faculty-student relationships, such as Swarthmore, Carleton, Oberlin, and Bryn Mawr. However, these students also are naturally highly grade conscious. (Reed College is an exception, which does not give grades, although it will prepare an appropriate transcript for graduate school, as will the two St. John's Colleges at Annapolis and Santa Fe.) But it is a self-serving mistake for professors, for example in the humanities, to see themselves as necessarily providing a liberal arts education as distinct from a disesteemed vocationalism. A musicologist or a philosopher who is seeking to recreate in his or her students a specialized professional scholar of his or her own 'school' and subspecialty, is in fact providing vocational training. The readings may be in principle emancipating, but they may be read in such a dehydrated way, with all the reductionist capabilities of which renowned scholars are capable, as to make the work of the undergraduate an exercise in tunnel vision.

I should make it clear that I do not criticize our Harvard undergraduates, and those in similar predominantly liberal arts colleges, for running scared before the uncertainties, occupational and global, of the future. Nevertheless, I am dismayed by their herd-like behavior. They lack any knowledge of demography, or of the ways in which the composition of the labor force is changing; hence, they do not realize that, by the time many of them have finished their graduate training, there will be job shortages in fields they have not entered, while there are already looming surpluses in many medical specialties, as well as in the law, and in some fields of management which our business school students now seek.

It is in my view unfortunate that many students at the Harvard Graduate School of Business Administration and at other similar schools are aiming to become general managers, moving on what they term the 'fast track' of consulting or via such specialized areas as finance or marketing, without reference to any particular product. Their analytic skills and the theories they carry away with them concerning organizational psychology and decision-making draw them away from any sense that they need hands-on experience with an actual product. Here again there is a contrast with the undergraduates at Carnegie–Mellon University who, as a matter of course, would be prepared to start in some actual production process, including new modes of production already with us in small measure and much in the air at CMU, such as robotics. (In my more gloomy moments, though I prefer business school cases in their intricacy and complexity over filtered appellate court cases which are the stuff of much legal training, I am inclined to believe that our business schools are one of the reasons for our inability to compete effectively with the Japanese or South Koreans who may send middle management executives to short-term executive programs at American business schools, but start their employees off after their baccalaureate degrees learning their way around a company in all its many different divisions by working at what Americans would consider lowly positions.)

**IV**

I see no inherent distinction between a liberating education in the traditional liberal arts and sciences and a liberating education in such professional fields as engineering, management, or applied art and music. However, faculty have an easier time teaching some subjects in a liberating way than others. In a field like anthropology, and in those parts of sociology and urban studies influenced by anthropology, there is an opportunity, lacking in other disciplines, to use an individual's, or several individuals', special gifts of observation of a certain group or ceremony or event, seen from many angles, and its possible interpretations, whether aesthetic, causal, or prophetic as one basis for teaching a subject.

From 1958, until my semi-retirement in 1976, I directed a course in Harvard's General Education Program on American Character and Social Structure. The course proceeded on two levels. On one, we read and discussed books about America ranging from Alexis de Tocqueville's remarkable ethnography of the United States during 1831, up to contemporary community studies. On another level, which I think might be considered professional at CMU, students were required to write a long term paper, the course's only formal requirement; a piece of original work, preferably field work which would provide them with at least a sample of what a certain kind of social research is like. Thus, students sometimes used their vacations in their home communities to study, through observation and interviews, small businesses, or the situation of teachers in the local high schools, or the ethnography of their own school, or workers in a small factory.

The problems I faced with students majoring in the natural sciences lay in persuading them at the outset that a judgment sample of a particular segment of life, reported on with as much objectivity and detailed observation as one could muster, was 'science,' even though its methodology differed from their ideology of what the natural sciences are like.[4]

I sought to train students to write up their observations fully, so that I could have access to the basis on which their interpretations were made, while they learned the difficult art of putting together in a paper observations of experiences with some assessment of what these may have meant for the participants, sometimes including the student researcher. Since outside of creative writing courses and some history courses, little writing is required of students at Harvard apart from our now required freshman course in expository writing, it was a surprise to students that I was going to judge their papers on the basis of their skills in exposition as well as their skills in discovery. I was told many times that I was not a professor of English but of sociology. I explained that to be able to describe what one has observed in clear language was an integral part of the requirement, as it would be for any professional presentation. Many students sought to protect their self-image as people capable of self-expression, even if they could not communicate in an organized written form. In response, I offered students the opportunity to turn in preliminary drafts of their papers which would be returned to them, with criticisms of substance and style, so that they could improve on the final draft.

To the degree to which I responded to student interests in what was a voluntary course, chosen among many other options in the General Education Program, I was not a teacher of would-be professionals, but of amateurs; since they lacked professional motivation, I needed to engage their interest if I was to make unaccustomed demands on them.[5] However, in another sense, the experience I was giving the students in writing these papers was that of doing a small-scale thesis, a preparation for a possible professional thesis for those going on to graduate school.[6]

## V

Among the natural scientists I have known, there are a number who are outstandingly capable of conducting a liberating professional education in their own fields. They teach students more than how to 'do' chemistry; they teach the epistemology and history of the natural science they are seeking to convey. But at a liberal arts college such as Harvard, they labor with the fact that there are many fewer students than there are at CMU who are prepared to accept the possibility that to be educated requires some grasp of technology, of demography, and of industrial organization.

To be sure, the largest single major among our undergraduates is economics. For the most part this is taught in an intramural way, heavily mathematical, focusing on aggregate data in macro-economics, and not looking at particular firms in micro-economics. Students of economics do not have much opportunity to link economic issues to broader philosophical questions, and entrepreneurial history is primarily taught at the Harvard Business School, a domain which Harvard College undergraduates rarely explore.[7] In contrast, engineering is taught as an applied field at Harvard, which does not have a regulation school of engineering, and students may be exposed, for example, to issues concerning workplace participation and democracy, changing definitions of the quality of working life, and the roles of unions and managements in response to new approaches in these areas.

Implicit in what I have said is a theme repeatedly emphasized by Herbert Simon in intramural discussions at Carnegie–Mellon University: that before engineers or economists can teach their subjects within a wider intellectual context, they themselves must become more broadly educated, maintaining not only the mastery of their subspecialties but transcending these in a continuous process of self-education along the arcs of their individual talents and institutional compatibilities. If faculty are working in fast-moving fields and are seeking to contribute scholarship in those fields, they cannot be expected fully to master other fields — not necessarily their neighbors in divisional organization — which have a bearing on their specialty. However, they can be expected to learn how to read the literature in these additional fields with the benefits of judgment they have already gained in their specialties.

I am saying something less obvious than that someone teaching genetics in a biology department may want to discuss with students the ethical dilemmas created by the discovery of the genetic code and recombinant DNA. Rather, I am saying that someone teaching genetics can do both a needed task of training in the appropriate skills and also find time to acquaint students with the interrelatedness of academic departments themselves, which makes it more difficult today than it was a few decades ago to separate physics from chemistry, or biology from either of these or from sociology.

## VI

It is hardly necessary to rehearse the deliquescence of much of our precollegiate education so that, even for students who score relatively well on the verbal SAT, it is not possible to assume either that they can write passable prose or that they have any basic cultural background. Their vocabularies and their personal libraries are often impoverished, irrespective of social class origins. The international comparisons are familiar: although there have been declines in the strict severity of the French lycée, the German gymnasium, and the British grammar school, and even the Japanese middle and high schools, their graduates are often at the academic level, even outside their specialized fields, of an American sophomore or junior at a reasonably selective college. It is perhaps not widely recognized that the sharpest drop has been in women's verbal scores, so that now for the first time (so far as I am aware) it is possible to find a number of colleges where men's verbal scores are somewhat, although not greatly, higher than those of women, while their quantitative scores remain forty points or so higher than those of women. To put it differently, girls in school have been brought down to the level of boys in their once traditional verbal facility, without being brought up to the level of boys in quantitative skills. As Martin Trow has studied in detail at Berkeley, selective institutions as well as those where there are either legal or *de facto* open admissions must devote immense resources to remedial work in quantitative skills as well as in basic literacy. But this compensatory education does little to repair the cultural *lacunae* of a population where, unlike Japan or Korea or Iceland or other west European countries book reading, especially among boys and young men, has never been a major sport.

When I taught from 1946 to 1958 at the University of Chicago, partly in the College and partly in the sociology department, the College had a core in which everyone took the same courses and had identical readings for the first two years, so that discussions after class, and in the student dormitories, revolved around a common set of intellectual concerns. Nothing could have been less professional in the CMU sense, and Chicago was and remains attractive to that small minority of students in the United States today who desire this intensity, irrespective of its eventual outcome for one's career. I should add that I was constantly at odds with much of the ideology of the program in which I taught at Chicago because (like Herbert Simon) I believed and still believe in sampling rather than in coverage, and was skeptical of any canon of Great Books as the sole staple for discourse. In fact, it led to a somewhat dehydrated, almost excessively cognitive, verbal–intellectual atmosphere.

Robert Hutchins believed that his ideas were carried out much more completely at St. John's College in Annapolis, with its branch in Santa Fe sharing the identical curriculum, including the Great Books. I recall on a visit to St. John's in Annapolis a number of years ago, sitting around with students in the basement coffee shop which was the center of the College's intellectual life, and asking a young man sitting next to me whether anyone ever painted a picture at the College. Quietly, one of them took me to his room and opened a closet filled with paintings — these had never come out of the closet since he painted them, in that atmosphere at once intellectually invigorating and at the same time oppressive.

In a way, St. John's College is more interesting for its expectations of and demands upon its faculty than upon its students. It stands at the very extreme of the American college in that it does not permit leeway for the individual interests of a faculty member, although a few of the more energetic ones pursue these extramurally. New recruits to the faculty go through a program of intense teacher training because they are each required to teach every course given in the College, in many of which, understandably, they will be neophytes and the students, in comparison, old hands. In the seminar discussing the selected Great Books, students and faculty are in a sense on an equal footing since all are learning from the same authorities, much as in a symphony orchestra the conductor and the concert master are simply the instruments of Bach and Bartok — all are subordinate to the score.

## VII

Not so long ago, engineering students came from the declining rural population, from the upper working class and the lower middle class. Engineering was something that parents who had not themselves attended college believed they understood, and their children were not mistaken to think that (except for ups and downs as in aerospace engineering) an engineering degree would provide them with a reasonably secure and well-paying occupational future.

However, as I look in a not too systematic way at the social origin of students at technical schools which are seeking to introduce a larger component of traditional liberal arts, such as Clarkson, Rochester Polytechnic Institute (RPI), Illinois Institute of Technology, and, over a much longer period, California Institute of Technology (Cal Tech), I have observed a rise in the social origins of engineers. Middle and upper middle-income families have encouraged their children to pursue a career for which a baccalaureate degree may suffice, thus reducing the demands on family income.[8]

I would like to return sometime to Georgia Institute of Technology which I visited over two decades ago, and talk to undergraduates in the various engineering programs. At the time of my visit, engineering students viewed others who had gone into the Industrial Management program as softies, studying supposedly easy subjects such as organizational psychology, rather than really tough topics such as fluid mechanics or the newly expanding fields of electronics.[9] As capable students from college-educated families see engineering as one of the few reasonably safe harbors in a chaotic and uncertain world, the position of engineers may become greatly altered and become on a par with that of engineers in Europe, and Latin America.

## VIII

As one wanders around the academic landscape, it is still possible to find students who are 'collegiate' in an older style, using fraternities and sororities not as an occasional safety valve *vis-à-vis* intense and generally internalized curricular pressures, but as the chief aim of one's college years. I have seen this in the sun-belt state colleges and universities, both predominantly black and predominantly white. And at some of the great state and land-grant universities, such as the University of Texas at Austin, and Pennsylvania State University, one can find both students who are working hard in the demanding curricula they have opted for, and very different types of students who assume, in the way that I believe President Reagan's own style of life (as distinguished from his hortatory rhetoric) would encourage, that, in America, one can be at once hedonistic, carefree, indifferent to the obdurate details of one's task, and rich. Even at CMU as recently as 1977, Herbert Simon found some students he termed 'sociables,' and one can find similar exceptions among undergraduates at such demanding colleges as Swarthmore, Amherst, Wesleyan, or Carleton. At my own institution, for the last decade I more commonly have seen undergraduates who have been as pre-professional as the great majority of professional students at CMU. I am speaking of both men and women; if anything, the women are more driven than the men. One can hear around Harvard College now the expression, 'science jocks,' as at MIT one can hear the phrase, 'engineering jocks,' a designation which is rich with symbolism, suggesting that, in an earlier day, only in sports did students fully extend themselves.

What differentiates the majority of our student body at Harvard from that of CMU is the lengthened trajectory of professionalism among the majority of our students, perhaps 80 per cent of whom are planning to go on for further post-baccalaureate education, with about one third of the class appearing to opt, on arrival, for medicine, and a third for law. On graduation, in the last several years, an increasing number of students have postponed for a year or two going on to post-baccalaureate study, wanting to be sure of their choice, or perhaps to try a second time for medical school or a top-flight national law school, although something close to 90 per cent declare that they will enter post-baccalaureate study eventually.

In contrast, at CMU a little over a quarter continue for further education. There, a baccalaureate degree provides a passport for the engineers and managers into top industrial and consulting corporations, and at least an embossed hunting license in fields such as architecture, or in the applied arts where prospects are chancy, as I have earlier indicated.[10]

Even though at Harvard College only about half of those who enter with the hope, perhaps parentally instilled, of medicine end up in medical school, the pre-meds help to create the climate in which other students work. In my judgment that climate makes Harvard a less than optimal college for students interested in pursuing careers in the natural sciences, except in fields such as astronomy or geology which are outside the set of calculations to secure top grades.

The competitive atmosphere among students at such colleges as Harvard who are spreading their energies among their courses as a cautious banker would, so as to secure the maximum return in honor grades, rather than considering the advantages a liberal arts college offers for exploring new areas of interest, tends to create a climate of guardedness among students. It is difficult to persuade students who are concerned with how their transcripts will look, knowing that many law and business schools (like Harvard's) do not encourage interviews,[11] to make use of what in the past has been one of the great virtues of the liberal arts college in contrast to the more vocationally oriented one: namely, the opportunity to fail at something or do less well than the top performers, either because one is trying out a field in which one is uncertain of one's talents, or taking a route on a term paper which may appeal neither to the definition of science nor of society held by one's likely readers; some students feel they cannot afford to make use of the pass/no credit option which was intended in part to encourage such experiments, because anything less than an A will reduce one's chances for *Phi Beta Kappa*.[12]

In this climate, students become guarded with each other. They develop an all-too-adult diffidence of specialists who hesitate to reveal areas of weakness *vis-à-vis* those who claim expertise in other areas. In a sense, this is no different from the position of the American public at large when faced with expert opinion, which it either accepts according to its own ideological and intellectual preferences and styles, or rejects out of hand in favor of an outlook which is not simply anti-scientist but intellectually Luddite, illustrated by reliance on astrology columns, plausible preachers, and politicians who dismiss all of science as mere opinion or as just another vested interest.

In every kind of academic institution, faculty members who care about their subject matter and wish to convey their enthusiasm for it to their students, can be wounded by those students who see them purely as gatekeepers to preferred post-baccalaureate opportunities. In a sense, all professors are service professors, whether they are teaching biochemistry to pre-meds or a core course in moral reasoning and analysis to students who would prefer to get on with their specialties and be done with requirements which they believe have no professional significance for them.

To avoid overspecialization and provide a general, if not always liberating, education, many liberal arts colleges set up distribution requirements. Harvard College has achieved a great deal of publicity for what it terms its Core Curriculum, publicity which may be useful in stimulating faculty action at those institutions which have followed a completely *laissez-faire* policy and abandoned requirements altogether. But the Harvard 'core' includes some one hundred courses, a number of them departmental courses altered in part by becoming a way of meeting the requirement for students not majoring in the area. The difficulty with all such efforts is that individual students can only by good luck share a particular course with roommate or friend as a topic of discussion carried over from the formal curriculum to the students' social life. As I have already suggested, students tend to be guarded *vis-à-vis* each other; and, coming from disparate fields, they often do not know enough about each other's areas of competence to converse seriously even if they wanted to. In a small liberal arts college of high selectivity and serious academic demands, perhaps especially colleges in non-metropolitan areas, students and faculty are thrown on each other's resources for company and the ethos is one of greater camaraderie, among faculty, among students, and between faculty and students. Students tend to be less afraid of each other's specializations, and readier to discuss topics in which they are not experts. They are not so afraid of being shown up as naive. Students' self-confidence tends to be somewhat higher (although this may change when they enter graduate or professional school and find themselves in a larger pool of talented and highly competitive fellow students).

This kind of still somewhat relaxed undergraduate education is a testimony at once to American affluence and American individualism. In university systems with more limited access, for example in the United Kingdom, students come to university already having spent the years of the Sixth Form in specialized preparation. If they then drop out, the British refer to the result as 'wastage,' rather than our more neutral term of 'attrition.'

However, it seems from my American perspective that this attitude of the British (and other systems that are more similar to the British than to our own) is unfortunate. To learn something about a subject, even if it does not become one's life work, is 'wastage' only if one is so desperate for the product that one cannot afford to pay attention to the process by which students who in statistical terms end up as wastage may have profited greatly, even from learning what it is that they do not like to do or cannot do.

In the American context, in the selective liberal arts colleges and university colleges (as in the Ivy League or Hopkins, Chicago, or Stanford), a number of students, despite their fears for the vocational future, lack professional commitment, having for example no firm career destinations. If these students change their majors, sometimes several times, as frequently happens, or drop out to finish their college educations elsewhere, as also frequently happens, I would not regard the result as 'wastage' in the British sense. Everything depends on the context. If the student believes himself or herself to be a failure, then 'wastage' becomes a self-confirming prophecy. If a student believes that he or she has had a fair chance, and has surrendered largely voluntarily, then one is simply adding to the market of those who, having had some education, are the best candidates for further and adult education.

Still, as Alexander Astin's studies demonstrate and as our own observation confirms in a less systematic way, residential colleges make a difference because of what students learn from each other. And it is here that fears to reveal areas of weakness outside one's specialty or even within it minimize the opportunity students have to learn from each other, that is, to be resources for each other's education.[13]

## IX

When one studies catalogues of liberal arts colleges, one finds many which emphasize that students will be exposed to multi-disciplinary perspectives.

But since they rarely find a single faculty member who has joined multi-disciplinary perspectives in his or her own mind, students seem to be asked to join together what the faculty has retained in separate compartments. To illustrate: Alan W. Howell, who teaches English at California Polytechnic State University at San Luis Obispo, is prepared to accept the utilitarian argument for undergraduate professionalism, but he goes on to insist that a general intellectual atmosphere is particularly essential in a polytechnic institution, in order, in his words, to free 'the minds of both students and faculty members of the disabling habit of compartmentalization.'[14]

There are of course many occasions where faculty members from adjoining disciplines jointly teach a course, but I have observed a number of these where faculty members take turns at expounding their own fields, but do not attend the lectures of their colleague or colleagues with whom they are supposedly giving a joint course. The Federated Learning Communities of the State University of New York at Stony Brook are a notable exception. In a program run by a professor of philosophy, Patrick Hill, faculty are drawn from their departments on an *ad hoc* basis: for example, a course on world hunger might be jointly taught by an anthropologist, a nutritionist or specialist on tropical public health, and a political scientist. The syllabus is jointly arranged; those giving the course listen to each other's lectures. A more novel arrangement is the provision of a mentor, a senior faculty person whose task it is to see to what extent the students are learning what the faculty members believe they are teaching, and to report back to the faculty so that self-corrective measures can be taken both among the students and among the professors. Since the faculty members are drawn only temporarily from their departments, they do not endanger their standing in their disciplines — a standing which, in some of the fastest-moving natural sciences, can attenuate in as short a time as two or three years.

Furthermore, most liberal arts colleges have honors programs which are usually college-wide, and offer students in large institutions an invaluable opportunity to meet each other and to discover that they are not alone in their intellectuality and academic interests. Honors programs often also arrange special courses or sections of large courses which can employ more sophisticated readings and modes of inquiry, and encourage freer discussion and more student writing because of the smaller classes. What is often the best opportunity is provided to a student by a senior research project or long essay which, given the proper climate, can enable a student to bring together perspectives from different disciplines.[15]

Two phenomena have joined in recent years to limit the scope of undergraduate opportunities, particularly in the social sciences, but also in other fields. On the one side are the students' vocational fears, which make individuals hesitate to take risks that might not prove acceptable to the faculty. Students' fears are heightened by attitudes found especially among younger faculty members, although there is no definitive chronological boundary here, who are often less broad in their own educations, and define appropriate work in their own department in terms of the subspecialty to which they cling in hopes of retention and promotion in hard times. Another limiting factor, notable in sociology, anthropology, and occasionally in history, political science, or even in English, are ideological preconceptions on the part of faculty, and the frequent exaggeration of these by the student grapevine. Thus there are some departments of sociology where students would hesitate to submit a senior essay that did or did not carry a deference to liberal-left preconceptions, whereas in some of the humanities one of the structuralist perspectives may either be anathema or unassailable dogma.

Nevertheless, given all these hazards, one's undergraduate years provide to those students brave enough to take advantage of them the opportunity to try things out and fail at them — failure either by their own or by faculty definition — with minimal penalties. As students often say, college is not 'the real world,' although the personal behavior of faculty and students *vis-à-vis* each other sometimes exhibits some of the less attractive features of that world.[16]

As the MIT Undergraduate Research Opportunities Program (UROP) illustrates, institutions that are primarily professional can also offer opportunities for relatively riskless undergraduate experiment. But it may be that the cultural backgrounds of their students, and the general atmosphere of professionalism among the faculty as well as the students, minimize actual use of such potentialities. In contrast, some liberal arts colleges encourage risk, as Reed College does by not reporting student grades but rather providing faculty comments on student work. To graduate, all Reed students must write a senior essay and pass a qualifying examination at the end of junior year before being permitted to proceed. (Students who quail before what are termed the 'Quals' are apt to transfer out of Reed — certainly not 'wastage' in the British sense, but transferring often to a state university where an equivalent amount of work will bring a virtually certain, if not always satisfying, 'A'.)

One might contend that a liberating education is one in which students attempt a number of things at which they have previously done badly, or not as well as in other things — that they have been willing to repair the *lacunae* as well as to build on the strengths of their previous records. And at best they have had some chance to do a small-scale piece of original work which, in fewer cases than would be desirable, can be published in professional journals along with their professors, or in the small number of undergraduate journals created to give visibility to the quality of undergraduate writing and scholarship.[17]

## X

I am not aware of any research that examines carefully the relationships among liberal education, professional education, and intelligent, non-spasmodic concern for social issues. Any such inquiry would have to hold other factors constant, such as the educational and socio-economic backgrounds of under-graduates in professional programs within liberal arts colleges, those in programs which are in primarily professionally oriented institutions such as CMU, and those in colleges with a long tradition of social concern which continue to attract such students (examples would be Swarthmore, Oberlin, Carleton, some of the outstanding women's colleges, and, in recent years, Wesleyan University).

I had direct experience of some of the problems of student self-confidence concerning their competence to deal with difficult technical issues as a result of bringing my principal civic interest, namely arms control, to extra-curricular activities I helped inaugurate at Harvard College. My own concern had begun with the indiscriminate mass bombings of German cities and the firebombing of Tokyo and Osaka, even before the first atomic bomb was, in my judgment, needlessly dropped on Hiroshima and the second one even more unjustifiably on Nagasaki. Toward the end of the 1950s, along with the historian Stuart Hughes, then at Harvard, I organized a group of graduate and undergraduate students who called themselves TOCSIN, in the sense of the word meaning a sounding of the alarm. In that day of wider job opportunities it proved possible to bring together for mutual enlightenment students in physics who knew something about radiation hazards and nuclear weapons, along with students in international relations who previously had closed themselves off from the natural sciences, much as the scientists had closed themselves off from examining, for example, the internal politics of the Soviet Union. The interest in a common problem made it possible for students to learn from each other and to break down the barriers of compartmentalization. For example, when a few students with limited training in science realized that an issue in achieving a test ban with the Soviet Union might depend on establishing that one could distinguish between earthquakes and underground nuclear tests, these students went off to Fordham University's seismic laboratories and learned enough about how earthquakes were registered on the Richter scale to give three of them the confidence to go to Geneva at their own expense to present their assessments in arms control negotiations then under way there.

Today I am skeptical as to whether or not it would be possible to organize such a group among Harvard undergraduates. This is not because, contrary to much that is commonly said, idealism has disappeared. It emerges whenever any issue of racism or sexism arises, and currently in what I regard as mistaken opposition to registration for the draft. But many things have obviously changed in the last quarter century. Scholarship in general has become more specialized, and faculty members also feel inadequate when it comes to areas outside their own specialties — areas that may endanger younger faculty from securing tenure if they do not adhere strictly to the themes considered central in their own departments, whether or not of any interest to a college-wide audience.[18]

Students, frightened of the occupational future, are unwilling to invest the time to investigate issues beyond their own undergraduate fields of specialization, being in this respect similar to young, untenured faculty. Moreover students share with other Americans a sense of incompetence in the face of highly specialized expertise. In some of the most superior academic institutions, they come to recognize that experts often differ so greatly among themselves that a certain passivity ensues: there is no point in even seeking to follow their convoluted trails. After what the students regard as a hard spell of work, an increasing number seek relief in heavy drinking and hard drugs, as well as recreational sex. Women students, who suffer, as various studies show, from greater stress both academically and in more general terms, have become almost as addicted as men students to alcohol and drugs.[19]

Students at Carnegie-Mellon University and at those other institutions that prepare undergraduates with a strong sense of professionalism in fields that are undeniably complex may be less afraid of venturing outside their professional bailiwick. They have a greater self-confidence concerning issues which appear arcane to those in liberal arts colleges who may regard themselves as humane because, as C.P. Snow pointed out long ago, they neither know nor care what the Second Law of Thermodynamics is about (thus perhaps contributing to global entropy!), and have focused their interests on the 'softer' social sciences and humanities.

At the Massachusetts Institute of Technology there is a tradition extending back to the end of the Second World War of an interest in applying technical and professional competence to issues of national and international survival and wellbeing. This has been true of successive presidents and other top administrators at MIT, of senior faculty and of graduate students and some undergraduates. There is a deep concern with the assessment of technology and not merely with its advancement. There has been a continuous preoccupation with the hazards posed by nuclear weapons, their vastly increasing numbers, the dangers of their proliferation, and the self-defeating nature (as Professor Kostas Tsipis of MIT's physics department has frequently observed) of efforts to make them more capable of more rapid deployment and launching, more accurate targeting, and the belief, despite Murphy's Law, that there can be developed an invincible and hence destabilizing arsenal. MIT nutritionists have been concerned with such matters as overuse of pesticides both in developing and technologically advanced countries, with the destruction of rain forests in Brazil and South East Asia, and, along with scientists at Harvard and Tufts and other New England and Canadian institutions, with acid rain and its long-term consequences. A number of these individuals, as is true also at the California Institute of Technology, Cornell, and the University of California at San Diego, have moved back and forth between government and governmental advisory commissions and their universities. In this atmosphere, professional competence in one's scientific area encourages undergraduates and graduates to develop focused, technically sophisticated concern for social issues. The sense of professional competence, it would seem, is transferable to the larger political arena.

I know that some individuals on the faculty at CMU share these concerns, and I talked to a few students who were also involved. But I have the impression that at CMU as at RPI or other 'tech' institutions, there is not sufficient 'critical mass' (in both senses of the term 'critical') to engender a sizable undergraduate concern which can build on the sense of professional competence cultivated by the CMU curriculum and the high degree of motivation students bring to that curriculum.

## XI

I would like to step back now from particular university settings and raise a broader and more inchoate question concerning the bases on which American universities and those who inhabit them justify involvement in larger social concerns, going beyond the question of competence to the question of the sense of legitimacy. In the 1960s, with increasing vehemence and even violence towards the end, students and a number of faculty in leading liberal arts colleges and universities protested in the first place against violation of civil rights for blacks and then against the Vietnam war. Although in the early years of both these movements there were thoughtful and informed leaders both among faculty and students, by 1965, when the first so-called teach-in was held at the University of Michigan, a concern for scholarly knowledge was rejected in favor of what was often a mindless activism; expertise indeed was often seen as the liberal enemy of the increasingly revolutionary Left. Teach-ins belied their name; they were forums for mobilization, sometimes for camaraderie as well. Although occasionally experts on South East Asia were initiators of teach-ins, as at Michigan, it was not their knowledge that was drawn upon, their awareness of the complexities of South Vietnamese society, culture, and politics, but their passion and indignation at American governmental policy. For undergraduates and graduate students alike, the draft was sometimes a sufficient motivating factor for opposition to the war, and paradoxically against the universities which, in the earlier years, sheltered most of them from the draft. In the civil rights movement, students and some faculty put aside any knowledge of historical and social-class differences in background and experience, wanting to identify with those they defined as oppressed, whether the latter were prepared for such mutuality or not — it later became evident that many were not. Similarly, because American policies were regarded as evil, students and faculty anti-war activists, both seeing themselves as anti-elitist, were so certain of their moral righteousness that they offended many, particularly women, who were also opposed to the war and who did not want to be identified with the counter-cultural and anti-American tactics of the visible and flamboyant leaders of the anti-war movement. In those years students talked frequently about mobilizing what they referred to as the working class, and refused to consider — as I know from many arguments and discussions — the possibility that they should listen to what working-class people were actually saying before they started to preach to them what they thought were the obvious moral horrors of the war.

In large part, those days are behind us.[20] But the harm done to the universities as centers of disinterested inquiry remains, and was evident in the long-delayed counter-attack by the Radical Right which provided part of the support for the election of Ronald Reagan as President.

## XII

Computers and machines are beginning to have their place in the teaching of more and more subjects, and some faculty are likely to worry about their use and possible narrowing effects. However, the machines that most endanger our teaching and learning today are not personal computers, but machines involved in television, in long-distance direct dialing, in the jet plane; these latter minimize the need for letter writing, as does the automobile, in linking friends and families without written communication, and absorbing, like television, immense amounts of time and fantasy among adolescents (and of course adults also). And one could think of second-order effects, such as the emphasis that we place on summer jobs even when there is no dire financial necessity for them, partly because it is the thing to do and partly because youngsters want money to buy machines such as stereo sets, computers, and cars.

All this leads to our asking, as Peter Stearns does in 'Impacts of Mechanization' (in an issue of *Focus*, a bimonthly journal published by Carnegie-Mellon faculty as a continuing dialogue about educational and cultural issues), whether a student today possesses skills equal to those of the previous generation. At Harvard, the students I see do not achieve up to the level of the parental generation, certainly if one holds amount of education and social class fairly constant. However, Stearns says, speaking of robotics, that the work students are committed to do at a professional level today may be made obsolete by the kinds of technological changes CMU itself is helping pioneer; and professors may not be able to re-train or may not have the resources or time to devote to adult education that will be needed. Young people of varying ages do not understand what is happening to them, let alone possess the consolations of literature or philosophy or art (though they are likely to have the consolations of listening to music and even of making music).

## XIII

In the student newspaper at CMU, Professor Richard L. Schoenwald has a brief comment concerning a topic that has long troubled me in the most *avant garde* institutions.[21] He remarks that he was saddened to hear cries of 'weirdo!'

and 'we don't need any weirdos here!' slung at two young bearers of signboards with Christian messages. 'It is clear that one subject we do not teach enough about is tolerance.' I should say that this is my experience at my own institution and at most of the highly selective cosmopolitan universities. I sometimes speak of the attitude as the 'tyranny of the enlightened.' It is likely that such evangelical students come from Protestant sectarian denominations. What matters to them is the social cement that, through liturgy and mutual commitment, ties genuinely devout people together in a community that appears more secularized than in fact it is. I wonder whether I need to remind readers that the United States is much the most religious of any of the major industrial societies. These devout students would regard a life of professional self-advancement, with a flavoring of social conscience thrown in, as not the kind of life they value. It is by symbols as small as this that the provincialism of strenuous pre-professional education is illustrated. The 'real world,' concerning which students like to talk, and to which they in some aspects are introduced when they make use of internship possibilities, is all around them among their fellow students, if peer pressure did not repress the actual differences among students who do not overtly appear different either in terms of color or conduct, but whose inner life may contrast sharply with that which is regarded as the student, and often also as the faculty, norm.


## XIV

Students', and indeed, common public thinking about careers has an inevitable lag built into it, similar to what farmers would recognize as the corn-hog cycle, or what Richard Freeman terms the cobweb cycle, which means that by the time someone has graduated in a field that now looks promising, the situation may be very different indeed.[22] Even now, this country has too many doctors, although poorly distributed in terms of geography and specialty. It has such an oversupply of lawyers that students of Japanese society, where there are hardly any lawyers and few issues are litigated in an adversarial milieu, believe that American productivity suffers not only from inflation and other obvious hazards, but also from our increasingly litigious climate and what I have sometimes referred to as our imperial judiciary.

However, the notion I hear frequently among my own students that there are 'no jobs' in academic life is a vast over-aggregation, and, as such, quite false. The ablest students are not entering PhD programs in fields for which, at the moment, there appears no immediate market. President Richard Cyert of CMU would probably agree that there is a comparable deficit of capable academic administrators who have had a thorough scholarly training, as well as having learned something about problems of management and decision-making.[23] One is unlikely to find students in schools of management (as compared to graduate schools of education) planning careers in educational administration, although some newly developed schools of public policy do concentrate on management in non-profit sectors of society. In any event, the chances are that the undergraduates in college at the moment will, if we avoid a nuclear catastrophe, achieve or endure great longevity. No doubt there will be corresponding shifts in the demand for capable people who can think of their careers as a series of choice-points on a decision tree with many branches, some branches not yet sprouted. While the future of the economy looks bleak for the unskilled and uncredentialed, I am inclined to think that, understandable as is student fear of the vocational future, it is somewhat excessive, and that a capacity to read difficult material and to write exemplary prose (as well as to present it orally) will not be rendered obsolete by computers or robotics.

A liberating education which broadens horizons and enhances curiosity can provide students both in programs termed vocational and those in the traditional liberal arts with the ability to cope with unforeseen and indeed unforeseeable change; all we can say with confidence about the future is that it will surprise us.

### Notes

1 There is a full but considerably less sympathetic account of Carnegie-Mellon University (CMU) in the *Insider's Guide to the Colleges, 1981–82*, edited by the staff of the *Yale Daily News*, (1981) New York, Perigee Books (G.P. Putnam's Sons) pp. 97–100, emphasizing differences in the quality of instruction in the various schools and within otherwise outstanding departments.

2 For a fuller but slightly dated discussion, see D. RIESMAN, (1979) 'A conversation with Simmons College' (1974), *Journal of General Education* 31, no. 2, Summer, pp. 79–108.

3 Whereas the standard *Comparative Guide to American Colleges* by J. CASS and M. BIRNBAUM, (1981) New York, Harper and Row, 10th edition, reports that 22 per cent of graduates from CMU pursue full-time post-baccalaureate study after graduation (2 per cent going on to medical school and 2 per cent to law school), while 75 per cent of graduates go to work immediately, another college guide, J. McCLINTOCK, (1982) *100 Top Colleges: How to Choose and Get In*, New York, John Wiley, p. 50, reports that 42 per cent plan immediate graduate study and 25 per cent declare that they will undertake some graduate study later. This latter figure, while probably high, may reflect the increasing proportion of upper-middle class students attracted to CMU's science, management, and engineering programs with an eye to attending medical or business school. To the extent that this is the case, CMU will become less professional at the undergraduate level and more like other selective liberal arts colleges, the great majority of whose students plan to go to graduate and professional school either directly on graduation or after a year or two of identity-search, relief from school, consolidation of plans, and, increasingly, taking temporary positions to make money to pay for further education.

4 In some instances, it was easier to persuade students majoring in astronomy or geology, for instance, to take an experimental attitude toward 'science' than to work with students majoring, for example, in sociology or economics, whose determination to follow what they believed to be the natural science model and to

show that they, too, were 'hard' and rigorous scientists, was less experimental and open.

5   There is a difference in the degree of professional motivation at CMU between the required core courses which everyone must take and where some students regard themselves as a captive audience prepared to put out some effort but not fully to extend themselves, and the elective courses (chosen to fulfill the humanities and social sciences requirement) where students can be guided by the grapevine toward more evocative teachers, and by their own interest in particular topics. When one considers these students, it becomes evident that there is no absolute or sharp line between professional and amateur undergraduate education — what makes a difference is whether one pursues subjects which attract one as an amateur with the purposiveness and involvement of the professional.

6   Students in the social sciences who took the course prior to their senior years were encouraged to see their term papers as prolegomena to potential senior essays in their respective departments, and many made use of them in this fashion. Some even carried the topic into graduate school with them as one basis on which to build an eventual dissertation.

7   See A.O. HIRSCHMAN, (1977) *The Passions and the Interests: Political Arguments for Capitalism Before Its Time*, Princeton, Princeton University Press; HIRSCHMAN, (1982) *Shifting Involvements: Private Interest and Public Action*, Princeton, Princeton University Press, and HIRSCHMAN, (1967) *Development Projects Observed*, Washington, DC, Brookings Institution; and D. LANDES, (1969) *The Unbound Prometheus: Technological Change and Industrial Development in Western Europe from 1750 to the Present*, Cambridge, Cambridge University Press.

8   It is still rare to find a student of upper or upper-middle class background from a private residential preparatory school attending an engineering school or any institution as professionally oriented as CMU.

9   A sociologist friend who has been teaching at Georgia Tech has recently written me that it is basically unchanged. The engineers are the real 'macho' types, the Green Berets of the academic contest, while those in the less demanding fields are more like civilians sitting behind comfortable desks. I had said to the Georgia Tech students that they would find themselves working for the people who had gone into the management option, and as already suggested by my reference to business schools, this is probably even more the case today than it was in 1960. Indeed, except for the most highly talented and specialized engineers at the frontiers of research and development, engineering has not quite achieved the status of an autonomous profession; no matter how highly paid they may be, engineers remain employees.

10  However, administrators of relatively unselective colleges have often been surprised to find how great is the interest of perhaps 5–7 per cent of their students in majoring in the arts when the bulk of the student body is crowded into career programs in business and management (including accounting), health technologies and services, a still sizable number in education and social work, and criminal justice. Even in a time of retrenchment, these colleges have been under pressure to expand their offerings and facilities available for the arts. Many factors are involved in these risky choices, including the glamor purveyed by television and other mass media. But I think that one neglected element is that there are virtually no 'boondocks' left in the United States: there is hardly a sizable town which does not have a little theater, a chamber music group or even a local amateur

symphony, and an art gallery which sometimes hosts visits from *avant garde* artists.

11 The refusal to place much reliance on interviews may in fact be a wise one. My own observation of admissions practices has been that faculty as well as admissions personnel, alumni and alumnae, can be gullible and at the same time insensitive interviewers, whose judgments distort the admissions process. An experienced interviewer can add something to a judgment based exclusively on test scores; a less equipped interviewer will in many cases prove a less reliable guide. *Cf.* my discussion (1980) of the vocal critics of the Educational Testing Service in *On Higher Education*, San Francisco, Jossey–Bass, pp. 123–36.

12 In making such judgments, undergraduates often exhibit the kind of mild paranoia that is endemic among graduate students and untenured faculty concerning what routes will provide them with security.

13 See, for example, A. ASTIN, (1977) *Four Critical Years: Effects of College on Beliefs, Attitudes, and Knowledge*, San Francisco: Jossey–Bass.

14 See A.W. HOWELL, (1981) 'The Polytechnics' dangerous way of apportioning the student mind,' *Chronicle of Higher Education*, XXIII, no. 3, 16, September p. 56.

15 Marlboro College, a tiny (200 student) liberal arts college in south-eastern Vermont, provides a two-year plan for upper-division students in which an essay or other project is the culmination of two years' work with one or more faculty members. The Massachusetts Institute of Technology, through its Undergraduate Research Opportunities Program (UROP), offers students the opportunity to work on a research project of a senior faculty member at any point when arrangements can be worked out. Of course, a great many colleges and universities, public as well as private, offer comparable opportunities to the pertinacious student — or at least they claim to do so in their catalogues.

16 See A. CHASE, (1980) *Group Memory*, Boston, Little Brown/Atlantic Monthly Press.

17 The *Reed College Journal of the Social Sciences* existed for a time under the leadership of Professor John Rock of the sociology department. Recently, the *Pittsburgh University Undergraduate Review* has been started as a forum for undergraduate work. A number of more or less fugitive journals of the same sort have been started at Harvard College, including in an earlier day the *Adams House Journal of the Social Science* and currently the *Harvard Political Review*.

18 See the contribution by D. CAMPBELL, (1979–80) to a symposium in the *Syracuse Scholar* 6, no. 1, p. 208.

19 For discussion of student stress, especially among women undergraduates, in selected colleges, see the report to be published by the Medical Foundation of a conference held at Harvard in January 1983 of deans of students, student health service personnel, psychiatrists and psychologists. One of the predisposing sources of student stress emphasized at the conference was the consequence of the increasing divorce rate, which affects not only students whose parents have been divorced or are on the edge of divorce, but students from intact families who are anxious about the precariousness of their parents' family ties. This source of insecurity was rare in previous student generations.

20 These lines were written prior to episodes in which Jeane Kirkpatrick, then United States Ambassador to the United Nations, invited to give two lectures at Berkeley, found that the first lecture was so continuously interrupted from the floor that she halted, and the hall had to be cleared of non-students before she could continue, and her second lecture was canceled because the University could not guarantee an

adequate measure of security from disruption. Similarly, Smith College was forced to cancel an invitation to Kirkpatrick to speak at Commencement in 1983 on similar grounds. I suspect that we have few such incidents because of the cautious and conciliatory attitude of the great majority of college administrators today.

21  See the *Tartan* 81, no. 24, 28 April 1981.
22  See R. Freeman (1976) *The Overeducated American*, New York, Academic Press.
23  See, for example, R. Cyert, (1980) 'Managing universities in the 1980s,' in *Leadership in the 1980's*, Cambridge, MA, Institute for Educational Management, Harvard University, pp. 39–66.

# Higher Education in an Urban Context[1]

*Henry R. Winkler*

The twentieth century has been the century of the city. In 1850, as Alvin Toffler has observed, there were only four cities on the whole earth with a population in excess of one million. One hundred years later, there were 141 such cities. We have changed from a rural, agrarian society to an urban one. Only a little more than one hundred years ago, 85 per cent of the people in the United States lived on farms. Today, 85 per cent live in cities.

This shift to an urban basis has radically changed the character of American society and has brought with it a variety of problems: crime, poverty, racial tension, decreasing tax bases, substandard housing, deteriorating transportation systems, inadequate educational programs, the catalogue seems endless. How to deal with issues such as these has increasingly absorbed the attention of politicians and public alike. However, these problems must be addressed as well by the urban universities of our nation. Failure to do so could have as devastating effect on the future of our cities as on the future of higher education in the United States.

It is vital to examine what the urban universities are well equipped to do — and what they are not. In 1972, the Carnegie Commission defined the urban university as 'an institution that takes its responsibility to urban society in general and to its own urban locale in particular as a dominant force in determining institutional objectives and allocating institutional funds.'[2] The definition is so elastic as to encompass almost any university which chooses to label itself urban. Title XI of the Higher Education Act of 1980 offers a more stringent and useful definition:

> 'Urban university' means an institution of higher education which (A) is located in an urban area, (B) draws a substantial portion of its undergraduate students from the urban area in which it is located or contiguous urban areas, (C) carries out programs to make post-secondary education opportunities more accessible to residents of such urban areas or contiguous areas, (D) has the present capacity to provide resources responsive to the needs and priorities of such urban

area and contiguous areas, (E) offers a range of professional or graduate programs sufficient to sustain its capacity to provide such resources, and (F) has demonstrated and sustained a sense of responsibility to such urban area and contiguous areas and its people.[3]

The focus here on present capacity and demonstrated commitment limits the definition of the urban university and enables us to go beyond the customary bromides of too many public pronouncements.

The heterogeneity of the student body is a distinguishing characteristic of the urban university. In every classroom there are likely to be students who represent a variety of racial, ethnic, socio-economic and age groups, who bring a variety of perspectives and experiences to the educational process and who need an education that recognizes and addresses these differences.

The heterogeneity of the student body reflects the heterogeneity of the community around the university. Unlike the students of a traditional residential university who come from diverse geographical locations and are insulated from the local community the students at an urban university live at home and are members of the local community. Most of them work, often for long hours, and some are rarely on campus except for classes. Urban university faculty must devise programs to balance the fragmented nature of their studies.

The concept of an urban university grew out of these differences and the need to develop programs to address them. At first, the urban university was modeled after the land-grant college. In 1958, at the meeting of the Association of Urban Universities, Paul Ylvisaker proposed that the land-grant college principle be applied to urban universities and that federal assistance be made available for those universities to meet their responsibilities to the urban communities of which they were an integral part.

Between 1959 and 1966, the Ford Foundation made approximately four and one-half million dollars available to a handful of universities and to some non-academic institutions, to carry out experiments in applying university resources to the problems of urban America. It seems to me that the results of the extension experiment, whatever they may have appeared at the time to be, were not encouraging, although they did lead to the inclusion of Title 1, which provides some support for community services and for continuing education, as part of the Higher Education Act of 1965.

The present concern with the urban university commenced as a direct result of social unrest in the cities during the sixties. Writers on the subject began to envision the university as an agent — sometimes almost the only agent — for social change, primarily through the education of previously underserved populations. As early as 1965, J. Martin Klotsche described the urban university as located in a city *and* dedicated to the education of primarily working class students. Klotsche identified the now familiar hallmarks of the urban university — its concentration on urban related research, its obligation to function as a responsible neighbor, its mix of the student body (which has subsequently and regrettably disappeared from discussion of this subject) and its responsibility to foster the creative and performing arts. Klotsche also included a caution which has been too frequently overlooked in the last fifteen years:

> The urban university must not . . . become so committed to the affairs of the city that the purposes for which it exists will be compromised. There is always the danger that a university can become too immersed in the problems of its community. It would indeed be fatal to its historical mission were problem solving and local politics to become its primary goals. Implied in the term 'urban university' is a quality of cosmopolitanism and sophistication that makes it a part of the city while it remains apart from it.[4]

Then in 1968, Clark Kerr expanded upon the urban concept. While he still focused on the need to resolve urban problems, he also emphasized the need to educate those who were previously excluded by American higher education. Cities are inhabited, to a large extent, by American people who have migrated from rural areas, Appalachians, Blacks, Puerto Ricans, Chicanos, and other minorities, and he argued that equal access, therefore, to higher education on the part of all of these urban residents was equally important as solving urban problems.

Given the composition of our cities, access remains a crucial issue. It reflects the evolution of what Arnold Grobman, chancellor of the University of Missouri at Saint Louis, terms the 'three guiding philosophies about study at American colleges and universities.' Grobman points out that at first our colleges and universities were considered aristocratic institutions serving primarily the children of wealthy families. With the expansion of public higher education and the development of various standardized achievement tests we entered a period which he labels a 'meritocracy,' in which the goals seemed to be to make a college education available to those who were prepared to profit from the experience. This was followed by a third stage of egalitarianism, with the goal that everyone should have an opportunity to attend college, regardless of prior preparation.[5]

While urban universities have responded to the egalitarian principle, recent actions on the part of the federal government, and indeed on the part of a number of state governments, indicate that these groups may be unconcerned, or perhaps even opposed, to the strides that have been made in the area of equal access to higher education. They have assumed a private sector model for financing the university that simply does not fit the urban institution. Whatever the tortured comparisons in some of the literature, universities do not provide a service that can easily be fitted into industrial analogues of efficiency. The reduction in real dollars of federal and state funds for higher education and the expectation that individual students bear a larger share of the cost of their education threaten gains that have been made. They may ultimately signal a return to the days when colleges and universities were only for the children of the rich. Such a development would be disastrous, not only for our institutions of higher learning, but for our entire society.

Most of what I have written so far has focused on the relationship between the urban university and students it serves. There is another equally important relationship that needs to be discussed. That is the relationship between the university and the city in which it is located. As part of its service function, the urban university needs to be involved in programs or services within its field of expertise which are requested of it, or which are negotiated between it and the local governments, or by various of the businesses and other groups in the metropolitan area. There is one important *caveat* that I would issue in regard to this relationship. The urban university must not duplicate services that put it in competition with state or local governments.

The Carnegie Commission's report of 1972, entitled *The Campus and the City*, remains probably the most influential publication in molding the programs of the seventies and eighties and outlines the general shape of many of my own University's efforts. While delineating the potential of the university's impact on the city, the authors conscientiously point out some inherent limitations, arguing that service must relate to teaching and/or research, that the university should not attempt to do what other institutions can do better, and that it must be wary of political and economic vested interests. By the middle and later seventies, the programs generated by the publication of *The Campus and the City* had demonstrated pragmatically that universities could indeed interact with their urban milieux for the profit of both, but they had also revealed the existence of problems previously unforeseen. A facile and simplistic identification of 'urban problems' with 'black problems' surfaced in the less thoughtful programs, while the temptation to do too much and thus dissipate limited resources in a patchwork approach was pervasive and probably remains so. Thomas Murphy and M. Gordon Seyffert pinpointed a fundamental problem of faculty resistance to urban programs and the concomitant lack of academic and budgetary support for them. The failure to perceive an inherent conflict between faculty values (theoretical and applied research) and community needs (immediate services) created disappointments and unmet expectations. Murphy and Seyffert suggested enlarging or reforming the outdated faculty rewards system to include urban projects.[6]

Clark Kerr, foreseeing the potential for disputes over faculty values and community needs, offered a caution designed to minimize them:

> When you deal with urban problems, you deal with urban controversies and with urban politics. And so, for this university to work effectively, there will have to be a considerable amount of public understanding — especially understanding of the distinction between service based on applications of knowledge and positions taken because of partisan politics.[7]

The academic community must be especially sensitive to that understanding, also, if objective inquiry and the university's traditional role as social critic are not to be compromised.

What urban universities are well equipped to do is to assist local governments in attempting to resolve urban problems. They could conduct research on problems and issues faced by their metropolitan area. They could provide advice to cities, and continuing education for personnel in the various local governments. They could use cities for intern and experimental purposes where needed.

What urban universities are not well equipped to do is to be in the business of providing or delivering services directly to the public, other than those related to the provision of higher education within the context of the particular institution's teaching and research goals. As with any general rule, there are exceptions, such as the delivery of health care services by universities that operate medical centers.

This is not to say that such cooperation is a natural state for either of the parties involved. Peter Szanton, the author of *Not Well Advised*, a recent book on the relationship between universities and cities, cites several areas of friction that can exist between the two entities, including the following:

* professors seek answers that are true and general, city officials need answers that will work;
* scholars work on long-term projects, government officials need quick answers; and
* scholars focus on the internal logic of a problem, politicians focus on the external logic, that is, the problem's political and bureaucratic ramification.[8]

Although these are overgeneralizations, there is at least enough truth in each of these observations to demonstrate why the potential exists for conflicts to develop between the university and the city.

There is another element in all of this. The emphasis on meeting the needs of an urban area, often to the exclusion of research, has caused some urban universities to be considered less important or prestigious than many of the traditional universities. Ironically, this bias is sometimes shared by the very people the urban university is serving.

Despite these difficulties, the urban institution must consider its urban-related activities to be an equally important part of its performance with those traditional areas of teaching and research with which all of us are familiar and to which we are committed. Nevertheless, certain warning flags must be raised. After fifteen years of practice, universities are becoming aware of the limits of effective action in pursuit of the urban mission. The land-grant analogy, first promulgated in 1958, is seriously misleading. Social scientists' impact on cities does not at present equal the agronomists' impact on agriculture since passage of the Morrill Act, and the problems of the cities appear to be more complicated than those of the countryside. Universities

THROUGH TRUTH TO FREEDOM

AUGSBURG COLLEGE 1869

**BOARD OF REGENTS**

Ryan Caldwell

v Pol. Sci. faculty

have also learned that they cannot, nor should they try to, replicate the work of social service agencies.

In order to enlist new reserves of intellectual and creative power, then, the urban mission must be redefined, partially expanded and partially contracted. And to do this, that is to work toward a reconceptualization of the urban mission, it is imperative to dismiss once and for all the false dichotomy between the liberal area and professional/vocational education. For it is within the urban institution that the dichotomy — the differences — are being and must continue to be eliminated. In the largest sense, the purpose of this chapter is to discuss the ways in which the urban university can redirect or redefine the interaction of theory and its application to the community, while continuing to emphasize the limits of such an approach.

What I want to argue here is that the very location of an institution squarely in an urban environment inevitably will have a profound effect on its character. To be sure, each of us has his or her own Platonic ideal of a university. It may be Cardinal Newman's, it may be Clark Kerr's, it may even be Oral Roberts'. But whatever the ideal, the very physical location of an institution in the urban area — at the center of society's most intractable problems — has drawn even liberal arts faculty into attitudes which cause them to interact with their environment rather than to observe it — or if the latter, to observe it very differently. The study of economics in the shadow of the slums elicits insights and understandings very hard to come by in even the most brilliant of chaste pages of academic analysis. The response to a novel by Saul Bellow will be substantially influenced by the student's own experience of the metropolis, whether it be Bellow's Chicago or any other such city. Urban institutions can and should, then, capitalize on their location where that is appropriate for the teaching of all subjects and not simply those in the conventional 'applied' areas.

Urban-related instructional programs at city-based institutions share a fundamental asset: metropolitan areas offer a superb laboratory applicable to courses in many fields — planning, architecture, economics, transportation, engineering, history, linguistics, geography, sociology; the inventory can go on and on. Even the list I have used here is composed of some fields customarily labelled 'liberal studies,' others 'vocational or professional.' My point is that the dichotomy is often a false one. Whatever the rubric, the manner in which learning takes place is equally important with the matter itself.

The city as laboratory should be employed but not exploited. Instructors must not confuse teaching with 'service' and must not claim, either to themselves or to others, that students can offer professional expertise. To do so is to raise expectations that will not be fulfilled and to sully the image of the university in the process. Student internships in social service agencies, for example, are designed to benefit the students; and student planning projects, while they may offer incidental benefits to the communities under study, are academic exercises. To pretend otherwise, to label these as 'service' activities, is to engage in deception. Educating is what a university does best; we should take pride in our instruction and not seek to make it do double duty as service. The opportunity to shape public policy by educating the city's future professionals is central to the urban mission. It can be further enhanced by the development of interdisciplinary and intercollege degree programs, such as planning-law programs, certificates in historic preservation, engineering-business options. Because urban problems, by their nature, require an interdisciplinary approach, academic planning should actively encourage the development of such courses of instruction.

Urban-related teaching is often beset by problems. One problem is that many urban university faculty members went from suburban high schools to suburban or even rural colleges and graduate schools, never really lived in an urban environment and quite simply do not understand the milieu into which they have been thrust. A second problem derives from the wide variety of instructional programs that are offered and the lack of coordination among them. At my own university, for example, a Council on Academic Urban Programs (CAUP) has made only the most tentative steps towards coordina-tion, and the problem is complicated by issues of 'turf' and varying levels of quality and commitment in these instructional programs. In addition, the purposes and values of the participants in these programs differ widely. At the one extreme, the School of Planning in our College of Design, Architecture, Art, and Planning stresses high selectivity of students and research activity of faculty, while the former College of Community Services accepted marginally qualified students, demanded only minimal research activity by its faculty, and emphasized the practical rather than the theoretical in both teaching methods and faculty reward system. Other urban-related instruction falls within the spectrum of these extremes.

A third problem involves a lack of urban focus where it would be useful, most obviously in Colleges of Education, some of which offer no courses in urban education or in the special problems of inner-city schools and teachers. Often, past recruitment practices ignored the need for faculty with expertise and interest in city school systems, and specific projects in cooperation with the city schools were at best infrequent. Of course there are exceptions, but the opportunities in too many cities have been inadequately seized.

A fourth problem of urban-related instruction, less well defined, concerns the danger of confusing academic and non-academic activities. This tendency surfaces most clearly in programs such as those in Women's Studies. Most such programs are interdisciplinary and usually articulate relevant courses from other departments into a planned sequence. Although faculty may have definite and well considered guidelines for the kinds of public service activities appropriately offered by an academic unit, these guidelines are too frequently not consistently applied in practice. They include academic objectivity and control by the program or its agents. Such a unit appears quite vulnerable to the confusion between academic and non-academic pursuits and can be inclined to function as an advocate for certain causes. A planned forum on day-care, for example, may not include opponents of the concept. There is a fine line between public service activity that offers expertise and a public service activity that provides merely the imprimatur of the University, but it is an important distinction, especially for an academic unit. A program on women and Social Security renders *instruction* to the community, an appropriate public service activity by an academic unit, whereas the use of the official imprimatur to justify political activism in the community would seem questionable. There are, of course, any number of instances in which academic units throughout the university misunderstand the differences between the academic and non-academic, but the point is that the urban mission is *best* served by appropriate instruction. It is imperative that for all academic units public service *per se* should remain subsidiary to instruction broadly defined and should occur as a function thereof.

I suspect that increasingly faculty members in all but the most recondite of studies will find that the urban environment colors their research in a broad variety of ways. The student of language and literature cannot help being influenced by the sounds of the streets, the rhetoric of urban intercourse, the ambiance of the shops, the places of entertainment, the corridors of business and trade. Some, of course, will continue to insulate themselves — and indeed should. But history studied in the shadow of a vast city is, almost inevitably I think, differently perceived than from within the pale of a sheltered academic environment. And I am inclined to think that even in the sciences — above all in the biological sciences — scholars will ask themselves different kinds of questions because they are suggested by one fact or another of the urban experience.

I am not suggesting that there are no differences between liberal studies and professional or vocational education in the urban context. That would be absurd. I am suggesting, however, that in such an environment the likelihood is greater that liberal and vocational/professional scholarship will share common concerns and certain common assumptions — and that both will in some ways be affected by the milieu.

The scope of such urban-related research is somewhat easier to comprehend than the scope of teaching, if only because it involves fewer people. Like instruction, research in this area tends to suffer from minimal coordination and the potential for an excessive duplication of effort. Substantial duplication in research is a necessity, not a luxury, since the advancement of knowledge and innovation requires multiple approaches and various scholars exploring their subjects from differing theoretical stances. However, more than most academic research, urban research occurs primarily on an *ad hoc* basis, stimulated either by the award of a grant or contract or simply by the interests of the individuals who may not always be aware that others are working in tangential areas. Because of its dependency on outside funding, this research serves a limited constituency, namely those who can pay for it. Urban related research at a University consists of service paid for by the establishment to guide policies of the establishment. Given the financial situation of the 1980s this limitation appears necessary. It raises the question, however, of whether the University should grant its implicit sanction to what are essentially independent consulting organizations, such as the various Institutes for Governmental Research. Although Directors argue that these units provide a 'university presence' at City Hall, the benefits of this visibility are doubtful. This is where coordination could be useful. The dependence of urban-related research on outside funding greatly diminishes the possibilities of long-term basic research, as those who can and will pay are generally interested in short-term efforts that promise quick answers to specific dilemmas. Scholars of urban problems, however, need the freedom of their counterparts in the physical sciences to pursue questions that may have no immediate applicability but that may eventually result in the amelioration of complex problems.

As Clark Kerr predicted, the complex issue of advocacy particularly besets urban-related research. Academic scholarship ideally synthesizes or discovers information and then provides it to concerned parties in an accessible form. However, when research is funded by a source outside the academy, which may or may not be disinterested, and is applied to a specific urban problem in a specific location, the distinction tends to blur between identifying the alternatives for action and suggesting a proper choice among them. Work on air pollution patterns or questions in a university poll regarding nuclear power or a mental health tax levy, for example, will inevitably supply information which may then be used by the providers of the funds for their own purposes. University affiliated researchers must remain constantly cognizant of the difference between procuring information, an appropriate activity, and overtly or covertly employing it to influence policy.

The question of advocacy is not easily resolved. At some point, an expert, academic or otherwise, has a moral obligation to place his or her knowledge in the service of policy formulation. The shelter of the academy does not neutralize this obligation, but the institution itself can suffer from ill considered advocacy positions adopted by some of its members. Urban planning will inevitably involve conflicts between transportation requirements and housing displacement; efforts on behalf of historic preservation must bump into questions of land usage and population density in the inner city. Academic experts may well be the most judicious voices on these and similar issues, but their voices should not be confused with that of the University. The urban scholar who chooses to adopt a public stance on a controversial issue must, of course, be free to do so, not only as a citizen but as a highly qualified expert; however, he or she should take particular pains to separate that stance from the institution which, quite properly, may have provided the research facilities to create and enhance that expertise.

In addition to problems connected with advocacy and funding, urban-related research often suffers from the insularity engendered by collegial and departmental organization. Quite simply, in many cases we do not know what our colleagues are doing, let alone care. Each institution needs, therefore, a voluntary clearing house for urban-related research. The emphasis here must lie equally on 'voluntary' and 'clearing house'; no one can really be required to register his or her investigations, and no one should be invested with the power to approve or disapprove a given project, save according to traditional standards concerning use of human subjects and equitable access to facilities. However, faculty members can be encouraged to file project descriptions with this clearing house, whose mission would be simply to place people with mutual interests in touch with each other. Such a clearing house might facilitate the dissolution of present barriers to cooperation by resolving or transcending old quarrels — every institution I know has its share of them.

It is generally accepted that public service comprises an essential part of an urban university's mission, but there is no agreement in the literature on the proper definition and scope of a university's obligations in this area. Perhaps the most fundamental disagreement concerns the constituency to be served by a university's public endeavors. Some Continuing Education Directors appear to believe that this constituency should consist primarily of the poor and deprived, those people who are most immediately afflicted by the problems of the cities. For others, the University's public service should work toward the creation of a more just society, enlisting the influential and powerful, when necessary, only as a strategic tool for assisting those in greatest need. Others within the University community believe a University is best suited to serve political and governmental entities, and still others implicitly regard public service as public relations, the cultivation of the well-placed and the influential in order to enlist their efforts on behalf of the academic institution. All these definitions are, in their own way, legitimate, and they should not be regarded as mutually exclusive.

We need to expand our concept of what university activities contribute to public service. Ideally public service activities would be part of the professional life of all faculty members as instruction and scholarship are today. At my own university, our guidelines for the annual public service award insist that 'Public service eligible for recognition through this award should relate directly to the professional interests of the faculty member involved and be compatible with the service, teaching, and research interests of the department or unit with which the faculty person is associated.' This guideline attempts to distinguish those public service activities members of the university community undertake as professional specialists and those they assume as citizens. The distinction is an important one and has always to be borne in mind by those who act as representatives of the institution. Observation of this distinction will enable us to concentrate our public service on activities that a university can do best; it will help us to avoid the temptation to render services best delivered by another sort of agency.

The criterion of professional expertise embraces a wide range and permits a workable definition of public service as any activity most suitably performed by a university which enhances the quality of life in any metropolitan area. Thus the library's reference service, a College of Music's free performances, a School of Design's donations of surplus art materials to the schools, and a

67

College of Law's Legal Clinic all offer exemplary public service. To relegate this responsibility to a single administrative division is to encourage other units to divest themselves of their own accountability for public service and to risk what George Spear calls the 'poverty of definition' whereby 'the words "community" and "urban" refer only to minority people, their neighborhoods and their problems.'[9]

Expanding the definition of public service might contribute toward alleviating faculty distrust and skepticism about the concept. The prevailing faculty view is that administrators talk a great deal about public service but that it counts for little in tenure and promotion decisions. The view cannot be dismissed as mere cynicism. The best faculty members at urban universities are unwilling to compromise traditional standards of excellence in teaching and scholarship for the sake of public service. No matter how committed they may be to an institution's urban mission, when they evaluate their colleagues they do so in terms of excellence in documentable research, and, occasionally, in teaching. Public service is often even less amenable to evaluation than good teaching. How does one assess how much preparation goes into a speech to a civic organization, for example, and how effective the speech was? When promotion and tenure decisions must be made with utmost stringency, faculty members cannot rely on *pro forma* thank-you notes from program chairmen. Should the effectiveness of the service rendered even weigh as a consideration in assessing its value? In addition, some faculty members have little opportunity to render professionally related public service because their disciplines preclude it; an astronomer cannot offer his or her talents to the city as readily as an economist or a transportation engineer. While we can mandate *university* service, therefore, as a prerequisite for promotion and tenure, we cannot mandate public service. However public service can certainly be encouraged and rewarded.

Just as the proper constituency for and definition of an institution's public service are ambiguous, so is the problem of funding. If service to the community comprises a part of the University's mission *distinct* from teaching and research, it should be distinctly funded. However, given a financial situation which is likely to remain bleak, the question of the user fee, or fee-for-service, merits serious consideration. Should individuals or groups receiving non-instructional service from the University pay for it? At some institutions, those most involved with public service answer no, arguing that a user fee would impair community relations and it would be inefficient because it would mean collecting small sums of money for the Division's many programs. Others argue the opposite, insisting that the University has no obligation to place its expertise in unpaid service to the city and that non-instructional functions should be required to pay their way. The argument is persuasive but depends on a flexible definition of educational functions to distinguish them from service activities. For instance, helping a neighborhood group to formulate its problems before seeking City assistance may well constitute legitimate extension teaching. Activities which are clearly non-instructional, however, would move toward financial self-sufficiency.

One question no one ever asks about University public service is, 'What's in it for the institution?' It sounds crass, but in a period of chronic financial pressure and the resulting need for reassessment, the question must be posed. The answer is that public service gains for the university a stock of intangible goodwill in the local community and local government, an important consideration but one not translatable into dollars. And of course what is learned in performing public service enhances all the other activities of the institution.

Finally, there is the question, already alluded to, of how best to organize public service. A few years back, William Donaldson, the former city manager of Cincinnati, had some advice in this regard. He suggested hiring someone to spend six months wandering around the city agencies talking to people about what interested them and what they thought the problems were. Then he thought that person should spend another six months circulating in the university seeing who knew what and who was inclined to be helpful. Above all else, Mr. Donaldson said, 'I would tell the guy that if he ever held a meeting of more than three people he'd be fired.'[10]

While we have not followed Donaldson's advice to the letter, we have been experimenting at my own university with what we call the matchmaker project. This is a small group of people whose role, under the leadership of our continuing education office, is to bring together various of the offices of municipal government and the university. Some faculty members may have a project in mind that involves cooperation with government offices downtown; the matchmaker's role is to try to put these people together. Somebody in the division of finance of the municipal government needs some kind of expert help. Again, the matchmaker's role is to put people from the division in touch with those members of our faculty who have the expertise that is needed. This is just one possible approach, but it demonstrates that methods can be worked out for making the university more effective in its urban community.

A major uncertainty is whether our faculties are adequately prepared to meet the opportunities afforded by their urban location. Nowhere is the question more importunate than in the area of continuing education, particularly in regard to services to the business community. To be sure, most urban institutions have been involved in continuing education for many years, and the market is not illimitably elastic. However, there exists now the prospect of a greatly-expanded clientele of people returning to the academy not only for job upgrading but to widen their vision, increase their understanding of world affairs, and improve their leisure time.

There are indeed real opportunities ahead, but they will have to be addressed more systematically if we are to take full advantage of them. Teaching older people is different from teaching people of conventional college age. One reason evening class instruction has been criticized is that it is done in the same way — often as an overload — by the same people as inhabit the day-time enterprise. In many cases, they have learned little — or nothing — about the needs of older students, and have thought little about differences in motivation, experience, work habits, and physical endurance between older adults and youths. These teachers have learned nothing about such issues because those who taught them were either themselves insensitive to the issues, or, if they were sensitive to them, were unable to teach their students ways to handle them. I am convinced that college instruction in my own field of history is often bad because we have persisted in the curious belief that inexperienced people somehow will become knowledgeable teachers by virtue of the fact that they have learned the nuts and bolts of scholarly research and writing.

Here I want to emphasize that academic departments have a chance to develop some expertise in continuing education, to help train people who can move into the area with more expertise and more knowledge, not just use it as a dumping ground for surplus graduate students, young PhDs, or senior faculty who seek extra income. Let us remember the two-year college experience. For years, county and community colleges were regarded by the academic establishment as almost unworthy of notice. With the job crunch, university faculty members suddenly discovered their existence, particularly since they had grown as rapidly — in many cases more rapidly — than the four-year colleges and universities. Faculty members tried systematically to place their graduate students in these institutions. I served for a number of years on the Advisory Committee of the History Department of a distinguished university. I witnessed just such a development. And what happened? University faculty discovered, as others of us did, that the professionals in two-year colleges found our products ill-trained for the job required of them, bewildered by the mixture of vocational and general education, and altogether unsuited for their task. The result has been a series of programs, in various disciplines, to prepare students consciously for careers in two-year colleges. The same thing could be done for those who plan careers in continuing education.

A somewhat different set of issues is posed by the business–higher education relationship. This is not the place to explore the advantages and the dangers of university–industry partnership. It is inevitable; it is desirable; and it must be carefully controlled. Here I want to focus on what Ernest Lynton has called 'the missing connection' between business and education.[11] While employment patterns have shifted dramatically — and will shift even more — in our post-industrial society, the institutions of higher education have done an increasingly smaller share of the training and education of the work force that makes up our 'human capital.' Larger companies have increasingly elected either to develop their own training and upgrading programs for employees or have turned to the burgeoning training industry of proprietary and not-for-profit concerns for employee-development. Whether the purpose is to prepare individuals for effective entry into first level positions or to bring employees up to the mark about changes in technology, organization, or legal issues, colleges and universities appear to be doing a proportionately smaller share of the job.

Why should that be the case? For one thing, faculty members at universities lack flexibility because they have, for the most part, been prepared in postwar universities whose graduate curricula were oriented toward narrowly specialized courses and research instead of toward breadth of educational experience. Such training seems to inhibit flexibility, thus reducing the ability of the faculty and the institution to respond to new challenges, new demands, and new ways of delivering educational services. If universities are better to serve the educational needs of business and industry, Lynton insists, they will have to develop procedures for rapid design, review, and approval of new courses, be they for credit or not. They will need more flexible and responsive admission and registration procedures. They will have to adapt time, place, and format of instruction to be more convenient for prospective students. And they will have to develop fresh mechanisms to make faculty readily available in increments of time considerably less than a full course for a full term. Parenthetically, the rapid advances in telecommunications technology may well drive reluctant academicians to try new experiments that they currently regard with indifference if not contempt.

All of this makes it appear that I am suggesting we must be more concerned with vocational than with more broadly conceived preparation. Quite the contrary. Recently there has been much talk and even some movement in institutions concerning the revitalization of the liberal arts. In particular, we have had a good deal of structural revision centering about what are called core curricula. Most such revisions have been essentially minor. A few years ago, I commented that

> Undergraduate education needs a thorough overhaul, not just a few Band-Aids applied here and there .... Few of us have done much to foster those exchanges that might encourage student motivation and inquiry and to promote the notion that our compartmentalized offerings might not always be the adequate or proper way to stimulate effective undergraduate learning.[12]

It may be that the latest revisions of core curricula will serve merely as a smoke screen to protect the various faculties from dealing with more deep-seated, pervasive issues.

What is really at issue is a misunderstanding of the world of work. John Dewey clearly stated — it seems a very long time ago — that education and society are fundamentally integrated. The idea of vocationalism and the liberal arts being the opposing sides in some post-secondary dualism is a gross oversimplification of the current debate. Today young people — and older people as well — are concerned about their futures: jobs, careers, and lifestyles. One should welcome the stability and the initiative this interest indicates. It is evident also that when the liberal arts are taught and considered as 'subject matter' separate from the very questioning of life's fundamental values, they become dull and lifeless — the material is studied by these earnest students, quickly forgotten, and not necessarily incorporated into their lives. The liberal arts are not there for their own sake, to provide some elegant gingerbread, some enrichment that is removed from social and political concerns. Quite the contrary, the basic purpose in higher education is to develop men and women as effectively functioning beings in society. David Saxon has noted that 'We are quite unable, as a society, to distinguish between sense and nonsense when it comes to science.'[13] And, too frequently, I would suggest the same is true of our understanding of politics or of other cultures or more generally of that amorphous and crucial area of study we call the humanities.

From time to time, chief executive officers of large companies have offered their advice on what industry needs in the way of new college graduates. They have always indicated that the business world needs individuals who have received well-rounded education — those young people with scope, who are grounded in their disciplines, but who are able because of the breadth of their educational backgrounds to analyze, correlate, be open to change, and to appreciate other points of view. The top executives are calling for well-educated people, not well-trained people. Yet, too frequently those who do the hiring for their companies look almost exclusively for the special skill. They give lip service to concern for what the prospective employee will be doing in ten years' time, with how well prepared he or she has been by education to grow in the face of often dramatically changing circumstances. In actuality, a balanced education is frequently a handicap, not an advantage to the young person seeking employment in many of our large corporations and smaller businesses. Academicians should insist that there not be a narrow approach to any occupational training — be it for laboratory technician or a medical doctor. Whitehead said, 'The antithesis between a technical and a liberal education is fallacious. There can be no adequate technical education which is not liberal and no liberal education which is not technical . . . .'[14] This same idea was also expressed by J.B. Conant — perhaps his explanation is more complete because he describes the process of integrating the world of work and the world of the mind at every level of the educational process:

> I must record an educational heresy, or rather support a proposition that many will find self-evident, but that some professors of the liberal arts will denounce as dangerously heretical. I submit that in a heavily urbanized and industrialized free society the education experiences of youth should fit his subsequent employment. There should be a smooth transition from full-time schooling to a full-time job whether that transition be after grade ten, or after graduation from high school, college or university.[15]

What is important to keep in mind is that we not short-change genuine education when the going gets tough. No doubt, as many have suggested, we can train people to do any of a variety of operations, technical, specialized, limited, in a shorter time and with fewer so-called irrelevant distractions than we presently require. We have been told this so often that it has become stale in the repetition.

In recent years especially there has been a polarization of views in the minds of the public and even among academicians themselves, about what constitutes legitimate higher education. In times such as ours, there is a tendency to stick to tried programs and approaches that most directly guarantee a job, an income. Despite substantial and sometimes shrill rhetoric about liberal learning, in institution after institution, the emphasis has been on professional, vocational, and technical programs and in the process the notion of the well-educated individual has fallen by the wayside. It may be that our society has become so complex, so technologically sophisticated that all we can anticipate is compartmentalization of our knowledge, fragmentation of our world of work. If this is so, I am afraid that we must also anticipate increased inefficiencies, declining productivity, and most importantly a society whose citizens will be unprepared to make rational judgments whether in public affairs or in private enterprise.

Higher education can be a mixture of professional training and the cultivation of attitudes of mind that can make professionals — or anyone — more productive in whatever they do, more responsible, and more flexible. The kind of professionals we produce need a good deal more consideration. Effectively educated human beings cannot be so narrow that they have no breadth of vision, no benchmarks to help them gain perspective about everything that they undertake. A few years back, students complained bitterly about the lack of relevance in their studies — their lack of contemporaneity, the lack of involvement, the absence of any direct application of what they learned to what they saw about them. I might argue, perversely, that we need more irrelevance — not relevance — but irrelevance — in education. The university is the one institution in society that has a prime responsibility to understand, to analyze, to provide theories and principles, to offer benchmarks for the actions that must be taken by all of us in society. It may well be that the study of Victorian cities in the nineteenth century is more relevant to an understanding of problems of modern urban complexes than is a superficial internship in one or another agency. Knowledge that may seem irrelevant, of history, of the classics or of the scientific notions that underlie so much of the dominant technology of our times, in the long run may enable us to be more effective in the community at large than studies that respond to the latest whim of a society that too often has no sense of where it came from — let alone any sense of where it is going.

Altogether, then, the task is to provide both general and vocational education because both are vital to the well-being of our institutions. A society such as ours needs many people whose varying skills demand more or less extensive periods of training. Institutions of higher education fairly explode with teaching directed toward technical competency and with applied research relating to economic growth, to national security, to peaceful social progress. As a people we still tend to think in terms of problem solving — and to assume that with enough technological knowledge any problem can be solved. Experience suggests that society will always value and thus emphasize the practical, the applied. The attitude seems unlikely to change. I am a strong advocate of beginning what I have called vocational training early. Of course it is important to provide the information and the skills for an occupation. We live in a world of work, as well as in ourselves — and indeed most education has been in one fashion or another, 'practical' — for if it was not preparation for an immediate job then it was more and more frequently preparation for a professional school or, as I have noted, a graduate school.

We in higher education must be responsive to the needs of the community, the demands of the job market, and the career goals of the individual, but we must also help our students integrate their specialized knowledge in such a way as to pursue a life of dignity and responsiveness, not one of exploitation and disintegration. A liberal education encourages us to provide a sense of direction to our lives, to raise the big questions about existence, to explore our own relationship to the world and its inhabitants, to think in terms of our own contribution to the greater well-being of individuals and of society. None of these attitudes or goals is promoted by vocational or specialized education alone.

Just as in the case of business leaders, lip service is paid to breadth of education in all quarters of the University. Our schools of business, for example, speak proudly of their 'liberal' curricula. After all, their students must take courses in the colleges of arts and sciences — which apparently proves to them that they are being liberally educated. Then it turns out that the courses are more work in statistics, in mathematics, in applied economics. Far from broadening, the tendency is to increase the specialization and to increase the narrowness of the largest single group of undergraduate majors we currently prepare.

Similarly, how often has one heard professors of engineering complain that the physics and mathematics courses their students had to take in the liberal arts college were too conceptual, too abstract for such pragmatically-oriented programs as they were following.

And the same is true of potential historians whose knowledge of the world of business or of science is nothing short of deplorable, of social workers whose perception of the dynamics of society is severely bounded in time and in place, of medical students for whom the rat race toward admission to professional school has meant single-minded concentration on so-called pre-medical subjects. We do a poor job of liberal education. We shall have to do better if the promise of our colleges and universities is to be fulfilled.

Let me turn back for a moment to the comments I made about access to higher education. There are people, perhaps a substantial number, who believe that in order properly to serve populations that have hitherto been denied access to our colleges and universities we will have to pay less attention to the needs of the intellectually gifted among our students. Looking to the future, I think we need to raise the question: Is there a clash between equity and excellence in the educational world? Excellence is often played down in our society, particularly in recent years. There is a curious notion — usually among those who don't make the grade — that everyone could do well if only certain conditions were different. Of course our environment plays a role in our accomplishments — it may be that proper childhood nutrition is more important educationally than proper schools or even parental attitudes. But if our society is to survive in an increasingly competitive world, we are going to have to get the utmost in leadership from those we perceive as gifted and who understand that achievement rests upon large doses of hard work. It is no accident that the rate of growth of our productivity declined almost in exact parallel with the growing indifference to intellectual discovery and creativity. And that indifference comes not simply from the proportionate decline of federal or state or private resources devoted to university research. It is a reflection, fundamentally, of the mistaken notion that to emphasize quality, intellectual performance, innovative thinking is somehow a form of 'elitism' that is inappropriate in our democratic society. Yet in such a democratic society, whose institutions try to serve all of us as fully as possible, educational accountability and standards must be of a higher order if the system is to realize its intended purposes. The challenges are broader and the need for the contributions of the best trained minds is greater, not less, than in a more structured social order.

Given the tension between these educational challenges and the economic realities facing higher education today, it is vitally important that we do not settle for the line of least resistance as we plan for the future. I realize that we cannot ask people to go hungry while we ponder higher truths. But we need to be sensitive to intellectual, to political, and indeed to ethical realities as we struggle to survive.

All of which brings one full circle to the discussion of the role of the urban institution in today's educational spectrum. To be sure, the urban university is in many ways more concerned with dealing directly with urban issues than perhaps are other academic institutions. The contributions it can make to an appropriate balance between the development of knowledge and its applications, between liberal learning and vocational preparation are clearly evident. That balance can be encouraged by a more flexible reward structure that makes public service as I have defined it a significant service of urban faculty members. But if the urban university does not remain, like universities of quality wherever they may be located, primarily an academic institution, if it does not remember always that its central tasks are teaching and research, then its ability to be effective, other than as another agency of government, will be seriously compromised. And that is hardly the function of a viable institution of higher education.

## Notes

1  I am grateful to Drs. Jill Rubenstein and Janice Long for valuable help in the preparation of this essay.

2  CARNEGIE COMMISSION ON HIGHER EDUCATION, (1972) *The Campus and the City*, New York, McGraw-Hill, p. 21.

3  U.S. CONGRESS, 96TH CONGRESS, (1980) *Public Law 96–374*, October 3, 94 Stat. pp. 1492–3.

4  J.M. KLOTSCHE, (1966) *the Urban University*, New York, Harper and Row, p. 29.

5  A. GROBMAN, (1980) 'The missions of urban universities,' *Liberal Education*, 66, Summer, pp. 203–7.

6  T.P. MURPHY and M.G. SEYFFERT (1975) 'The future urban university,' in *Universities in the Urban Crisis*, T.P. MURPHY (ed). New York, Dunellen, p. 395.

7  C. KERR (1967) 'The urban grant university — a model for the future,' Lecture delivered at the Phi Beta Kappa–Gamma Chapter-Centennial meeting of City College, New York, NY, October 18, pub. (1968) in *City College Papers* 8, City College, NY, p. 13.

8  P.L. SZANTON (1981) *Not Well Advised*, New York, Russell Sage Foundation and Ford Foundation.

9  G.E. SPEAR (1975) 'The university public service mission,' in *Universities in the Urban Crisis*, T.P. MURPHY (ed)., New York, Dunellen, p. 97.

10  M. SCULLY, (1981) 'When it comes to taking advice, town rarely gives heed to gown,' *Chronicle of Higher Education* 3 pp. 19–21.

11  E. LYNTON, *The Missing Connection Between Business and Education*, mss. to be published by the MacMillan Company and the American Council on Education.

12  (1979) *The Great Core Curriculum Debate. Education as a Mirror of Culture*, New Rochelle, NY, Change Magazine Press, p. 56.

13  D.S. SAXON (1983) 'The place of science and technology in the liberal arts curriculum: conference on science and technology education for civic and professional life — the undergraduate years,' *American Journal of Physics*, 51, 1 January, p. 12.

14  A.N. WHITEHEAD (1929) *The Aims of Education and other Essays*, New York, The MacMillan Company, p. 24.

15  J.B. CONANT (1961) *Slums and Suburbs*, New York, McGraw-Hill, p. 40.

# Higher Education — The Contenders*

*Harold Silver*

A crucial difference between our understanding of higher education since the 1950s and everything that went before is in the kind of questions that we are able, but also willing, to ask. Social and behavioral scientists and educators have, especially in the past quarter of a century, wanted to know who enters higher education, and why, correlations between access and social background, between school performance and later achievement. They have investigated learning success and failure, choice and methods of admission and assessment. They have even been interested in the opinions of students on some questions, and increasingly frequently those of employers of university graduates. We have an economics and sociology of recent higher education, we have research into higher education topics unknown even twenty years ago — Expectations of Higher Education, Higher Education and the Labor Market. . . .

Writing about British universities and the state at the end of the 1950s, Berdahl concluded that further encroachments by the state on the autonomy of the universities were unlikely — and he was, of course, proved to be wrong.[1] It is not only the role of the state, but also the landscape of higher education, that has changed. One of the main novelties under recent scrutiny has been the emergence and awareness of the 'system' or 'systems' of higher education, and attempts to define what Ashby in 1974 called the 'inner logic' of the different sectors.[2] In England and Wales, with the new universities mainly of the 1960s, the thirty polytechnics created in the late 1960s, and the sixty or so colleges and institutes of higher education of the 1970s — together with the equivalent Scottish colleges — new complexities of scale and style have needed attention. The polytechnics, mainly urban, with traditions inherited from their progeni-

* This chapter is an adapted and extended version of a public lecture given at the University of Edinburgh in June 1983, as part of the celebrations of the University's 400th anniversary. The original was published in Nicholas Phillipson (ed)., (1983) *The University in Society: Past, Present, and Future*, Edinburgh, Edinburgh University Press.

tors of technical and applied studies, and part-time students, suggested a new range of higher education images, and began to aim at identities paralleling partly the European technological institutions and partly the American urban state universities. The colleges and institutes of higher education, generally smaller, often out of traditions of teacher education, residence and strong student support services, stretched the new definition of 'higher education' even further from the mid-1970s, as the American state colleges had done already. Once upon a time there just had been universities. As little as twenty years ago ('little,' of course, to an historian) books were still being written and debates being conducted in which British 'higher education' was equated with 'universities'. The common assumption here was that institutions — even if promoted — would remain a rank or two below the universities — which in Britain are alone able to grant degrees — with the exception of the Council for National Academic Awards, created in 1964 by royal charter with the ability to award degrees for non-university institutions. Inside the universities these perceptions remain. The point for the moment, however, is that in all this expansion and diversification there has been much to discuss and research.

But what about questions asked of the first half of this century, the nineteenth century, and before? It is not easy to generalize about the ways historians have approached the history of Edinburgh or St. Andrews, Cambridge or London, Harvard or Virginia, still less about the national and cultural contexts, traditions of ideas and social purpose, in which they have tried to situate and explain the patterns and differences. But, and always with exceptions, historians — certainly in Britain — have asked their questions mainly about provision, about the relationships between provision and ideas and intentions, provision and providers, provision and national economics and international relationships, the motives for and forms of provision, the debates about what to provide. That may be less true of historical work on medieval or Enlightenment Europe or some American work on Revolutionary or Great Awakening times — and in such cases the experience of the scholar has attracted interest. It is largely true, however, of the way historians have approached the nineteenth century. In the last century or so they have conducted their explorations largely in the frame of institutional and curricular responses to 'industrialization', 'modernization', scientific and technological advance, the interests of new classes and new professions. The record is predominantly focused on the public spokesmen for the liberal defense and the scientific prosecution, with obvious differences to explain between England on the one hand, and Scotland, continental Europe and the United States on the other hand. Our understanding of the last century and a half of torment — particularly in England — about a liberal education and its alternatives remains substantially conditioned by the interpretations of John Stuart Mill or Cardinal Newman or Matthew Arnold, with sideglances at the more moderate spokesmen for science, and encompassing perhaps the *Edinburgh* and *Blackwood's* magazines and the reports of the relevant royal commissions.

What we know about the nineteenth century, therefore, is a function of the questions historians have asked — and on the whole they have not asked questions about the nineteenth century universities within their communities, the employers rather than the founders, the experience of students rather than parliamentary controversy and reluctant reform. It may not be easy but, for example, Michael Sanderson in the one case and Sheldon Rothblatt in the other, have shown the directions and the possibilities.[3] We know little, however, about how the emergent professions, industrial, managerial and commercial occupations viewed the universities and their functions, their procedures and standards. We know next to nothing about student expectations or opinion, about liberal values as interpreted within the new institutions, as translated into practice by academics and in their encounters with students. Historians have certainly shown little curiosity about the views and activities of those seeking to challenge, to re-interpret or to adapt the liberal traditions under debate -the industrialists, the European-or Scottish-trained scientists, the technical staffs of the new English university colleges, universities and late-nineteenth-century first generation of 'polytechnics'. The very conception of a university, as autonomous and hermetic as possible, has made such questions irrelevant. The history is therefore resistant to non-institutional implications — except as seen from elevated positions. It is very often a history in which the contenders for truth or for position include few or no students, and only those intellectuals with access to the pulpit or the publishing house. Historians are capable of easy and wild assumptions about how policy is made and how institutions receive and interpret messages and act, or decline to act, on them.

These historical deficiencies help to define our version of the past and the dilemmas of our present. But we do not have a ready made 'history' that tells us how to discern, let alone to solve, the problems of the dichotomies and polarities which have been under discussion here, as often before. There is not *a* history which tells us how to handle, for example, the conceptual and practical difficulties of the 'vocational' and the 'liberal', the 'specialized' and the 'general', and overarching all of these past and present debates, the question of the relationship between the university and whichever wider canvas you prefer to use — government, the state, society, the world outside. At the same time as interpreting those relationships, there is a confusing history to be interpreted also.

Having defined the near-impossibility of the task, let me try to stand for a while at some intersections of what we ask of the present and what we think we know of the past. I would like to select a small number of the directions in which universities and others have to look in determining their future courses of action. We continue to agonize in the present about the dichotomies to which I have referred, and they are a good place to start. In the past thirty or so years we have located those dichotomies in the strains of expansion and of contraction. In the 1950s and 1960s we were familiar with controversies about the universities and the world outside — Kingsley Amis and his team versus A.D.C. Peterson *et al.* on 'the threat of the practical'[4], debates about two or more cultures, technology as humanism,[5] or, in terms peculiar to England, as low-status intrusion — with the UGC and others valiantly attempting to define the controversy out of existence.[6] We went on looking over our shoulders at the world as explained to us between the wars by, among others but outstandingly, Abraham Flexner, distinguishing between professions, which belong in a university, and vocations, which don't. A case could be made, he told us in 1930, for a university faculty of law and medicine, but 'certainly not at all for business, journalism, domestic "science", or library "science". In the British universities, which he rather liked, he discovered nevertheless:

> such short-sighted and absurd ... excrescences as the School of Librarianship and course in Journalism at University College, London, the Department of Civic Design at Liverpool and the work in Automobile Engineering at Bristol. This technical development is slight, as compared with that in America, but is none the less deplorable and, we may hope, the defects of youth, for it is of neither liberal nor university quality.[7]

What a battle, thirty years later, Ashby and others had to wage! And, in whatever versions, and with whatever publicity, the problem has accelerated as the world has pressed in upon the universities and upon that newly diversified artefact labelled higher education. *The Sciences, the Humanities and the Technological Threat* is a book title only nine years old[8], and in it 'technological totalitarianism' is firmly confronted.[9] As the technological and the economic have become more salient, as expansion and national planning for it or for its opposite forced institutions more firmly into dependence on the state, so have the meaning and the relevance of the 'liberal' become more elusive. In a powerful American book on the subject Earl Cheit summarizes a view increasingly explicit among many academics on both sides of the Atlantic:

> Now colleges and universities are no longer defined by liberal education. Liberal education lacks the power to define. It lacks coherence; it lacks definition itself. Liberal education has become splintered, specialized, and, to some extent, eroded.[10]

Behind that comment lies the curriculum search of Harvard and other American institutions, lies the confusion of a recent past in Britain about where to put, and what to offer, an increasing number of students, and of course, where to put the 'excrescences'. Revise or abandon the liberal? Liberalize the vocational, as became official British policy in the late 1950s, or vocationalize the liberal — as David Hawkins persuasively suggested to us in the United States.[11] And then, having botched up some answers — how to sustain them in contraction and a disappearing 'age participation rate'?

The basic problem in Britain has been the implications of the creation of the 'binary' division in the late 1960s, by which the emergent system or pattern of higher education was segmented, in part by tradition, in part by vague and ill-defined intentions. The universities retained their traditional 'autonomy' — financed through and at the time loosely overseen by the University Grants Committee. The new 'local authority' institutions — at first the polytechnics designated in 1968, and joined in the second half of the 1970s by the colleges and institutes of higher education — were funded through and controlled by local authorities, and emerged from traditions which include a larger percentage of employment-related courses, part-time degrees and teacher education. This 'public sector' looked more 'practical', 'professional' and 'vocational', but although the propulsion of this other side of the binary divide into higher education status expanded the system, it made it neither tidy nor rational nor stable. Many universities, or departments in universities, resented the inference that they were other-wordly, impractical and unprofessional. Universities also had their changing responses to the needs of the outside world as they interpreted them, and there were voices insisting that the binary concept was based on outdated conceptions of the work of the universities. The polytechnics and colleges themselves did not stand still, and carried their changed status in directions which brought them into competition with the universities, or at least into the difficulties of definition of frontiers and futures. 'Binary' had to do with structure and sources of finance, with the extent and style of power, with prestige and hierarchy, and in confused and uncertain ways with curriculum and purpose.

It was in this 'public' sector that I spent some years teaching 'liberal studies' as an additive to technical and science students and am still, much though *I* enjoy it, not sure with what justification. I am not as sure as I once thought I was that Ashby was wrong to argue that brewing — and by implication almost anything else — can be a liberal education if properly approached. I am certainly not sure that a core study of great books à la Hutchins or Lord James, or a compulsory core study of the 'civilizing' disciplines, is a useful approach to education after secondary school. There are, of course, important national differences here, including Scottish attempts to defend the tradition of broader curricula, or to reconcile that tradition with the common pressures to refine and to specialize. Nevertheless, the actual or potential danger of losing purchase on familiar models of the liberal remains a matter of anxious debate — especially when the contenders for influence and position outside the institutions appear to threaten to impose new and unacceptable conditions and values — though of course there is nothing new in that. What we have to be sure about is that we know clearly what we do before we defend it. Alain Touraine recently suggested that the idea of general culture needed to be 'unequivocally defended', but by 'reviving it, to start with'.[12] Are we sure whether teacher education, and if so all of it or some of it, and by implication the mission of the colleges where it still forms a significant fraction of their work, are easily identifiable as 'vocational'? The Committee of Directors of Polytechnics thought so when one of their spokesmen told a House of Commons committee that 'we have also had the colleges of education that have been highly motivated vocationally and in a sense have existed in order to meet the needs of a particular profession'.[13] On that basis I am scarcely able to find a course of study in higher education that does not have some major element of the vocational or the professional — the vocabulary here is difficult to disentangle (and certainly before the late nineteenth century the argument would not have had much meaning). Theology, architecture, medicine, the law ... raise intractable problems of definition in the context of vocational motivation and the needs of particular professions. As, indeed, do all those courses of academic study which have in the past pointed towards employment in academic life.

Amidst the pressures we face, therefore, is this complex question of what it is to which we are wedded, in the face of strong pressures for change, including for change in the focus of policy, and decision-making. If the universities and others are going to have to accommodate such pressures from various directions, they will need to understand them — and that is far from easy. They will also retain choices. I do not agree, for example, with the conclusion reached by the Committee of Directors of Polytechnics at the end of quite recent evidence to a House of Commons select committee: 'Traditions of academic freedom and of permitting local judgments on nationally allocated educational expenditure must both bow to the over-riding need to achieve greater national purpose and prosperity.'[14] That seems to me to be abandoning too many fields, unnecessarily, to too many enemies. I prefer the kind of conclusion reached by Maurice Peston that the role of higher education is likely to increase in relation to the economy, but the task of becoming more responsive to national needs can best be accomplished by the institutions taking the initiative themselves.[15]

The problems of curriculum, of the profile of teaching and research, and the traditions and values associated with them, are inextricable from another set of problems to do with institutions, with the expansion of the system since the second world war, and with the reasons both for that expansion and for the forms it took. I would like to discuss just one component — the purposes and implications of the expansion. Broadly speaking, in Britain we did not give much attention to the implications of expansion for higher education. We had a silly debate about whether more means worse, and in 1963 Robbins attempted — in less than four pages of the report on *Higher Education* — to discuss aims and principles. We discussed, hotly, a 'pool of ability', academic governance, and student participation, and occasionally such matters as whether, at the end of the 1950s, the elevated Colleges of Advanced Technology should be technological universities or plain universities. We did not much care how many new universities were in suburbs or green fields, and there was little debate about the UGC preference for sites of not less than two hundred acres. There was discussion of and report on degrees broad and narrow; single-honours and modular, on what a Nuffield research group rightly called 'The container revolution'. Having aired our prejudices about numbers and size and structure or even democracy, most of us went on doing what we thought we knew how to do best. We did not really discuss higher *education*. If that sounds unduly cynical, may I summon two witnesses in my support — only two, but worth calling.

Richard Hoggart, then still a university teacher, said in a lecture in 1965: 'Like most people in the educational world, I am engaged almost to the point of pre-occupation with expansion and its effects — and don't get enough time to think about them.'[16] That may seem light years away now, but it is how it was in most places and for most people. If the history of the nineteenth century cannot be written confidently around Newman and Arnold, neither can the history of the past quarter of a century be written around the new universities and the Robbins report. That things were happening at new universities in Falmer or the outskirts of Norwich, or that the UGC was publishing them did not alter the basic national picture, and a host of good intentions did not alter the realities of institutions accomplishing much expansion and little thought. In most places, as with Hoggart, there was not the time. More important, I doubt if there was the will.

Sir Frederick Dainton, from a quite different point in the higher education spectrum, wrote a note on science in higher education in the period 1945–60, though what he says has implications well beyond that date. He describes the rapid growth in the proportion of the gross national product placed at the disposal of scientists, and he asks:

> So what did the scientists in universities do? They enjoyed a bonanza. With money and research students in plentiful supply they 'pursued research', winning approbation whatever the quality of the product ... possibly because would-be critics were bemused by the sheer quantity. There was no need to change courses; all that was necessary was to produce more chemists, physicists or whatever, cast in the same mould as their teachers, acquainted with as much of the latest rapidly growing information as students could tolerate through an undergraduate curriculum determined in its essentials by research scientists using primitive pedagogic methods.[17]

And not just scientists, of course. The world did not stand entirely still. The Hale Committee on university teaching methods did, in 1964, point to weaknesses and suggest remedies, including operational research, training and experiment.[18] Dainton tried to move the schools and Swann to move the universities to think about new approaches to science and technology.[19] Things did happen, but Hoggart and Dainton were basically right.

If we plunged into expansion without too much concern about the validity of what we were expanding, the same is true for the institutional implications. This is particularly the case of attempts to describe differences amongst the sectors of institutions which, in the late 1960s and 1970s, entered the new-named territory of higher education. How complex that territory became is something — if I may be autobiographical for a moment — I encountered at close quarters. I taught in a College of Commerce, which was a College of Further Education, and which became part of Hull College of

Higher Education. I then taught in a Technical College which is now Huddersfield Polytechnic. I then moved to a College of Advanced Technology — which then became a school of the University of London (having almost, in combination with what is now Hatfield Polytechnic, become an independent university in Hertfordshire). I then became principal of what started life nineteen years ago as a Teacher Training College, became a College of Education and was, when I arrived, a College of Higher Education. Since Bulmershe has almost nothing but degree level students, including masters' and PhD students, my visitors from Japan or Kuwait want to know how we differ from a university and — even whilst explaining the Council for National Academic Awards — I am hard put to tell them. My point is not that we have indulged in troublesome, unsystematic or unnecessary developments. The point is that we have not really thought about and discussed the educational implications of what we have been doing. On the rare occasions that purposes have been declared, they have not been the subject of serious debate — least of all in the universities. The invention of the binary system, as Peter Scott has rightly shown us, combined two parallel and conflicting motives. Were we seeking to build a bright new technological future, or were we protecting the universities from too many encroachments on their traditional pattern of activities? The history is at least ambiguous, and if Scott is right in suggesting that 'the binary policy was never intended as an instrument of radical change in higher education' we are guilty of never having seriously debated why not, or what would be.[20]

In terms of the institutions rather than the system, the difficulties of definition are enormous. By what criteria do you judge the difference between a university and a polytechnic? If one takes such criteria as research and teaching, part-time and full-time students, the curriculum and its content, size, students' motivation, either the overlap between them is too great to make sense, or there is — in Maurice Peston's words, 'no reasons *a priori* why (one) sector should have certain characteristics'.[21] The polytechnics, even given their own differences from one another, have often laid claim to a common concern for vocational content in their courses — but the claim is equally valid for some if not all of the British universities, according to how you resolve the ambiguities of the definition. There is certainly considerable overlap in curriculum, research is as much a commitment of the polytechnics as it is of the universities, and no institution or kind of institution has a monopoly of good or bad teaching, of part-time students, or of anything else I can detect.[22] The polytechnics, needless to say, have had to overcome resistance and ignorance. Sir Lawrence Bragg once considered it impossible for the higher technological education to take place in 'any institution which is under the direct tutelage of the Ministry of Education or the local education authorities' — which were competent only to control 'technical schools serving local interests'[23] — a view that has not entirely disappeared over thirty years and many developments later. With that hurdle surmounted, the question then had to be faced of whether the Colleges of Advanced Technology and the polytechnics could or should teach in areas considered traditional to the universities. There were questions as to whether they should conduct research at all, and if so in more than narrowly specified areas. The very existence of their degree work, or their postgraduate teaching and research, was widely ignored or misrepresented. As with the development of state colleges in the United States, there were attempts to view the universities as 'critical' and the rest as 'service stations', and — however the relative positions were allocated — the universities as first-tier, and the others as second- and third-tier.[24] And then, of course, when the colleges and institutes of higher education entered the picture in the 1970s, there was not only massive misunderstanding of their roles and standards within the universities, but also self-defensive positions by the polytechnics, alarmed at having to protect their tenuous hold on higher education against a new wave of immigration. It all sounds a bit like Boston in the nineteenth century.

Critics of all these policies and outcomes have argued that if the intention was to create, in the polytechnics particularly, a British higher education sector somehow similar to the technological institutions which emerged in nineteenth-century mainland Europe or in the United States, the policy signally failed. It is not only the directors of the polytechnics who have argued that they have been underfunded to achieve such a purpose. In 1950 the UGC described the continental system of establishing technology outside the universities in high-status institutions, and the American system of establishing a 'great range of work both in technology and in technical studies' inside the universities.[25] It could be argued that the way decisions were implemented in the 1960s and 1970s achieved the worst of both worlds.

My contention is that it is impossible to discriminate between the university and other sectors of higher education on the basis of defensible criteria. You can, of course, discriminate in providing resources and thereby introduce or strengthen differences in quality and inevitably of standing. The transfer of the UGC to the Department of Education and Science, however, together with the search for new forms of accountability, the likely and growing similarity between the new National Advisory Body for the main-tained sector and the UGC in their agency functions on behalf of the government — all of these have eliminated major differences with regard to institutional autonomy, public accountability and outside influence or control. This does not mean that institutions enjoy parity of prestige. That is a different and long story, but it would be helpful to consider for a moment two related aspects of how the different sectors of higher education are viewed by two constituencies — by employers and by students.

First, what is it that employers want of higher education? Do they want different things of different kinds of institutions? Without attempting to summarize the available research I would like to underline how contradictory or ambiguous are the declared expectations of employers. Again, there are national differences, and Michael Sanderson has described, for example, the nineteenth- and twentieth-century involvement of Scottish professors and their research in engineering, electrical physics and shipbuilding.[26] With the slow growth of willingness by English employers to employ university graduates — in many cases the reluctance not being overcome until the past quarter of a century — no unanimity or even clear pattern has emerged in the qualities employers seek in the graduates they employ. There have been pressures for greater specialization, and especially for greater practicality in higher education courses, the outstanding example being the argument of the Finniston report on engineering in favor of students gaining 'an understanding of engineering practice within the working environment'.[27] Employers in certain industries, or more precisely those who do the recruiting at certain levels in certain firms or services, have a clear picture of the particular skills they require of certain graduates in certain situations. But that is only part of the story. There are also employers who want something very much less specific from graduates, in order to complete the specific requirements themselves. Over the past couple of decades this employers' lobby seems to have been consistently strong. It is less than twenty years since *The Times* 'Review of industry and technology' reported that some firms took graduates because 'bright people nowadays go to university'. A representative of a steel company at that time said: 'If there were other alternatives we would go for them'.[28] A year before, in a debate preceding the publication of the Robbins report, the chairman of the English Electric Company called for encouragement to be given 'to a general education with a proper balance between science and the arts', and the chief education office of ICI hoped that the problem of overspecialization would be tackled.[29] At the beginning of the 1970s the chairman of Shell Transport and Trading and of Shell International explained that 'tomorrow's executives will have to be competent in a much wider field than at present, and in Shell we are applying more scientific methods in order to find them in good time and then equip them for their future responsibilities'.[30] There are of course many interpretations of what constitutes a broad education, but Sir David Barran's 'then' is important and not untypical. The Swann report on the employment of scientists, engineers and technologists argued in 1968 for 'a more general scientific or technological education with specialism grafted on later', and specifically for a broad first degree to be followed by 'continuing education and training, beyond graduation and throughout the career.'[31] Touraine, looking at the international crisis in university education in 1980, suggested that big firms in fact prefer future employees to have a general knowledge precisely because the firms 'prefer to supervise the training of members of their staff ... so that they themselves remain in direct control of what is most closely connected with their own particular operational system'.[32] At an OECD conference in 1982 a Japanese representative concluded, as Maurice Kogan summarized him, that 'Japanese industry probably prefers students with general knowledge and vitality to people with specialized knowledge'. Kogan underlined that in both Japan and Britain 'the stereotypes of industry knowing what it wants and students and higher education failing to meet industry's expectations must be seriously modified'.[33]

There is continuing evidence that many employers have no clear view of any existing or desired relationship between undergraduate studies and what is required of graduates in employment. Evidence from the employers themselves to parliamentary committees and elsewhere reveals constant stress on personality characteristics, extra-curricular activities and general education, together with diverse views about and interpretations of specialization and broadly-based study. The Fulton committee on recruitment to the civil service reflected but certainly did not end the debate about a change from the recruitment of 'generalist' administrators and 'intelligent all-rounders' to the recruitment of people to 'do a specified range of jobs in a particular area of work, at any rate during their early years.'[34] There is evidence from within the Council for National Academic Awards, from the 'Expectations of Higher Education' project based at Brunel University, and elsewhere, that the confusion amongst employers about what they want — even in highly specific areas of expertise — is not less now than it has been. The range of views is likely to remain as wide as ever, the interpretation of vocabularies just as confused, and the job of higher education in reading the signals — whilst crucially important — no less difficult.

If the employers' expectations are so complex and uncertain, in a sense those of students seem more clear. The findings of the available research seem very similar for Britain and other countries. In explaining their presence in higher education students over the past couple of decades have tended to use more rather than less vocational arguments. The figures and the arguments are consistent and revealing both of secondary school and of higher education students. As one researcher put it, some 80 to 90 per cent of sixth formers (in this case aspirants to a university or a college education) tended to 'eschew the "academic" and espouse the "applicable".'[35] Another researcher found that students expect priority to be given to a combination of intellectual and vocational goals.[36] Other researchers found that in a sense (the phrase is important) vocational goals are relevant to all students.[37] The question is, in what sense? The researchers in this field have tried to break down the question and explore students' perceptions of more or less specific vocational goals, and although there are obvious differences between, say, engineering and English students at the level of specific expectations and links between courses and precise job destinations, there are consistent vocational emphases across the whole range. Researchers have therefore suggested a clash between the practical/vocational orientation of a majority of students and the academic/ research orientation of a majority of those who teach them. What students expect is therefore not what they often find. One research conclusion is that students expect better teaching than they get, expect a greater relationship than they find between the staff's research and the quality of their teaching, and even where students expect to participate in the academic culture of the institution and try it, they are frequently disappointed and opt out.[38] On the reverse side, therefore, staff expect students to achieve excellence by criteria students often do not share or understand.[39]

There are other elements in what students expect of their subjects and institutions. They see hierarchies in both — for instance, a higher status for science than for technology[40] and often have uncertain expectations of differences between, in particular, universities and polytechnics. Not surprisingly, parents also see disparities between expectations and realities. One project which looked at parents' goals for their children's university life discovered three main goals. The parents thought that universities should (a) work students hard, in a few specialized subjects, with 'a supporting cast of academic counsellors'; (b) provide career guidance, and (c) develop skills for dealing with other people. Among their lowest priorities was learning for its own sake. Parents were, however, least satisfied that their highest priorities were being successfully attended to by the universities.[41]

Although the vocational target of many students and their parents is no more precise than getting 'a more interesting job', and the aim of employers something as vague as to detect 'qualities of leadership' in potential employees, questions are being asked of these and other constituencies, and institutions are expected to respond. These attitudes and expectations are difficult to discover, to interpret and to respond to — given the basic conceptual ambiguities. But while we are responsive to change in the economy, in technology, and in various public agencies, we have also to take into account those other publics whose involvements can and must be made explicit.

Let me summarize the implications I see for the universities in the conflicts and dichotomies I have discussed so far.

*First*, universities will inevitably continue to be drawn into debates about the relationship between their curriculum and structures and processes and methods on the one hand, and employment, the professions, the labor market, on the other hand. Internationally, the literature of the past decade has been busy with these debates. If the autonomy of the universities appears undermined by this, then it is no good looking for solutions in Newman or Flexner. If there are traditional values that appear to be at stake, then these will need to be scrutinized and redefined, knowing how relative they in fact look across national boundaries and across time, and how far they have already been transformed in the late twentieth century.

Employment is not part of the world outside, it is in the motives, aspirations and expectations of students inside. I would argue that universities will need increasingly clear understandings of the relationships between what they offer and how it is perceived by the largest possible range of constituencies and contenders. Their dialogue with the forces of social and economic pressure will need to be less symbolic and rhetorical, and more open and explicit. In contraction, expansion or steady state, the learning/employment relationship is bound to attract increasing attention, and needs to become a permanent feature of university research and policy analysis. I am not predicting how universities will or should react, I am describing a situation in which their functions, their definitions, their activities, have become negotiable, and their success (in their own terms) will be increasingly dependent on entering the negotiation with maximum clarity and awareness of the processes in which they are engaged.

*Second*, I would select as priority in that process a much clearer understanding by universities of the world outside as it is brought inside in the shape of students. I believe now as I did in the 1960s that students were at that time being radical about the wrong things. Leaving aside the wider political concerns of some students, in relation to their own institutions, student debates about university government and membership of senates and academic boards and committees and so on were either wrongly targeted or unduly narrow. What students really needed was to be seen as members of their institutions, as integral, as counting in some fundamental sense, not as customers, as guests. To return to one of my earlier points — the history of universities is very often a history without students, except as statistics. Psychologists and sociologists and others have shown us more clearly in recent decades that students are *there*, with analyzable characteristics, as participants in processes. The history of universities needs to become also a history of adolescence, of student expectation of academic, social and adult life — including employment. You cannot talk about the purposes of universities in modern society, in my view, without asking what students want of them, and without discussing the implications for the institutions. It is not enough, and it certainly will not be in the future, to assume we know, to identify students with the institutions' unchallengable values and purposes. They need to be asked, as do all the partners and contributors who have historically been, not silent, but not heard.

*Third*, British universities will have to learn far more clearly than they have done so far, that society has altered the landscape of higher education without consulting them, and the world out there now contains two major components with which they are still fairly unfamiliar: first, a hundred or so institutions which are not universities but which are doing things barely, if at all, distinguishable from what universities do; and second, the need to think in terms of a national system, or at least pattern, of higher education, with consequences that need sustained discussion. I have been in many places where it is clear that university teachers do not understand that the newer institutions now share the landscape with them, share an interest in good teaching and research, provide courses which require students to enter with similar profiles and to reach similar destinations, share the same system of external examiners, the same anxiety to exert institutional control over the curriculum, over staff development, over the whole range of institutional operations. Many university people do not begin to know what polytechnics and colleges actually are and do, and the nature of their share in the new, if still incoherent, structure called 'higher education.' Approximately one third of all undergraduates in Britain are reading in degrees not of universities but of the Council of National

Academic Awards, in polytechnics and colleges; and large numbers of others are taking degrees in colleges validated by universities. In defining themselves universities are now doing so in competition for students and resources in a total system, and most discussions of universities have little meaning unless they are located in that wider context.

One disincentive to considering the whole pattern of higher education has been the underlying anxiety about autonomy *vis-à-vis* government. Are we, by admitting the existence of a 'system' weakening the UGC, lessening university autonomy, increasing the power of national and local government, streamlining higher education ready to be controlled all the more tightly by the exchequer, the needs of national finance and economics, the busybodies of politics, industry and commerce? These dangers are no less real today than when our Victorian spokesmen worried about them or than when Thorstein Veblen in the United States railed so splendidly against them. The Americans are tormented by them — with Burton Clark and others explaining how inefficient is European-style central control of higher education, and a flurry of academics and administrators agonizing over creeping or rampant dependence on or interference by the federal government since the mid-1960s.[42] In Britain we have experienced, in different ways, the same phenomenon. Edward Shils has recently talked of the United States and British governments moving 'steadily forward towards making the universities the instruments of their social ideals of efficiency, of justice and of the pre-eminence of government over all other institutions.'[43] Shils starts from the point that 'the autonomy of universities in the face of governments has been genuine but it has never been complete',[44] and it is important that without hysteria and blinkers we should look both at the history of that incompleteness, and at the nature of the experience of non-university institutions that are now part of the landscape of higher education.

This is not an appeal for some easily packaged 'rationalization' by which 'functions' or characteristics or quality are carefully distributed throughout the system (when the criteria for doing so are, in any case, elusive and ambiguous, liable to political over-simplification). It is an argument for recognition that higher education has become a new, complex concept and reality — within which older interpretations of 'the university', 'vocational' and 'liberal' education, have to be — and already are being — fundamentally re-evaluated. In one similar form or another the same is true of West Germany or the United States or Australia or Britain. The economic hazards of the 1980s cannot disguise the distance run by the new higher education 'systems' of the two previous decades, and the traditional, or even the new and innovative, universities have to understand the impact of the recently admitted runners.

There are solutions to the British higher education tensions that have been canvassed but little discussed, and could be feasible even within present difficult realities. Peter Scott has argued for the acceptance of between 80 and 100 universities.[45] Robbins argued twenty years ago, after the report, for 'more and more university institutions with limited areas of activity.'[46]

Charles Carter wants more higher education but fewer universities, each a centre of excellence.[47] Some polytechnic directors have proposed chartered status for their institutions in parallel with the universities. My own preference has been, not for a large number of separate new universities, but one new federal National University, incorporating polytechnics, the main colleges, the CNAA and the Open University.[48] My point is that we are inevitably, with the trends of the past few years, and with the emergence of the National Advisory Body for local authority higher education, or whatever succeeds it, in a new world, a world of imperatives we cannot escape. An opportunity for the would-be controllers is also an opportunity for those intended to be controlled — as social control theories too often ignore.

Establishing a coherent pattern of relationships in higher education is a chance to make something more acceptable of our present unsystematic system, to relate and to respond on the basis of better understandings of our present and our future than we have at the moment.

The third implication of my discussion, therefore, is that we need to pay a great deal more attention not just to the separate sectors of higher education, but to '*higher education*' with its wide domestic and social dimensions and concerns. There are historical and contemporary components to that argument. Without attention to them the issues facing universities or other institutions of higher education seem to me narrowly defined, intractable, and in the end insoluble — issues of the vocational and liberal not excepted.

## Notes

1   See R.O. BERDAHL (1959) *British Universities and the State*, London, Cambridge University Press.

2   A. ASHBY (1974) *Adapting Universities to a Technological Society*, San Francisco Jossey-Bass, p. 138.

3   See M. SANDERSON (1972) *The Universities and British Industry 1850–1970* London Routledge and Kegan Paul; S. ROTHBLATT (1976) *Tradition and Change in English Liberal Education: An Essay in History and Culture*, London Faber and Faber, and ROTHBLATT (1976) 'The past and future freedom of the British university,' *Minerva* XIV, 2.

4   A.D.C. PETERSON (1961) 'Degrees for living,' *The Observer Weekend Review*, January 8, 17; K. AMIS et al. (1961) 'The threat of the practical,' *The Observer Weekend Review*, February 26, p. 21.

5   A. ASHBY (1963) *Technology and the Academics: An Essay on Universities and the Scientific Revolution*, London, Macmillan [First edition, 1958], pp. 81–5.

6   UNIVERSITY GRANTS COMMITTEE (1950) *A Note on Technology in Universities*, London, HMSO pp. 3–4.

7   A. FLEXNER (1930) *Universities: American, English, German*, New York, Oxford University Press, pp. 255–6.

8   W.R. NIBLETT, ed. (1975) *The Sciences, the Humanities, and Technological Threat*, London, University of London Press.

9   *Ibid.*, p. 19.

10   E.F. Cheit (1975) *The Useful Arts and the Liberal Tradition*, New York, McGraw-Hill p. 136.

11   D. Hawkins (1973) 'Liberal education: a modest polemic,' in *Content and Context, Essays on College Education*, C. Kaysen, (ed.), New York, McGraw-Hill.

12   A. Touraine (1980) 'Decline or transformation of the universities?', *Prospects*, X, no. 2, p. 193.

13   House of Commons (1972) *Minutes of Evidence Taken Before the Expenditure Committee* (education and the arts sub-committee) London, HMSO, memorandum of evidence by the Committee of Directors of Polytechnics, examination of witnesses (N. Lindop), p. 135.

14   House of Commons (1980) *Minutes of Evidence Taken Before the Select Committee on Education, Science and Arts*, London, HMSO, memorandum submitted by the Committee of Directors of Polytechnics on the Planning and Control of Higher Education, p. 122.

15   M. Peston (1979) 'The future of higher education,' *Oxford Review of Education* 5, no. 2, p. 131.

16   R. Hoggart (1965) *Higher Education and Cultural Change: A Teacher's View*, Newcastle Upon Tyne, University of Newcastle upon Tyne p. 3.

17   F. Dainton (1975) 'A note on science in higher education: the era of certainty, 1945–1960,' *The Sciences, the Humanities and the Technological Threat*, W.R. Niblett, (ed.) London, University of London Press p. 36.

18   University Grants Committee (1964) *Report on the Committee on University Teaching Methods*, London, HMSO.

19   See Council for Scientific Policy (1968) *Enquiry into the Flow of Candidates in Science and Technology into Higher Education*, London, HMSO, and Committee on Manpower Resources for Science and Technology (1968) *The Flow into Employment of Scientists, Engineers, and Technologists*, London, HMSO.

20   See P. Scott (1979) *What Future for Higher Education?* London, Fabian Society p. 7, and P. Scott (1981) 'From binary to pluralism,' Opening Address to the Residential Conference of the Standing Conference of Principals and Directors of Colleges and Institutes of Higher Education, Stoke Rochford, Mimeo., pp. 3–9.

21   Peston, 'Future of higher education', p. 130.

22   See H. Silver (1980) 'Enforced conformity or hierarchical diversity?', in *Education Beyond School: Higher Education for a Changing Context*, N. Evans, (ed.), London, Grant McIntyre, pp. 55–63.

23   L. Bragg (1949) 'The place of technological education in university studies,' in *Conference of the Home Universities: Report of Proceedings*, Association of Universities of the British Commonwealth, London, p. 75.

24   M. Trow (1982) *Defining the Issues in University-Government Relations — an International Perspective*, Berkeley, Center for Studies in Higher Education. Occasional Paper no. 27, p. 23.

25   University Grants Committee (1950) *A Note on Technology in Universities*, London, HMSO, p. 4.

26   M. Sanderson (1972) *The Universities and British Industry 1850–1970* London, Routledge and Kegan Paul pp. 389–90.

27   See Committee of Enquiry into the Engineering Profession (1980) *Engineering Our Future*, London, HMSO p. 84.

28   (1964) 'Does industry know what it wants?' *The Times Review of Industry and Technology* 2, no. 10, p. 83.

29  See contributions by LORD NELSON of Stafford and F.H. PERKINS (1963) in 'Robbins: The great debate,' *The Times Review of Industry and Technology* 1, no. 8, pp. 73–4.

30  D. BARRAN (1971) 'Industrial requirements from the universities,' in *University Independence*, J.H.M. SCOTT, (ed.) London, Rex Collings p. 122.

31  COMMITTEE ON MANPOWER RESOURCES, (1968) pp. 75–9.

32  TOURAINE (1980) *Prospects* X, no. 2, p. 192.

33  M. KOGAN (1980) 'Expectations of higher education within the policy setting,' p. 5. Introductory paper at OECD Conference on Higher Education, Hatfield, Mimeo.

34  COMMITTEE ON THE CIVIL SERVICE (1968) *Report of the Committee, 1966–8*, I, London, HMSO, p. 78.

35  L. COHEN (1970) 'Sixth-form pupils and their views of higher education,' *Journal of Curriculum Studies* 2, no. 1, p. 70.

36  R. OXTOBY (1971) 'Educational and vocational objectives of polytechnic students,' *Universities Quarterly* 26, no. 1, p. 88.

37  J.L BRENNAN and K.A. PERCY (1976) 'What do students want?,' in *Proceedings of the Second Congress of the EARDHE*, A. BONBOIR, (ed.) Louvain-La-Neuve, I, p. 150.

38  K.A. PERCY and F.W. SALTER (1976) 'Student and staff perceptions and "the pursuit of excellence" in British higher education,' *Higher Education* 5, no. 4, p. 466.

39  *Ibid.*; see also, H. SILVER (1983) *Education as History*, London, Methuen chapter 8.

40  See D. HUTCHINGS (1963) 'Sixth form scientists in search of an image,' *Universities Quarterly* 17, no. 3; and D. HUTCHINGS (1967) *The Science Undergraduate: A Study of Science Students at Five English Universities*, Oxford, University of Oxford Department of Education.

41  D. CHILD *et al.* (1971) 'Parents' expectations of a university,' *Universities Quarterly* 25, no. 4.

42  See, for instance, P.G. ALTBACH and R.O. BERDAHL (eds.), (1981) *Higher Education in American Society*, Buffalo, Prometreus Books and D. BOK (1982) *Beyond the Ivory Tower: Social Responsibilities of the Modern University*, Cambridge, MA, Harvard University Press.

43  E. SHILS (1982) 'Great Britain and the United States: legislators, bureaucrats and the universities,' in *Universities, Politicians and Bureaucrats: Europe and the United States*, Cambridge, Cambridge University Press p. 483.

44  *Ibid.*, p. 437.

45  P. SCOTT (1981) *What Future for Higher Education?*, London, Fabian Society pp. 22–5.

46  LORD ROBBINS (1966) *The University in the Modern World and Other Papers on Higher Education*, London, Macmillan p. 9.

47  C. CARTER (1979) 'Not enough higher education and too many universities?,' *The Three Banks Review* 123.

48  H. SILVER (1983) 'A national university — the next step?,' *The Times Higher Education Supplement*, April 22.

# For Whose Benefit? The Objectives of English Studies Today

*Mary Waldron*

'Now let us go through that once more', said Mrs. Garth, pinching an apple-puff, which seemed to distract Ben, an energetic young male with a heavy brow, from due attention to the lesson. '"Not without regard to the import of the word as conveying unity or plurality of idea" — tell me again what that means, Ben.'

(Mrs. Garth, like more celebrated educators, had her favourite ancient paths, and in a general wreck of society would have tried to hold her 'Lindley Murray' above the waves.)

'Oh — it means — you must think what you mean,' said Ben, rather peevishly. 'I hate grammar. What's the use of it?'

'To teach you to speak and write correctly, so that you can be understood,' said Mrs. Garth, with severe precision.

George Eliot, *Middlemarch*, Chapter XXIV.

By the time George Eliot wrote *Middlemarch* in 1871, Lindley Murray was already out of date;[1] looking back to 1829 the novelist could poke gentle fun at old-fashioned teaching methods. What was new in 1795 had very little relevance for Ben thirty-four years later, and in 1871 had become laughably pedantic. Nevertheless, Mrs. Garth still believed that the old standards, however little likely to have any message for the young, should be upheld; new methods and new theories would have seemed to her not only unreliable but dangerous. But even in 1829 there *were* new ideas in the air, as any educational historian will affirm. Since then much has been written about the teaching of English, and as this century progresses the output seems to grow by a geometrical progression, without the least sign of any consensus emerging. Seeking to remind myself, for the purposes of this chapter, of at least some of the research which had affected my own teaching career, I spent some time in the Library of the University of London Institute of Education. There, shelf after shelf, dauntingly stuffed with innumerable volumes on various aspects of this language of ours and its place in school curricula, made me feel that the subject I had chosen was altogether too large for the compass of a single chapter. But it is not only writers, imaginative and otherwise, who pay such close attention to the teaching of English; everybody feels entitled to have their say, and the only thing that they all agree about is that English is very important. In fact, anybody contemplating for any reason the present state of education in England will take it for granted that, however narrowly pupils at secondary level may specialize in chosen subjects as their school life progresses, they should continue to study English as a matter of course. Pressed for a reason for this assumption our theorist may be less clear, and the acknowledged truth may disintegrate in a welter of supposition and myth. There is something heretical, even to teachers of other subjects, in the suggestion that English is of anything less than overriding importance in the curriculum.

This state of affairs is not a particularly healthy one; it is the result and at the same time the creator of very high expectations — expectations which in the nature of things cannot be fulfilled to everyone's satisfaction. I should like in this chapter to examine the nature of these expectations and to show how they create dissatisfaction in the public mind and confusion in the minds of English teachers about what is required of them which serves neither the interests of the liberal arts nor those of commerce, industry and the professions. The variety and strength of the pressures exerted upon English departments in secondary schools are almost bound to defeat the most assiduous of organisers and it is inevitable that at any one time some omission or loss of emphasis will attract criticism, often of a very destructive and uninformed kind. I should like also to show how present-day theory may be offering us a chance to reconcile some of the pressures and resolve the conflicts.

Where, then, do these pressures come from? In order to give some kind of answer to this question we must examine the attitudes of the interested parties and discover what each group feels should result from the nine years (at least) of English teaching which every child in the country receives.

Perhaps the first and most important group consists of the pupils themselves. Their views are not often heard outside the classroom, which is strange, considering that they are the ones most directly affected.

Parents, too, have an attitude which must bear upon the teacher of English because it is to parents that teachers have personally to justify what they are doing and explain how it fits into the pattern of society as a whole.

Next comes a group of people who regard themselves as the true 'consumers' of the 'product' — the employers of school-leavers, and also those in charge of higher and further education (education which continues after the statutory school-leaving age of sixteen). Employers have always been most vociferous in their criticisms of the abilities in English of the young people whom they interview for jobs. Such criticisms are detectable far back into the mists of time. 'It is a great surprise and disappointment to us to find that our young employees are so hopelessly deficient in their command of English': thus Messrs. Lever Bros. in 1921; in the same report, Messrs. Boots Pure Drug

Co. had the following to say: 'the teaching of English in our present day schools produces a very limited command of the English language .... Our candidates do not appreciate the value of shades of meaning, and while able to do imaginative composition show weakness in work which requires accurate description, or careful arrangement of detail'.[2]

Almost exactly similar charges are brought today; the question is — are they more justified — as many assert — than ever before? And, indeed, what kind of English teaching would exactly measure up to the requirements of employers engaged in a wide variety of business activities? What 'shades of meaning' are being referred to by Messrs. Boots as essential to the communications of their clerks and storekeepers? Such critics usually have a fairly narrow range of uses of English in mind; what often arouses the fury of a teacher of English is their insistence that there is an easy way of providing just what is needed in the linguistic equipment of school-leavers who have had no experience of the business world. One complaint I received a few years ago from a departmental manager of a local firm was that their top-level recruits did not know how to write an inter-office memo. My reply that I knew of no definitive method and therefore left all that sort of thing to the firm's own induction procedures was received, to say the least, coldly. In fact, much of the dissatisfaction stems from a conviction that there is only one way to write well, and teachers of English should teach it. Employers seem unaware that they all have their own favored methods of stringing words together, some of which would find no favor at all with the school examining boards.

The complaints from teachers in higher and further education are perhaps more justifiable in that the linguistic competence they require is academic and should be familiar to school-leavers. But they complain that their students arrive from school deficient in the basic skills of oral and written language; they cannot explain clearly what they mean, and they cannot use the normal conventions of spelling and punctuation when they are required to write something down. It may be true that standards of this kind are falling, or at least changing; and yet a very little research among past commentators will reveal that they always have been 'falling'. It would be a fairly safe bet to say that few university teachers have ever been satisfied with the standard of English among their freshmen students. In the nineteenth century these deficiencies were probably put down to a surfeit of that undisciplined modern writer, Dickens; in the twenties of this century to an undue preoccupation with rag-time and popular songs. The universal explanation given nowadays is that something 'permissive' has been going on in the schools and that it ought to be looked into.

The average 'consumer' is, I suppose, only vaguely aware that never a moment passes but that someone *is* looking into it; that there is a continuous open-ended debate about content and teaching methods. There are a number of national and even international bodies dedicated to this activity: the National Association for the Teaching of English, the English Association and the English-speaking Union are among the best known. Books about English teaching pour from the presses; universities initiate research projects on the subject, and from time to time the government of the day will produce a report of which the state-funded educational system is expected to take notice. This battery of advice often conflicts fundamentally with the views of the badly-informed but far from silent majority. Furthermore, institutions concerned with the training of teachers will of necessity have to select from this avalanche of theory and information. As a consequence, newly-trained teachers will often differ very greatly from one another, depending on the particular emphases of their courses.

These, then, are the groups providing the pressures and expectations: students and their parents, employers and other 'consumers', and the 'experts'. I write from the point of view of one who for some years, as head of the English department of a large neighborhood comprehensive school, serving young people between the ages of eleven and eighteen, was responsible for bringing all these expectations together in the classroom. Those of us who take on this task need to understand and appreciate the flux of theory and ideal which takes place over the years and underlies teacher-training; know and allow for the difficulties which beset teachers at the 'chalk-face'; and — perhaps most difficult — come face to face with the society which pays us to teach their children in the shape of parents and employers. As well as all this there is often the need to justify to other teachers in a school the extra time allocated to English; because, although teachers will accept this in theory, in practice they often make very clear their dissatisfaction with what has actually been achieved. The question of grammatical terminology, for instance, has often been the subject of very acrimonious debate between teachers of English and those in charge of foreign languages during the past thirty-odd years. The requirements of public examining boards, too, press closely on English teachers and again sometimes conflict painfully with received opinion among educational theorists.

It will now perhaps be helpful to allow those groups of people responsible for the pressures upon teachers of English to speak for themselves. As far as possible I shall confine myself to what is happening now — in the 1980s — but it will be necessary to take some steps back into the past to indicate how we may have arrived at the present situation.

Let us first hear what pupils have to say about the matter. In England, until children are eleven years old, English is not easily identifiable as a separate 'subject'. In the six or seven years of their primary schooling they will have learnt how to decode written English and, it is to be hoped, to find enjoyment and information in reading; they will also have learnt to write with varying degrees of organization and success. When they transfer to secondary school they will find 'English' on their timetable for six 35 or 40 minute periods during the week, separated from history, geography, science and other traditionally defined subjects, in what will be, to them, a totally unfamiliar way. Pupils in their first and second year at secondary school are not always clear about what is going on in their English lessons. Much of what they do may seem eccentric and the result of the personal interests of the teacher they happen to have. There follow some comments written by such children when asked what their English lessons were supposed to do for them. The comments are in the children's own spelling.

This is Claire, now aged fifteen:

> In my first year at (secondary) school I had Mr. T. for an English teacher. He was alright — well, for an English teacher. He would sometimes get too excited, though. We had drama during our English lessons and this was when he would get excited, he would get us to join hands and skip round and round singing, in the middle of the playground. We occasionally did some work, though, usually reading and a lot of punctuation.

This is typical of the mystified acceptance of what obviously seemed activities of doubtful relevance, to say the least, though I must add that Mr. T. was a highly successful and popular teacher!

Melanie, aged twelve, is more specifically critical:

> There are some things I don't like about English and some I do. I don't like writing poems and I don't think that poems can help you really unless you're thinking about becoming a poet.... Word games are important to your vocabulary....

Mark is obviously very confused but disarmingly willing to accept whatever comes:

> English is an important subject in this world. When I was a junior (i.e. in primary school, to the age of eleven) I thought English was handwriting and punctuation, not reading, righting and games etc. When I first arrived at (name of secondary school) I didn't know what to expect from English. The first piece of English I did was a kind of puzzel. We did poems, short stories carols christmas cards everything.

The word 'everything' is very suggestive of the degree of vagueness with which pupils regard their English lessons, and their inability to pin down exactly why they are so 'important in this world'. A hint of some practical aim comes in the next extract from Greig, also aged twelve, although it is clear that tying in all the activities of the typical English lesson has defeated him:

> I think English is a very good subject and every school should teach it. And it is good because if you cannot spell words very well at all you would not get a job.... English is boring in some ways and good in other ways.... We do English to improve our reding, riting and speaking the laguge. This laungauge should be tourt in every school. We do many things like rite stories and poems, read plays. And we have discussions about polotics. And other types of things.

It is clear that Greig's job prospects are poor if they do in truth depend upon his spelling! To the teacher of English, however, it is even more serious to note that he is missing or failing to grasp any clear aim in his English studies. Perplexity is writ large in every line.

Karen, aged thirteen, perceives other possibly practical aims:

> Sometimes we are given books to read but often choose our books. I think the more you read the better you become at other subjects. . . . English is a good subject we have discussions because it helps your speech.

Employment prospects figure very largely in the comments of the older pupils. It should be explained for those unfamiliar with the system that a number of independent examining boards set General Certificate of Education 'Ordinary' and 'Advanced' level examinations each year for young people of sixteen–plus and eighteen–plus. These are intended to identify roughly the top twenty per cent of ability in each subject. Regional CSE (Certificate of Secondary Education) boards provide for those sixteen–year–olds deemed less likely to succeed at O-level. Although the system is divisive and unreliable, and long overdue for reform, these qualifications are used extensively by employers and universities in their selection procedures and are therefore taken very seriously by most young people. Here is Tim, aged fifteen: 'We get more lessons than in any other subject because in most jobs you need your English "O"-level besides other qualifications.'

Paul, also fifteen, agrees: 'I think we are justified in having more lessons in English because when you go to a job interview the main requirement is either a good CSE result or an O-level.'

Most of the comments from fourteen- and fifteen–year–olds took the same line, but there was no detectable attempt to explain how those things that were tested in the all–pervading 'exams' were linked to life outside school. There was in fact much less criticism of the curriculum than there had been among younger children. Older adolescents are perhaps prepared to accept even poetry if it seems — however oddly — to be one of the keys to success in life! But it is very clear that these pupils, although they expect that the study of English will somehow, however mysteriously, make them better and more acceptable to the world outside school, have abandoned the attempt to understand how their activities in English lessons will achieve this.

The parents of these same fourteen- and fifteen–year–old students are often less acquiescent. 'Will he satisfy the examiners?' 'Will she get into university?' are often among their main preoccupations. Examination success is seen as the main aim of the pupil's final years at school, but some skepticism is expressed about the way in which courses are being handled, especially if the parent's own experience of school was widely different. Concern is often expressed about the literary content of English courses; parents assert that their children hate literature, that it is in any case useless and only taking up time that could be used to improve their spelling. 'How can you seriously expect a boy of fourteen to read *Pride and Prejudice*?' I was asked once at a parents' evening. 'Easily,' I replied — silently adding the rider 'if you don't queer my pitch by suggesting otherwise.' Almost as destructive to the successful inclusion of literature in these courses is the 'medicine' approach. Many parents have a strong belief that it is part of everyone's education to become acquainted with the literary 'heritage' of Britain. It is frequently seen as an unpleasant but patriotic duty which will make their children better citizens, rather in the same way as cod-liver oil was once used to build their bones. The growth of the mind and spirit through the *enjoyment* of literature is often quite outside their comprehension; and furthermore, even its medicinal virtue is for the most part confined to the literature of the past; 'modern' literature is often seen as harmful — 'sloppy' in expression and morally depraved. A third attitude is often apparent at parents' evenings; many are glad to see their children reading anything in the shape of a book, believing that in this way their written English will gain in fluency and maturity. Though this has at least the virtue of making literature superficially acceptable, it does not really bear close examination and will not prevent such parents from blaming literature if the spin-off fails to occur. The view that literature is an essential sharing of the common experience of the species is rare indeed.

I have isolated parents in a group of their own for the purposes of this discussion, because although they may also be employers and colleagues of young school-leavers — they may even be teachers themselves! — as parents they are in a special relationship with those who are educating their children — a more intense and anxious relationship than they usually have with anyone else. As employers of young people, adults are able to take a more detached and often acerbic view. As we come to this group it may be helpful to quote from a leading article which appeared recently in a serious, somewhat right-wing newspaper, stating its view of the present state of affairs on the educational scene:

NOW READ ON, IF YOU CAN
The lost ability with words of children under eighteen, their helplessness with railway timetables and newspapers, their paralyzed incompetence with percentages, graphs, and concepts like the rate of inflation is a social tragedy of a growing order. Ten per cent of young adults now admit to technical illiteracy — that is, to be so unversed in reading and spelling that they cannot write a letter or read a job advertisement. The implied figure of two million illiterate Britons understates the reality, says the Adult Literacy Unit; even that is closing fast on peasant illiteracy rates in backward Mediterranean countries. What has gone wrong?

Nothing, blandly reply progressive teachers; modern children receive a visual education, their parents got a literary one. In many families this visual education means only the six hours lolling before the television of the average child in 1983, mindlessly viewing a flicker of images when his parents 30 years ago read books. But the problem goes deeper. Socialist teachers are full of contempt for literary English, as for anything which smacks of 'standards' or 'proper use'. So grammar is no longer taught, 'correct' English said not to exist, and children are democratically informed that one man's English is as good as another's and that the use of words is more or less up to them. Dictionaries since 1960 have been loyally compiled on the basis that the meaning of a word is no more than the majority vote at any time. All of this has devalued the importance once attached to language and to effective expression. . . .[3]

It can be fairly safely assumed that this article must have provoked a number of replies demolishing its specious and tendentious arguments. However, the ones that were actually printed joined in the criticism with considerable gusto — thus:

Sir — It would be pleasant to think that your strictures upon inadequate literacy could be confined to those held to have had inadequate opportunity to know better.

At this time of year I am the recipient of many startling letters from graduates. I have some before me as I write. One, with an upper second in English, is interested in 'persuing' a career in librarianship. . . . Another, similarly endowed, addresses me as 'The Principle'. . . .[4]

and in reply to this: -

Sir — Mr. —— 's letter on the inadequate literacy of graduates comes as no surprise to those of us who work in the field of technical publications.

Typically, an analysis of a report from an engineer engaged in commissioning a system installed in a large ship showed that out of 51 items mentioned, deficient information was the cause of 16 problems and a probable associated cause of a further 12. . . .

One cannot escape the conclusion that many English teachers rate the ability to communicate effectively and accurately lower than the ability to conceive an imaginary situation and embellish it with a hotch–potch of whimsical metaphors and flamboyant adjectives. They seem to live in a literary fairyland, far removed from the world of real people, few of whom will ever produce any published or substantial work that involves inventing a story; but most of whom would derive substantial benefits from being able to write powerfully, fluently and precisely.

The time has come to establish new criteria for the evaluation of literature. It is neither reasonable nor realistic that year after year a substantial part of the 'A' Level English paper is based on Chaucer, an author whose works are hardly ever read outside the educational establishment.

The inevitable result of such policies is the creation of an intellectual gulf between educational literature and reality, and the consequent abysmal level of functional literacy of which Mr. —— rightly complains. The failure to teach English in a way that is convincing and realistic results in many pupils, especially boys, 'switching off' at an early age. Meanwhile, the panorama of factual literature, from the writing of Copernicus to the biographies of our most eminent statesmen, together with the scintillating spectrum of personal qualities from which this literature stemmed, is virtually ignored. This seems tantamount to an intellectually supercilious disregard for the very human bedrock on which our present civilisation is founded.

Is it really unreasonable to suggest that the balance between factual and fictional writing in the educational system should reflect the balance between factual and fictional writing in society at large?[5]

Perhaps the most interesting thing about this correspondence is the fact that, though it took place over a period of little more than one week in the summer of 1983, and the letters purport to be responses to the same article and to agree with each other, the three writers are in fact saying quite different things. For example, the leading article complains that children do not read any more; the first correspondent dwells heavily on the poor spelling of two of his applicants as evidence of a total collapse of standards; and the second correspondent moves into a completely different area, almost contradicting the original article by suggesting that inaccuracy in communication may be due to too great an emphasis on imaginative writing and the study of fiction. In fact, any fairly representative group of critics at any time will present this muddle of analysis and solution; it becomes very obvious that while they all agree that something is *wrong*, they do not agree about the *causes* of their dissatisfactions. All have their theories on the cure for these ills, and all assert that it surely can't be too difficult to teach people to write and speak in good plain English that everyone can understand. Now the truth happens to be that it is very difficult indeed, that the interaction of language and society is almost impossibly complex, and that English teachers have never been able to do more than tinker with their pupils' use of a living, volatile and largely uncontrollable medium. The trouble is that teachers of English are somewhat coy about admitting this, and sometimes try to collude with their critics by claiming to have found a new and entirely reliable solution to the problem. I think it is true to say that these new methods and practices *never* sound sensible to people who do not teach English, and therefore the usual charge levelled at the teachers is this: that they have abandoned the search for a strategy which will dispose of these problems for good and all, in pursuit of some educational fad of the day.

It is clear, then, that one of the chief blocks in the interaction between society at large and education is the continuing and rapid flux of theory taking place in the various kinds of educational research. Partly because of the strong tradition of decentralization and independence in England, individual schools do not have to wait for central approval in order to experiment with new ideas; nor are teachers compelled to abandon old ones. The result is that any 'outsider' is likely to get a distorted view of the educational scene from experience of too small a sample. This freedom, valuable in so many ways, also bears heavily on people responsible for the organization of English courses, for they will have to accept a very wide spectrum of method and theory among their teams of teachers. In order to appreciate the complexity of this task the reader may like to be reminded briefly of the influences which are likely, in 1983, to be affecting a team of English teachers who may be up to thirty or more years apart in age, tradition and experience. In examining these influences I shall be dealing with the last of my 'pressure groups', whom I have called the 'experts'. I use this term in no derogatory sense; such people are nearly always very successful and experienced teachers themselves and differ from the majority of teachers only in their ability and desire to embody their ideas in writing. And yet there is no doubt that their message, necessary and salutary though it may be, often contributes to confusion and conflict both inside and outside schools. A glance at the period from Butler (the 1944 Education Act) to Bullock (the 1974 government report *A Language for Life*) may provide some evidence of this.

Teachers trained in the fifties, and obtaining their first experience then and in the early sixties were subjected to a particularly strong wave of change. This is not the place to go into all the structural changes which took place in English education in the fifties as a result of the irresistible egalitarian forces at work in society after the Second World War. Similar forces were producing a change in the approach to teaching in general. During the first part of the period under discussion there was a violent swing away from the vocational towards the liberal in education. This is not to say that there had been no conflicts before 1944 — the remarks of Messrs. Boots and Lever in 1921 make it quite clear that there had been — but that because of a restructuring of society it became possible to repudiate the idea that specific groups of children should be educated 'for' certain occupations. After many years of talking, writing and reading about democracy in education it at last became possible to do something about it. Schools began to concentrate on turning out well-rounded, well-adjusted and happy individuals who could *then* be trained to cope with any paid employment they might find within their mental capacities. The idea of education as instruction, the imparting of knowledge, was to be replaced by the exploration of children's own experience, which would gradually lead them to an understanding of the common experience of the human species. English studies were particularly affected by this new set of ideas, because it combined very well with the current theory of literature as a vital moral force, which stemmed from Cambridge University and the Leavisite critics. The great literature of the past and present and the practice of imaginative writing were to become central to the English curriculum. This basic ideal was very evident in teacher-training during the fifties and gradually found a voice in pedagogical literature, particularly in the sixties. The works of David Holbrook are well-known, but I should like to quote two short passages as a reminder of the all but religious fervour with which these views were held at the time:

> Our minimum aim is to develop powers of imagination in every child so that the school leaver has had some experience, in phantasy, of the major adult problems of living . . . . Every child should gather thereby that such problems are common to all mankind, and are met with varying degrees of moral quality. Even the weakest pupil should have at one time or another, felt deeply about a story or a poem, so that the experience provides a sense of balance, the enlargement of sympathy, and a grasp of values.

And again, this time specifically of Shakespeare:

> to ignore his work, or regard him as 'old-fashioned', or to fail to see all poetry . . . as a present spiritual force, an essential means to dealing with life in our own time, is virtually to deny the advances the human spirit has made since Shakespeare's birth.[6]

In 1963 a country school-teacher called Sybil Marshall wrote *An Experiment in Education*,[7] an account of the way the extreme simplicity of the equipment and surroundings in the tiny school wherein she was the only teacher led her to make use of her pupils' own observation and experience of their rural environment as a basis for their work in all subjects. Although she differed from such thinkers as David Holbrook in that she believed that the unifying activity should be the visual representation and interpretation of experience through drawing and painting, she eventually came to a similar conclusion — that the written word can also be the key to understanding. The chief contribution she made to the theory of English teaching was her collection of the spontaneous creative writing of children.

These works, reflecting as they did the spirit of the times, found much favor among teachers, and contributed to the altogether more liberal, less authoritarian regime in English classes. There was a new respect for children's writing, and several other collections were published.[8] The general atmosphere of the sixties fostered acceptance and a loving appreciation of children's work.

There was, though, another side to all this pleasant acceptance and optimism which was not agreeable to everybody: it also involved the abandonment of such things as schemes of work and syllabuses. The whole pedagogical ideal which was set up required spontaneity first and foremost, and Sybil Marshall herself admitted the possibility of spontaneity deteriorating into chaos in the wrong hands.[9] Moreover, the holy fervour which seized many people concerned with the teaching of English began to seem a little over-wrought even to some of the faithful, and to bring a hint of *folie de grandeur*. Here is Boris Ford addressing the National Association for the Teaching of English in 1965:

> As teachers of English we are now used to being reminded that the child's use of language, and sensitivity of response, and delicacy of perception, and grasp of moral values, and sense of cultural tradition, and spiritual maturity are in our care. . . .

and later: 'As teachers of English we are (we know) the custodians of a literary heritage that stretches from Chaucer to Wesker.'[10]

It was hardly surprising, if these were indeed the responsibilities that English teachers were taking on themselves, that those outside the profession, and some of those inside it also, began to feel that English teaching had reached a cloud-cuckoo-land from which practicalities were all but excluded. It was at this point that the very justifiable expectations of children, their parents, and employers that young people should leave school equipped to deal with the real world began to look as if it was being neglected. Certainly the seeds of reaction were already present, as we shall see. But the ideas expressed by Holbrook and Marshall had enough fundamental truth in them to have remained current long after the more extreme applications of them have disappeared; teachers in 1984 still try to exploit the moment — and though theory now demands a more structured approach, there are still teachers, trained in the mid-fifties, who doggedly refuse to produce schemes of work on the grounds that all work in English should have an element of surprise for both teacher and taught; the unprepared exploration of passing experience which cannot be expected from a structured work-scheme. This is all very well, but as reported by the pupils to their parents these lessons may appear to the uninitiated to be more dedicated to saving preparation time for the teacher than fostering their children's sensitivity of response. Many teachers of English are also prepared to uphold the theory that all work should be based, in different ways, on imaginative literature; they believe that it is only in literature that we can observe language being exploited to the full. This may sound like nonsense to the Gradgrind perceptions of the correspondent quoted earlier, who clearly believes that only facts can represent reality, and that nobody can write 'powerfully, fluently and precisely' unless they are writing about facts. No real consensus is possible in this situation, only compromise; and there is no doubt that by the middle of the sixties, a compromise was necessary. However, before we examine the nature of that compromise, there are two other causes of concern to be touched upon.

The first of these was the disappearance of formal grammar from the English curriculum. Almost from the turn of the century there had been a school of thought which believed that the categories used to describe classical languages were unsuitable for living languages such as English. Otto Jespersen was perhaps the first to formulate this theory,[11] but in 1923 the English Association published *The Problem of Grammar* which directly challenged the habits and traditions of the public and local-authority secondary schools.

'English . . .' it suggested, 'must not be tied down to a system of grammar which does not recognise to the full the fundamental facts of its structure'. Board of Education circulars tried to resist this new attitude, pointing out that teachers of foreign languages had a right to expect basic grammatical terminology to be taught by English teachers, and suggesting a compromise; it did not seem too much to expect, the writers averred, for pupils to have mastered 'the distinction between a relative and an interrogative pronoun, or between the main adverbial clauses'.[12] What a shock it would be for them to be suddenly translated to a present-day English school where a number of the teachers, let alone the pupils, would find such distinctions totally incomprehensible, the vocabulary being completely unknown to them. By 1955 in fact the teaching of grammar had almost disappeared from the English curriculum leaving a uneasy vacuum. P. Gurrey sums up received opinion of 1954 on the matter:

> We shall be concerned here only with language as expression, and with the pupils' training in language. We need not consider the teaching of facts and theories *about* language — with figures of speech, the history of the language, changes in meaning, derivations or grammatical classifications; because for the great majority of pupils in secondary schools the ability to *use* language effectively and appropriately is vastly more important to them than to be able to reproduce what they have read or have been told about language.[13]

From the mid-fifties, then, it became almost sinful amongst young teachers to breathe the words 'noun', 'adjective' or 'clause' in the classroom.[14] If instructed by heads of department to set aside a period for formal grammar they simply refrained. A generation of pupils grew up without a vocabulary with which to refer to the structure of the language. By 1965 a small segment of these had become teachers, and there was more and more evidence that the general public found the loss of analytical grammar, the relaxed attitude to such matters as spelling, handwriting and punctuation, and an apparent obsession with unfamiliar literature and classroom drama very alarming. Thus theory and what were seen as the practical needs of everyday life seemed to part company, resulting in a loss of confidence on all sides. Such doubts die very hard and are clearly responsible for much contempt for English teaching in the community at large, and the horrified reaction to quite predictable statistics about literacy and examination results. As with literature, there is an underlying, so far unresolved conflict of aims giving rise to these dissatisfactions. The public in general tends to see grammar-teaching as prescriptive — an important way of preserving 'standards of correctness', which they imagine to have been laid down for all time. Teachers, on the other hand have long since come to regard language as a much more volatile medium which may perhaps be described, but hardly controlled.

Connected with this was the apparently even more alarming abandonment of standards of spoken English. In this area, developments in sociology had begun to affect the teaching of English. Respect for the individual naturally involved respect for his or her mode of speech. 'Received standard' pronunciation or an approximation thereto had up till then always been required of children in school. From 1945 dialect had become increasingly respectable; Basil Bernstein's work on 'restricted' and 'elaborated' codes, imperfectly assimilated, begot a wariness and loss of conviction rather than a new certainty.[15] Nobody really knew whether dialect was a degraded form of speech or a complex and effective means of communication unfamiliar to, and therefore despised by, the mainly middle-class teaching profession. As with grammar, the uncertainties were not cleared up once and for all, but shelved. Today the reaction has arrived in the work of J. Honey, who holds that we seriously let down our children by encouraging them to believe that received standard is no longer required of them.[16] Professor Honey thinks that the pre-war prejudices are alive and well and damaging our school-leavers' employment prospects. His arguments may have some cogency, as the occasional irritated comment such as I have quoted earlier seems to suggest, but it seems very unlikely that any thoroughgoing change will now occur in the schools. Any obligation to correct children's speech habits would go seriously against the grain, and is one of the elements in the hostility between teachers and this quite vocal section of the public. Michael Marland's *Language across the Curriculum* very admirably presents a mean between these two attitudes which may gain ground — but for the moment there is undoubtedly considerable disagreement, which creates another element in the confusion of aims in English departments.[17]

The foregoing section seeks to sum up, all too briefly, perhaps, what constitutes by far the most persuasive wave of educational theory of the present century, and it remains the strongest influence in most English teaching today, although in a modified form. Its keynote was relaxation, a non-authoritarian acceptance of life and literature as educators. By the mid-sixties it was almost inevitable that a reaction should set in, and a new theory, stemming from the young science of linguistics, began to gain some currency among teachers of English who had one or two doubts about the universal efficacy of the charismatic approach advocated by the followers of David Holbrook. This new questioning of the objectives of English teaching was to have very far-reaching results, culminating in the adoption of the idea of language and its use as central to all education, and thereby throwing new and enormous responsibilities on to teachers of English.

In 1964 a Programme in Linguistics and English Teaching was launched by the Communications Research Centre at University College, London, under the direction of Professor M.A.K. Halliday. Successive working papers produced during the next four years got to grips with many of the problems perplexing English teachers at the time. Briskly, the first paper, *The Relevance of Linguistics for the Teacher of English*, written by Ruquaiya Hasan and Stephen Lushington, and published in 1968,[18] summarized the extreme unease generated by what Geoffrey Summerfield had referred to as 'a chronic non-coordination of learning and a non-policy of *ad hoc* excitements.'[19] Other papers in the series questioned the centrality of literature in the English curriculum, insisting on the broadening of the subject-matter of English to take in all modes of discourse in common use. It also advocated a training in descriptive linguistics and phonetics for English teachers. This was pretty revolutionary stuff, and it was only to be expected that, England being England, a sizeable number of practising teachers would resolve to ignore the movement. It did, however, throw the whole basis of English-teaching theory into the melting pot; a large number of books were published which quite properly found their way into teacher-training programmes, but the approach was so different that it was inevitable that conflict among English teachers at all levels should result.[20] One of the most unwelcome misunderstandings which arose out of the re-introduction of grammatical terminology was that some older teachers, for years frustrated by the outlawing of formal grammar teaching, simply reverted to the prescriptive, Latin-based grammatical categories of their youth. In fact, the distinctions between the old and new approaches were subtle enough to require retraining, of which there is a perennial lack in England. Thus organizers of English departments, whilst aware that Geoffrey Summerfield might well be right, had good reason to feel that the cure was worse than the disease. Moreover, there was as yet little agreement about which linguistic description of English might be most suitable in schools. (A welcome attempt to bring order to the chaos has recently been published under the aegis of the English Association called *English Grammar for Today*.[21] It seeks to bring all the relevant ideas in language research in recent years into a coherent and useful course for teachers. Even so it fails to take into account the presence of many teachers, trained from the mid-sixties onwards, who have *no* knowledge of traditional terminology.)

By 1970, therefore, an uncomfortable loss of direction was apparent in any English department seeking to do an efficient job. This and widespread public unrest about 'standards' led to the government's report *A Language for Life* in 1974. While offering reassurance about the general state of English teaching, (seen as mere 'whitewash' by some), the Bullock Committee used some of the findings about 'language in use' advocated by Professor Halliday's team of researchers to suggest a new approach to the handling of language skills in schools. The concept of 'language across the curriculum' is well known and has been thoroughly discussed by many eminent educationists.[22] From the point of view of heads of English departments it has meant a fundamental rethinking of the place of the English teacher in the work of a school, and almost insurmountable difficulties of leadership. It has always, as I hope I have shown, been difficult to organize and lead a group of people influenced at different times by different, equally plausible theories, and battered at the same time by the demands of the public; since the Bullock Report it has been expected that English teachers will play a leading part in the development of language over the whole range of subjects — so that the individual prejudices of even more people have to be confronted. How this will work itself out has yet to be revealed. On the evidence of the newspaper correspondence columns this new concept has so far done little to reassure the public. On the credit side, the theory of 'language in use', the movement away from the centrality of imaginative writing towards the practical and trans-actional, is definitely providing English teachers with a better opportunity to interface with society as a whole, if they find a way of making use of it.

But, though there is some satisfaction to be gained from the prospect of a closer connection with the practical side of life, and perhaps less hostility from the community, there is a danger now that in the process of reshaping courses and bringing other teachers into the dialogue, English teachers could lose sight of their cultural aims; that in slotting literature into an equal instead of a leading place in English studies we may lose sight of it altogether. 'Language across the curriculum' represents a compromise for teachers of English with those who maintain that facts are all-important; but it would never do to capitulate altogether. While we concern ourselves with the use of English in laboratories, workshops, offices and other such places, we should not forget that it is in literature that vocational and liberal studies meet and overlap: it is the most human of all the humanities. It is important that we should be prepared to explain and defend the relevance of literature in any discussion of language and its use. We may not share the vision of David Holbrook and other writers of the sixties, but we must never lose the conviction that literature is a vital component of education. It will survive if pupils can satisfy their parents as well as themselves that the study of the prose and poetry of the past and present offers real enlightenment; for this reason English teachers must be able to explain the nature of this enlightenment and show how it links up with life as we live it now. In the face of people who sincerely believe that good spelling equals good English, and that imaginative writing must necessarily lack power and precision, this is a difficult enough task; but there is no reason why it cannot be accomplished provided English teachers keep their objectives clear and the public informed. Educators in England are proud of their system's decentralization, the independence of individual institutions, and that of its teachers. If this results in so much whistling in the dark, then independence has become isolation, in which little can be achieved. Some rational agreement about the responsibilities and aims of English teachers would enable them to face their critics, as well as their classes, with confidence and assurance, bearing in mind vocational requirements, but giving due weight to those things which impress us so strongly with our common humanity — 'the very culture of the feelings'.[23] This agreement is a matter of real urgency; if teachers themselves appear to be unsure about their aims, they cannot complain if the center of decision is moved outside the profession itself.

It is important, too, to be honest about what can and what cannot be done in a school. It should be clearly understood that there is no strategy for English that will take care of every call made on everyone's linguistic competence. Failure in communication is bound to occur sometimes. Nor can anyone be taught a facility with language beyond the level of their intelligence. There will always be a range of competence — and there will always be some illiterates. As for spelling, punctuation, 'good' pronunciation and grammar, it must be accepted that habits will change and the expectations about what can be done in English lessons will have to change too. Education reflects social change, but it can neither create it nor hold it back. It is therefore quite unrealistic for anyone to expect teachers to extract from their pupils standards of convention-al 'mechanical accuracy' significantly different from those evident in the society in which they live. Perhaps an acknowledgement of these limitations will be hard for teachers to make — but it would be worse to ignore them. Those concerned with the welfare of young people, and the young people themselves, should be aware, behind the inevitable flux of methodology, of a clear set of honest, attainable aims adapted as far as possible to the require-ments of society as well as to a cultural ideal. Recent developments in theory have made this perhaps more feasible than ever before. The study of their native language ought to give our children confidence, interest and happiness in all the situations in which they need to use it. The joke against Mrs. Garth quoted at the beginning of this chapter is that her teaching material was too pompous and obscure to have a hope of producing clarity in the expression of the young. It may be true that teachers are often in danger of requiring blind faith in the efficacy of all their methods. It would be pleasant to think that the Ben Garths of the future might enjoy a more honest and enlightening dialogue with their educators.

## Notes

1  L. MURRAY (1795) *An English Grammar*, first published in York, England. Lindley Murray was born in Swetara, near Lancaster, Pennsylvania, USA, in 1745, but settled in York, England, in 1771. His work enjoyed extraordinary popularity throughout the nineteenth century. It should be borne in mind that 'grammar' at that time comprised most of what is now called English Language and Literature. The reference in the introductory quotation may be found on page 210 of the 1808 edition, under the heading 'Syntax: rule IV'.

2  Quoted in the Report of the BULLOCK COMMITTEE (1974) *A Language for Life* London, HMSO.

3  1983 *The Daily Telegraph*, July 25, p. 10, column 1.

4  1983 *Ditto*, July 28, p. 18, column 5.

5  1983 *Ditto*, August 3, p. 12, column 5.

6  D. HOLBROOK (1961) *English for Maturity*, Cambridge, Cambridge University Press.

7  S. MARSHALL (1963) *An Experiment in Education*, Cambridge, Cambridge Univer-sity Press. I should mention two other influential books of this period: F. WHITEHEAD (1966) *The Disappearing Dais*, London, Chatto and Windus; B. JACKSON and D. THOMPSON, (Eds.) (1964) *English in Education*, London, Chatto and Windus.

8  The best-known of these, R. JONES (1962) *Explorations*, London, Routledge and Kegan Paul, appeared before the publication of Sybil Marshall's book. I am aware that this movement in England came long after similar work in the USA — for example F.J. ARNSTEIN (1946) *Adventure into Poetry*, Stanford, Stanford University

Press.

9   S. Marshall (1963) *Experiment*, Cambridge, Cambridge University Press, Chapter 2, esp. p. 42.

10  B. Ford, Editor of *The Pelican Guide to English Literature* and prolific writer on literature and education. At the time of the address to NATE he was Chairman of Education at the University of Sussex.

11  O. Jespersen's most influential works were: (1905) *Growth and Structure of the English Language*, Leipzig, B.G. Teubner, and (1928–49) *A Modern English Grammar on Historical Principles*, parts 1–7, Heidelberg, and London, G. Allen and Unwin.

12  Board of Education, (1923) *Some Suggestions for the Teaching of English in Secondary Schools in England*, Circular, London, HMSO.

13  P. Gurrey (1954) *The Teaching of Written English*, London, Longmans, Green and Son. Professor Gurrey modified his views in (1961) *Teaching English Grammar*, London, Longman.

14  Some think this change occurred in the thirties. I am judging by the persistence of grammar questions on O-level question-papers well into the post-war period. See F.D. Flower (1966) *Language and Education*, London, Longman, esp. Chapter 19, 'What about grammar?'.

15  This research began in 1958 and has continued. For an analysis of Bernstein's work and its effect on educational thinking, see D. Lawton (1968) *Social Class, Language and Education*, London, Routledge and Kegan Paul, and for recent work on the subject, E.B. Ryan and H. Giles, (Eds.) (1982) *Attitudes Towards Language Variation — Social and Applied Variation — Social and Applied Contexts*, London, Edward Arnold.

16  J. Honey (1983) *The Language Trap*, National Council for Educational Standards, London, February. This body is partly funded by the Department of Education and Science.

17  M. Marland, (Ed.) (1977) *Language Across the Curriculum*, London, Heinneman, Chapter 4.

18  R. Hasan and S. Lushington (1968) *The Relevance of Linguistics for the Teacher of English*, London, Longman. These working papers were published in pamphlet form.

19  G. Summerfield (1966) *New Education*, Vol. 2, No. 3, March.

20  For example: F.D. Flower (1966) *Language and Education*, London, Longman. P. Doughty, J. Pearce and G. Thornton (1971) *Language in Use*, London, Edward Arnold, a source book for teachers; (1972) *Language in Education: A Source Book*, London and Boston, Routledge and Kegan Paul in association with the Open University Press; G. Thornton, D. Birk and R.A. Hudson (1972) *Language at Work*, London, Longman; M.A.K. Halliday (1973) *Explorations in the Functions of Language*, London, Edward Arnold, especially Chapter 5.

21  G. Leech, M. Deuchar and R. Hoogenraad (1982) *English Grammar for Today: A New Introduction*, London, Macmillan.

22  As well as M. Marland, (Ed.), *Language Across the Curriculum*, see, for example, E.H. Grundin and H.U. Grundin (1978) *Reading: Implementing the Bullock Report*, London, Ward Lock for the United Kingdom Reading Association; F. Davis and R. Parker (1978) *Teaching for Literacy: Reflections on the Bullock Report*, London, Ward Lock.

23  Quoted from J.S. Mill's *Autobiography* by D. Holbrook (1961) in *English for Maturity*, Cambridge, Cambridge University Press.

# Science, Technology, and The Liberal Arts: Educational Considerations for Human Resource Utilization

*Sheila M. Pfafflin*

Historically, mathematics and science have a legitimate claim to be part of the liberal arts. A knowledge of mathematics was considered part of the education of a citizen by the Greeks, and mathematics and astronomy were part of the curriculum of the medieval universities from which the liberal arts tradition derives. Superficially, this tradition may appear to have continued into the present day. Most universities still have mathematics and science departments in the arts and sciences college. Some colleges and universities still have requirements in mathematics or science which are justified on the grounds that an educated individual should know something of these areas. As David Saxon, a physicist and former president of the University of California, stated in his keynote address at a recent conference on science and technology education for civic and professional life, 'If the ability to distinguish sense from nonsense is an indispensable aspect of liberal education..., then in a technological society, science is an indispensable part of the liberal arts curriculum.'[1]

Practical considerations aside, science and mathematics have had a profound effect on the intellectual life of the modern world. Scientific developments, from the Copernican revolution to the theory of evolution, the theory of relativity, and recent discoveries in fields from physics to molecular biology and the social sciences, have done more than simply add to our store of facts. They have profoundly influenced the way in which human beings view themselves. Given this profound impact, it is difficult to imagine any set of humanistic disciplines which would not have the sciences and mathematics as core components. Nevertheless, further examination of the present day relations between the sciences, mathematics, and the traditional core of the liberal arts curriculum makes it clear that there is a division between these areas which is as profound as that between the liberal arts and professionally oriented schools and curricula.

To start at the most obvious level, the sciences and mathematics are not considered by most observers to be part of the liberal arts today. While there may be less than complete agreement about what fields should be included in the liberal arts, it is common to assume that they will be drawn from some combination of the humanities and the fine arts. The context of Dr. Saxon's remarks cited above is an example of this view. The conference he was addressing had been convened because of concern that the sciences do not, in fact, have the place they should in the liberal arts curriculum, despite the need which may exist for their inclusion.

Beyond the question of common perceptions, there are substantial differences which divide the sciences and the liberal arts in ways in which, say, English and history are not divided. Some of these have to do with the question of the content of the two domains. In the sciences, there tend to be natural relations between different areas. Biologists need to know chemistry, which is basic to the understanding of biological phenomena, and chemists need to know some physics. Virtually everyone in the sciences needs to know some mathematics. Similar interdependencies exist in the humanities. It is hard to imagine the study of literature without some understanding of the history of the period in which it was written, for example. Such direct connections between the sciences and the humanities are less common.

But more important than the question of overlapping domains of interest is the sense of belonging to the same kind of enterprise, which is common within the sciences, and the humanities, but which is not shared between them. This difference is less tangible, but it may be more fundamental. C.P. Snow, in his well-known exposition of the 'two cultures' caught the essence of the difference.[2] He took the view that scientists share attitudes, standards, and patterns of behavior, and that this common ground cuts across many other divisions. Similarly, shared values exist among humanist scholars, writers, and other 'intellectuals'. However, Snow perceived a gap of indifference, often bordering on hostility, between the two domains. He was deeply concerned about this gap, for he felt that a society which owed its pre-eminence to its technological accomplishments could not afford to have the leaders of its intellectual life indifferent to the intellectual tradition on which that technology depended. He made a strong plea for the need to help underdeveloped nations achieve technological sophistication. But he also warned against the smug assumption that the industrialized nations would always maintain their lead in the applications of technology. He predicted that they would find their pre-eminence challenged by other nations as they adopted Western technology.

Snow made these points in 1959, and he was speaking as an Englishman who was addressing primarily the situation in England, though he felt that his remarks reflected a reality which held for much of Western Europe and the United States. It is surprising, nevertheless, how contemporary much of his commentary sounds. Perhaps prophetic is a better word for it. He stresses the possibility that Asian nations, for example, could become major competitors of Western technology, and today we find ourselves scrambling to keep up with the Japanese. His concern over the transfer of technology to third world countries could have come out of many recent discussions on this topic.

I think most scientists in the United States today would agree that the different branches of the sciences share a common view of what constitutes science. This view may not be easy to articulate, but it is there. It is shared, to varying degrees, with other fields not labelled 'science' but these are most likely to be technical professions, such as engineering. The essence of this view was expressed by an executive of a major research laboratory who once said that 'Science is what scientists do.' The interesting thing about this remark, apart from the fact that it captures a unity which may not be apparent when most scientists give verbal definitions of science, is that it was made by an engineer, who automatically included his field of engineering in the scientific enterprise.

I have spent less time with scholars in the arts and the humanities than with scientists, but I sense that Snow is correct in perceiving among them a sense of common purpose. While it is true that scholars in the sciences and the humanities share a common commitment to the sphere of scholarship, it is no longer clear, as perhaps it once was, that the sciences and the humanities are part of a closely knit enterprise making up parts of a single tradition. The schism may not be as sharp in the United States as in Britain, partly because in the United States the 'third culture', which Snow identified in a later essay as consisting of the social sciences, and which he viewed as a potential bridge between the sciences and the humanities, has developed considerable strength.[3] Nevertheless, I believe that most observers would agree that the schism between Snow's two cultures does exist in the United States as well, and many would find it a cause for serious concern.

When did this division arise, and what caused it? Snow considered that it had existed in England since the beginning of the twentieth century, and he attributes it to the early start and high degree of specialization in English education. He believed that the greater emphasis in the United States on providing a broad education to all children had helped Americans to avoid the extremes of the division that he saw in England. Not all British scholars have shared his views on American education. T.R. Henn, a fellow of St. Catherine's College, Cambridge, has expressed his lack of faith in compulsory 'cultural spray' courses, for example.[4] One could also question the recent origin which Snow assigned to the development of the two cultures. Montesquieu's desire to remove the barriers to understanding scientific discoveries raised by technical jargon, forbidding language, and poor writing, suggests that eighteenth-century philosophers had a view of scientists that was not so far from many contemporary views.[5] Still, the leading scholars of the eighteenth century seem to have felt profoundly the excitement engendered by developments in scientific thought during the preceding century. A closer relationship between scientists and other scholars does seem to have existed in the past.

One factor which many have viewed as a major contributor to the maintenance of the two cultures, is the lack of communication which has developed as the sciences have become more and more mathematical. A working knowledge of mathematics is becoming essential for a person to comprehend many fields of modern science. Few individuals with training in the humanities possess such a background. Scientists are apt to perceive an asymmetry here, believing that they possess the skills necessary to understand the arts and humanities, while those trained in the arts and humanities do not possess the skills to understand contemporary science. Those trained in the arts and humanities will very likely perceive a symmetrical pattern of mutual incomprehension. Certainly, all fields of scholarship are becoming more specialized, and one result is that the skills required for professional understanding in another area are harder and harder to attain.

It is also true, at the practical level of designing undergraduate curricula, that the demands of a modern science curriculum, and especially its hierarchical pattern of prerequisites, tend to limit the availability of effective instruction for students who are not majoring in that field. The hierarchical nature is clearest in mathematics, where advanced courses usually will be incomprehensible without the necessary prerequisites, but it is a characteristic of many other areas as well. The same is true of some curricula in the liberal arts, especially foreign languages and the development of skills in the fine arts. Nevertheless, it is probably true that it is more feasible, without extensive prior coursework, for science majors to take advanced courses in the humanities, than for humanities majors to take advanced courses in the sciences. However, it should not be assumed that those who major in the sciences or mathematics will take advantage of the opportunity to obtain a solid grounding in the humanities, for the demands of specific majors make this potential difference less useful than it would at first appear. Thus, the implications of increasing specialization in all fields, and the increasing dependence of scientific and technological areas on mathematics, means that the 'two cultures' are likely to remain with us for the forseeable future.

In the context of this volume, the sciences appear to share characteristics of both the liberal arts tradition, and of training for a profession. The fundamental purpose of the sciences is to acquire knowledge. However, in the context of twentieth century American society, science is also big business. Figures given in the 1982 report of the American Association for the Advancement of Science analyzing the FY 1982 Federal Budget for research and development indicate that current federal support for R and D activities are running at about 1.2 per cent of the Gross National Product. Support for basic research is running over 0.15 per cent of GNP.[6] When one considers that, in addition to government funding, industry undertakes substantial R and D expenditures, it is clear that science and related technological research activities constitute a significant area in the United States.

The prominence of science and technology in modern society means that many young people will be attracted to careers in these fields. While many of them will be motivated by the desire for knowledge, the fact that science can provide good career opportunities is also a motivating factor. Studies indicate that individuals who major in the sciences show an early interest in science, and choose such careers relatively early. Although an undergraduate degree does not prepare students for professional-level work in the sciences, it can be a preparation for various kinds of technical careers, as well as being the basis for additional study in the sciences. As reported in studies by the National Science Foundation a substantial majority of majors in engineering and science, especially the physical sciences, go on to work in science or engineering.[7] Fewer graduates in the social sciences, which share a greater affinity with the humanities, remain in scientific professions. One must allow for the possibility that social science majors show a greater number of field changes because of limited opportunities in areas for which their training would be directly relevant. Nevertheless, it seems likely that these differences reflect the fact that most science majors are found to be working in science because they planned careers in science; relatively few students choose to major in a science simply because science is of interest to them *per se*. If one defines the liberal arts student to be one who is seeking a wide knowledge of the humanistic aspects of culture, combined with broad skills in expression and analysis, rather than seeking knowledge and skills relevant to a specific career, then few science majors would be included in that definition. Most science majors are seeking specific knowledge and skills.

Does this imply that the science-liberal arts dichotomy is primarily a liberal arts versus professional training decision? Certainly the question of whether to major in a specialized area such as science is an important one for students. Nevertheless, both the nature of the sciences, and the current concern over the role of the sciences in the liberal arts curriculum, suggest that the issues go beyond the question of providing sound career guidance to students.

In spite of their current independence, the sciences and the liberal arts both concern themselves with domains of knowledge which are part of the heritage of western culture, and which should, therefore, be part of the training of a broadly educated person. For the liberal arts, in particular, to write off the areas of human knowledge represented by the sciences would appear to be a fundamental departure from the ideal from which this tradition of education derives. There is the related concern that all citizens need to be adequately educated in the sciences, if they are to deal effectively with the demands placed on them by the impact of technology. The question of what constitutes 'adequately educated' has been the subject of much recent concern. However, on the part of the scientific community, at least, there seems to be little doubt about the desirability of the goal.

While the training of scientists may be conceived independently of the liberal arts, there are other considerations here as well. There are skills which are important for a successful career in the sciences but which receive little emphasis in most science curricula. The ability to write well, and to give organized oral presentations are among these, and it is commonly held that greater exposure to the liberal arts will improve these skills among scientists.

Beyond the immediate question of useful career skills, there is the need for scientists to have the breadth of background and experience to make humane policy judgments affecting society. While the vision of the mad scientist merrily brewing disastrous potions in his laboratory regardless of their consequences has hopefully always been more a product of science fiction than of science itself, it is clear that as science has come to play a larger role in our society, and as the technology deriving from science has become more important to us, the decisions made by scientists have become more and more significant. Decisions about the direction of future research, and the ground rules under which that research will be conducted, are no longer the concern of the scientific community alone, as the debate over recombinant DNA research showed, for example. The need for greater public understanding of science is certainly paralleled by the need for greater understanding by scientists of the needs of their society, and it is the liberal arts which are intended to provide this breadth of understanding.

### Career Implications: Science or Liberal Arts?

Nevertheless, there are career implications of a choice between the sciences and the liberal arts in our current society, which are relevant to the present discussion. Statistics on the entry-level salaries of individuals with baccalaureate degrees in various fields indicate that salaries are lowest in the humanities. These figures also show that in many fields, men receive higher salaries than women, and that this salary gap is greater for the humanities than for technical fields such as accounting or engineering.[8] Since women are less likely to major in the sciences than men, this difference contributes to the continuation of a salary gap between men and women. Unemployment also seems to be greater for those who majored in the humanities than for majors in many technical fields. It is true that not all areas of science show reduced salary gaps between the sexes, or relatively low unemployment figures. Some fields, such as the biological, behavioral, and social sciences also offer relatively poor career opportunities today. These are also the areas of science with the greatest numbers of women. The implications of this will be considered later in this chapter.

Entry-level salaries are not the only consideration in choosing a career, of course, and one of the arguments for a liberal arts education is the belief that it provides broadly applicable skills which are needed for advancement in many careers, and which provide some protection against the obsolescence of specific skills which is becoming a serious problem in our rapidly changing society. Engineering, despite its favorable entry-level pay and openings today, is considered by some observers to suffer from a relatively high risk of skill obsolescence.[9]

But will liberal arts graduates be able to obtain entry to professional level occupations in the 1980s? There is an excess of college graduates over openings for jobs which traditionally required a college degree for entry, and this excess is projected to continue throughout the 1980s.[10] As a result, it is expected that many college graduates will have to find employment in occupations which have not traditionally required a college degree, and, if the unemployment and underemployment patterns which now exist for different fields continue, it is likely to be liberal arts majors who are going to be disproportionately represented in the less desirable jobs. Whether the opportunity for future advancement will be as good for those who enter the workforce through such jobs as they have been for those who have gone into jobs which are now traditional for college graduates can certainly be questioned. So those who now choose a liberal arts education may face greater career hazards than in the past.

Advanced training in the liberal arts is unlikely to improve career opportunities for liberal arts majors, and could conceivably make them worse. The phenomenon of 'gypsy scholars' in the humanities already reflects the desperate employment situation for such scholars in the universities, and the absence of alternative opportunities to use their professional skills. While the reduction of opportunities in the universities has affected certain areas of the sciences as well, especially the social and biological sciences, opportunities in the physical sciences, engineering and computer science are expected to remain good in industry.

Thus, while we may have a need for those with the broad training provided by the liberal arts, in the sense that individuals with such training could make important contributions to society if they were given the opportunity to do so, it is by no means clear that they will have that opportunity during the coming decade. Given the investment in time and money which is implied by a college education today, students are already turning in increasing numbers to fields where the practical payoff is more certain. Pressures over the next decade seem likely to reinforce such choices. If our society wishes to continue to produce broadly trained individuals in substantial numbers, the question of how this is to be achieved in the face of these trends needs to be faced. Increasing the integration of education in the sciences and the liberal arts may help by providing a greater communality of background to both technical and liberal arts majors.

Greater integration of the science and liberal arts curricula also could have the beneficial effect of reducing the negative impact which the current division has on particular groups in our society. I shall be discussing women since I am most familiar with the issues which involve them, but other racial, ethnic and socio-economic groups may be similarly affected to varying degrees.

Women have participated in science and technology at much lower rates than men.[11] While this situation is changing to some degree, witness engineering, where women have gone from less than one percent of the bachelor's degrees awarded to over 10 per cent in the course of a decade,[12] the reality is still that most scientists and engineers are male, and this is especially true of those in senior, policy-making positions within the scientific community.

This difference in the numbers of women as opposed to men who choose the liberal arts versus the sciences, has several implications. One is that women will receive less return on their education than will men with equal amounts of education, since the technical professions tend to be more highly paid than those into which most liberal arts graduates are attracted. This situation is compounded by the greater salary differentials, favoring males, for graduates in the humanities, and by higher unemployment rates for women in these fields noted earlier. It also means that the projected shortage of jobs for college graduates during the next decade is likely to have a disproportionate impact on women, if they continue to major in liberal arts in greater numbers than men. It also means that the nation will suffer the loss of technical talent, since the technical abilities of women will continue to be underutilized.

Beyond the direct consequences of career choice, there is the question of the impact of technology on women. Science and technology have great impact on the lives of both men and women in today's society. However, because the roles and status of women differ from those of men, the impact on them of science and technology also differs. Much of the impact on women has been negative, despite the potential for positive change, and there has been concern that the absence of women from policy-making positions within scientific and technological professions has contributed to the negative effects, especially in areas such as the impact of transfer of technology to developing countries on women in those countries.[13] Recently, in this country, the implications of the introduction of microelectronic technology for occupations which have been predominantly female has also been a matter of concern. Both health concerns over the use of video-display terminals in word-processing equipment, and concern over possible 'de-skilling' of these jobs have been raised.[14] Again, decisions on the implementation of this technology are being made predominantly by men.

Furthermore, because so few women now go into science or technical professions, most women who will reach policy making positions in the future will have minimal exposure to science, and therefore may be disinclined to become involved in policy issues in this area. While males who are liberal arts majors may also lack formal education in science, there is reason to believe that males are more likely to receive informal education in science and technology than are females. In any case, there are many technologically trained males available for policy-making positions related to science, and few females.

The reason why so few women participate in science and technology has been the subject of considerable study. To some extent it can be attributed to barriers to entry into scientific and technical professions by educational institutions. For example, for many years, the percentage of physicians who were women had been in the range of 6–8 per cent. However, over the last decade there has been a dramatic increase in the percentage of women among graduates from medical school.[15] This increase coincides with the period when legislation such as Title IX of the Educational Amendments of 1972, made it much more difficult for schools to impose quotas against women. Thus the reduction in barriers to training must be considered a significant factor in this change.

In addition to explicit barriers, however, the stereotyping of science and technology as subjects which are appropriate primarily for males must also be considered a factor. Girls show less interest in science in high school than do boys, take fewer mathematics and science courses, and, although sex differences are not found in mathematics achievement in the elementary grades, by the time students have finished high school, sex differences in science and mathematics achievement are found in the graduates of some high schools. These differences carry over into the college years, when fewer women than men major in the sciences.

The perception of a dichotomy separating the sciences from other subjects exists well before the college years. Science is one of the least preferred subjects by 9 year-olds; 13 and 17 year-olds are somewhat more positive, but only a little over 10 per cent of these age groups indicate that science is their favorite subject. Mathematics is perceived more positively in the early grades, but enthusiasm for it falls off markedly in high school.[16] This situation is probably compounded by what many perceive as the present inadequacy of science and mathematics instruction at the pre-college level in the United States. The National Science Board Commission on Pre-college Education in Mathematics, Science, and Technology, of the National Science Foundation, has just completed a report which was highly critical of science and mathematics instruction,[17] and most of the recent reports concerned with pre-college education have identified the need to strengthen education in the sciences and mathematics. While concern over the adequacy of education in the sciences and mathematics has occurred before, particularly at the end of the 1950s after the Russians launched Sputnik, there is a difference in the focus of the current concerns. After Sputnik, the emphasis was on producing technical specialists. Today, however, there is concern with science literacy for the entire population.

One problem with most of the recommendations of these reports, which include prescriptions such as increasing the number of required courses in science and mathematics, is that they do not deal directly with the fact that many students lack interest in these subjects from the early grades. Improving the general quality of science and mathematics instruction may help in this regard, of course, as would remedial efforts in mathematics instruction comparable to what is now done in remedial reading programs. But unless there is a specific focus at the pre-college level on overcoming the low participation rates of women, minorities and other underrepresented groups, our colleges are likely to continue to receive incoming classes which already perceive the 'two cultures', and where disproportionate numbers of individuals in these groups will have opted out of the scientific domain.

## Achieving Change

It is easier to identify a need for a return to an education which provides greater integration of the sciences and the liberal arts than it is to specify ways to achieve this goal. In both areas, but especially perhaps in the sciences, the enormous growth of knowledge has resulted in the development of completely determined curricula. If one considers the demands of technologically oriented professions such as engineering, the problem is even greater at the undergraduate level, where virtually all of a student's time is allocated to career preparation.

The need to deal with the vast increase in knowledge has led to efforts to broaden the conceptual base of training even within technical professions. For example, an influential study of the engineering schools in the early 1950s concluded that there was a need to base engineering education more broadly on scientific principles, if engineers were going to have the breadth of background needed to keep up with the rapidly changing technology in their field. The Johns Hopkins University introduced an engineering science curriculum designed to respond to these concerns, and other engineering schools followed. While this development had no explicit concern with areas of study beyond the sciences, the analogy to education stressing broad knowledge and the development of reasoning ability as opposed to a more narrow, specific skills oriented training, is certainly relevant to this general issue.

Unfortunately for those who would like to see a broadening of education for students in the sciences generally, the engineering science effort found it necessary to compromise with the need of the profession for engineers trained with the specific skills which industry requires. While engineering education has not returned to the narrow focus of earlier times, the schools have found that there is a need to maintain a curriculum that is more specifically oriented towards engineering. The Johns Hopkins University itself recently re-established its engineering school as an entity separate from its arts and sciences school.

When one considers educating non-science majors in the sciences, there are even more formidable barriers. Despite a number of innovative courses in recent years, no one has come up with an accepted approach for teaching science to non-science majors which will leave them with useful skills. 'Physics for Poets' courses can be excellent, but they often have the same relation to training in the sciences that a course in art history does to the training needed to become a professional artist. The recent conference on this topic sponsored by the AAC and the AAAS, warned that too often at present, science courses for non-science majors are simplified introductions to the major field which fail to provide general knowledge about science and technology as enterprises.[18] Participants at the conference made a number of recommendations regarding desirable outcomes of an improved curriculum, including such goals as having students learn about scientific investigation and the nature of scientific knowledge from a curriculum which includes mathematics and laboratory courses in science, exposure to engineering principles and the concepts of modern technology, computers, and questions of personal and social values raised by science and technology. While these and other goals would appear desirable, however, it is by no means clear how new curricula are to be designed which will accomplish these goals.

Simply adding additional requirements in science and mathematics appears unlikely to make much change in well established attitudes about these fields. At a number of points in this chapter, two problems have emerged repeatedly: how to persuade students who have already formed negative attitudes about a particular subject that they should nevertheless study it, and how to find the time to fit additional courses into already crowded curricula. No one, to my knowledge, has developed solutions which are fully adequate, but some steps to overcoming these obstacles can be identified.

First, there is a need to define more precisely the goals of additional study in areas outside of one's major field. This is necessary for those majoring in the sciences and other technical subjects, but it is especially necessary for those majoring in the liberal arts and other majors not related to science and its related technologies. This is true in part because concern over educating professional students and those majoring in the sciences has existed for some time, and has already received considerable attention, and because providing useful education to non-science majors in the sciences raises a number of questions about which there is little consensus.

For example, is the goal of increased education in the sciences intended to insure that students have a knowledge of current facts in these subjects? If so, how useful is such knowledge, given the rapid rate at which new knowledge is required in these fields? Is the goal to give an understanding of the process of scientific discovery? If so, how useful are many of our present science courses, which concentrate on teaching facts and techniques which, at the undergraduate level, may be far removed from the realities of research? If we want non-science majors to be able to make informed judgments about science and technology in their role as citizens, what kind of knowledge about science and technology is needed? Efforts have been made to address these questions but more study is needed before we arrive at definitive answers.[19]

We need also to examine the arguments for the inclusion of the liberal arts in technical education. It may seem self-evident that an educated individual should know something of history, literature, and the arts, and it is a goal which, if considered in isolation, would probably not be questioned. However, the issue today is the priority that such education should receive, given the demands on students' time. Arguments are often made that the purpose of such study is to develop general skills in expression and analysis. These arguments have often been accepted uncritically in the past, but the stakes in developing generalizable skills, to the extent that this is possible, are much higher today. We need to examine carefully all claims that studying a particular content domain in fact generates such skills.

Recent developments in the cognitive sciences may shed light on these matters, where research seems to be yielding results which have the potential to increase the efficiency with which students learn. If this potential is realized, it could make a great deal of difference to the solutions of the concerns raised here. In part, of course, improved instruction could relieve the pressure on time to include additional material in the college curriculum. But, beyond this, major improvements in our ability to teach general learning and reasoning skills to students, could result in major re-evaluation of the role which the liberal arts and the sciences should play in the curricula of those not specializing in these fields.

If improvements in the training of students in mathematics and science at the high school level actually take place, they will also make redesign of the college curriculum for both science majors and non-science majors more feasible. If the planning takes place in a way that truly reduces the separation between the sciences and the humanities, and does so starting in the elementary grades, then the result could benefit education in both the sciences and the liberal arts, and could reduce the negative impact of the present division on segments of our population, such as women and minorities.

The danger in the present concern over education is that it will not have the effect of reducing the division between the sciences and the humanities, but will exacerbate it, by coming to concern itself primarily with improving the education of the traditional entrants into science and technology, who are a relatively small group of largely white, male students. This is not where our educational system needs to be improved, either at the college or the pre-college levels. This group of students is already receiving the education needed to produce highly skilled technicians. The need for this group of students is to find ways to increase the breadth of their education in the liberal arts while maintaining the quality of science and mathematics education. However, we do need to increase the numbers of able students who receive education in the technical areas for which expanded demand is projected: in the physical sciences, engineering, applied mathematics, and computer science. And we need to improve the ability of all of our citizens to understand the sciences. In order to achieve these goals, it is essential to eliminate the view that the sciences and mathematics are a specialized group of studies of interest only to a small group of future scientists and technologists, and to integrate these studies fully into the curricula in both our high schools and colleges, and, more generally, into the intellectual stream reflected in the study of the liberal arts.

## Notes

1   ASSOCIATION OF AMERICAN COLLEGES and the AMERICAN ASSOCIATION FOR THE ADVANCEMENT OF SCIENCE (1982) *Science and Technology Education for Civic and Professional Life: The Undergraduate Years*, a report of the Wingspread Conference, Racine, WI, June 1–3, 1982, Washington, DC, Association of American Colleges, (hereafter cited as AAC and AAAS, *Sci.* and *Tech. Ed.*), p. 14.
2   C.P. SNOW (1964) *The Two Cultures: and a Second Look*, Cambridge, Cambridge University Press.
3   *Ibid.*, pp. 69–71.

4  T.R. HENN (1967) 'The arts v. the sciences,' in A.S.C. ROSS, (Ed.) *Arts v. Science*, London, Methuen.

5  H. GUERLAC (1971) 'Three eighteenth-century social philosophers: scientific influences on their thought,' in G. HOLTON, (Ed.), *Science and the Modern Mind*, Freeport, NY, Books for Libraries Press. Reprint of the 1958 publication by the Beacon Press, Boston, p. 2.

6  W.H. SHAPLEY, A.H. TEICH, G.J. BRESLOW (1981) *Research and Development AAAS Report VI: New Directions for R and D: Federal Budget — FY 1982 Industry Defense*, Washington, DC, American Association for the Advancement of Science.

7  NATIONAL SCIENCE FOUNDATION (1982) *Women and Minorities in Science and Engineering*, Washington, DC, National Science Foundation, p. 21.

8  SCIENTIFIC MANPOWER COMMISSION (1983) *Opportunities in Science and Engineering*, Washington, DC, Scientific Manpower Commission, p. 29.

9  D. BRADDOCK (1983) 'Engineers — higher than average risk of obsolescence?' *Occupational Outlook Quarterly*, 27, pp. 9–11.

10  J. SARGENT (1983) 'The job outlook for college graduates during the 1980s,' *Occupational Outlook Quarterly*, 26, pp. 3–7.

11  NATIONAL SCIENCE FOUNDATION, *Women and Minorities in Science and Engineering*, pp. 1, 31.

12  *Ibid.*, p. 31.

13  See, P.M. D'ONOFRIO-FLORES, and S.M. PFAFFLIN (1982) *Scientific-Technological Change and the Role of Women in Development*, Boulder, Co, Westview Press; UNITED NATIONS (1979) *Women and Science*, New York, United Nations.

14  See, for example, D. WERNIKE (1983) *Microelectronics and Office Jobs: The Impact of the Chip on Women's Employment*, Geneva, International Labor Organization.

15  Discussed in A.B. JONES and E.C. SHAPIRO (1979) 'The peak of the pyramid: women in dentistry, medicine, and veterinary medicine,' in A.M. BRISCOE and S.M. PFAFFLIN, (Eds.), *Expanding the Role of Women in the Sciences*, New York, Annals of the New York Academy of Sciences, 323, pp. 79–93.

16  A. BUCCINO, P. EVANS, and G. TRESSEL, (1982) *Science and Engineering Education: Data and Information*, Washington, DC, National Science Foundation, p. 87.

17  NATIONAL SCIENCE BOARD COMMISSION ON PRE-COLLEGE EDUCATION IN MATHEMATICS, SCIENCE, AND TECHNOLOGY (1983) *Educating Americans for the Twenty-First Century*, Washington, DC, National Science Foundation.

18  AAC and AAAS, *Sci. and Tech. Ed.*, p. 22.

19  See, for example, AAC and AAAS (1981) *Sci. and Tech. Ed.*; Council for the Understanding of Technology in Human Affairs (CUTHA), (1981) *Technology for the Liberal Arts Major: A Workshop Summary Report*, Hoboken, NJ; NATIONAL RESEARCH COUNCIL (1981) *Science for Non-specialists: The College Years*, Washington, DC, National Academy Press; F.J. RUTHERFORD (1983) 'Sputnik, Halley's comet, and science education,' *The Forum for Liberal Education*, V, pp. 2–4.

# Insights from the Professions Regarding the Development of Expertise

*H. Bradley Sagen*

## Liberal Arts Education and Expertise

For years the liberal arts have tilted at the windmill of vocationalism. 'Premature specialization' and the 'provincialism' of technical studies have been the catchphrases employed against an enemy that now exists more in the minds of its critics than in reality.[1] In attacking vocationalism, the liberal arts have ignored the expanded role of specialized expertise in a complex society and the resulting restructuring of social roles.

The risks of ignoring a phenomenon of this magnitude are considerable. Over a century ago, the English liberal arts college ignored the advent of organized scientific research and the transformation of Europe through the resulting industrial revolution.[2] The English liberal arts college and Great Britain itself failed to provide the knowledge and educated manpower needed to participate in that revolution, and the German university and German science came to dominate late nineteenth and early twentieth-century Europe. Ironically, American higher education is often described as the combining of the English liberal arts college with the German university. That description fails to note that it was because of the failure of the English university to respond to social change that the German university, not the English, provided the model for advanced expertise in the United States. And one can now question whether at least some of the tenets of a liberal arts education derived largely from the English model represent more a self-serving ideology than a viable model for education in a complex society.

The class based eighteenth-century English model of education and of expertise emphasized wisdom as the province of the upper classes and technical skill as the province of the middle class.[3] This distinction was built into the British professions through internal differentiation, for example, between physicians (upper) and surgeons (lower) in medicine, and barristers (upper) and solicitors (lower) in law. For the upper classes, a liberal arts education to acquire wisdom followed by a brief apprenticeship to master a few techniques was the preparation for a life of service. The techniques and skills of the middle class professions were considered inferior and were typically acquired through apprenticeship without particular reference to wisdom and judgment.

The American concept of liberal arts education continues the disdain for 'technique' embodied in the English model. Graduates entering the job market with only a liberal arts degree are assumed to have developed adequate competency as a byproduct of studying the liberal arts. Specialized expertise is not seen as a responsibility of liberal arts education, except as that expertise develops through the study of one or more disciplines. The model is also supported to some degree by the American post-baccalaureate professions such as law and medicine which typically require an undergraduate degree as a condition of admission to professional preparation.


## The Failure of the Traditional Model

Lack of success among liberal arts graduates in the job market indicates that the traditional liberal arts model of career preparation is failing and that the failure may eventually undermine liberal arts education itself. The best estimate is that the supply of college graduates through the 1980s may contain a labor market surplus of approximately one fourth to one third or at least 250,000 graduates per year.[4] Studies suggest that the oversupply among liberal arts graduates may be about 40 per cent relative to their current opportunities, or perhaps 50 per cent greater than that of other programs.[5] The only factor likely to change this estimate is an accelerated movement of students away from the liberal arts.

The reasons for this larger oversupply of liberal arts graduates have to do with the market itself. Liberal arts graduates have typically gone into education, government, and sales and general staff positions in business; areas that are sensitive to the lack of growth in population and are among the first to be eliminated in difficult economic times. In addition, fundamental structural changes are occurring in employment opportunities and will have a long term effect regardless of economic conditions. The most significant change is in the increased demand for specialized expertise, especially in entry-level positions. Corporations are not seeking to build a pool of manpower from liberal arts graduates as they once did. Instead they are hiring directly for specialized positions. This is especially true in the current static labor market where hiring is primarily for replacements; but specialized hiring is likely to continue as the market expands in the future.

Three consequences of the liberal arts' failure to respond to changes in the job market deserve mention. First, students are enrolling in fields outside the liberal arts with better job prospects, such as business, and within the liberal arts are moving to majors such as economics and psychology where prospects are at least perceived as better. In response, less than affluent liberal arts institutions are emphasizing occupational programs in an effort to attract students. And because of this, the humanities and several social science areas in some comprehensive institutions are being reduced to service centers for professional programs. Even schools firmly committed to the liberal arts are unable to cope with enrollment increases in economics and computer science while the numbers of students in the humanities and other social sciences dwindle.

A second consequence of the failure to prepare students adequately for careers, and a further explanation for the enrollment shifts, is the pressure upon liberal arts students to pursue occupational specialization at the post-baccalaureate level. Liberal arts education in the United States has largely constituted the route to the post-baccalaureate professions and to graduate education in the arts and sciences. Most of the expansion in post-baccalaureate education can be explained by the demand for advanced expertise. Additional factors, however, are that a considerable proportion of the demand can perhaps best be described as 'remedial;' and that the additional cost appears to be forcing students away from the liberal arts at the undergraduate level. In discussions with placement directors at several universities, I found that MBA graduates with a liberal arts background are typically offered lower starting salaries than baccalaureate level business majors. (This is not true of the most selective MBA programs.) Similarly, many master's level programs in fields such as public administration and even engineering enroll liberal arts graduates and provide education and job opportunities comparable to that acquired by bachelor's level graduates. Perhaps the best illustration is found in law where the anticipated oversupply of lawyers can be explained in part by the lack of more immediate opportunities for liberal arts graduates. Obviously, if liberal arts education is no longer a reasonably certain preparation for work, those at the economic margin cannot afford to take a chance on their being accepted into or their being able to afford a post-baccalaureate program. Instead, the less than affluent must seek educational programs with immediate employment possibilities.

The likely consequence of the failure to address career preparation will be a sizeable impact on one of liberal arts education's most fundamental ideals — equality of educational opportunity. Clearly it is minority students who will be most affected by a lack of employment opportunities and the financial burden of additional education.[6] If liberal arts education is to remain the major path to the post-baccalaureate professions as well as a major component of the American educational system, it cannot become restricted to those of affluence. Society, if not the educational system itself, must eventually remedy that situation.

That liberal arts education's role in society is declining further because of its failure to cope with the issue of career preparation is illustrated by another development — the break in the heretofore monopolistic role of the liberal arts as preparation for the post-baccalaureate professions. Although the liberal arts continue to produce the vast majority of students for post-baccalaureate professional programs, the conceptual link between the two and the monopoly of the liberal arts has been broken. MBA programs and law schools, especially, are enrolling increasing numbers of students from the undergraduate professions of engineering and business. Such technical expertise when combined with a degree in management or law provides excellent preparation for the complexities of managing advanced technologies, or the legal problems of a business corporation.

Liberal arts education is clearly the loser today, in a society which emphasizes credentialism in a highly competitive job market. By credentialism I mean the legitimate task of verifying occupational competencies carried to the point of absurdity, where credentials are required that have little relevance to the work to be performed. In a highly competitive job market, those who are over-qualified displace those who are merely qualified. Graduates of professional programs thus displace otherwise qualified liberal arts graduates, who in turn displace those without a baccalaureate degree. Liberal arts education is at a particular disadvantage in this competition because it has not considered what career related competencies and legitimate credentials might be appropriate for its graduates. Certainly a listing of typical liberal arts courses provides little insight into the career related competencies possessed by students.

The irony is that the less attention liberal arts educators give to the acquisition and verification of appropriate career related competencies by students, the more the acquisition of credentials becomes a problem for them. Students then search for experiences such as internships and courses in economics which at least give the appearance of providing legitimate credentials.

Here then, in summary, is the list of actual and probable consequences resulting from the failure of liberal arts education to address adequately the issue of career preparation:

- loss of occupational opportunities for capable students;
- enrollment shifts away from the liberal arts to professional fields, and within the liberal arts to fields perceived as career related;
- a resulting financial instability in many liberal arts programs and institutions;
- the need for additional post-baccalaureate specialization at considerable cost to the student;
- likely losses in equality of opportunity among minority and disadvantaged students;
- over-reaction by students to the need for adequate career related credentials.

The fundamental problem for liberal arts education is how to incorporate specialized expertise into the undergraduate program for those students who will enter the job market directly with a baccalaureate degree. To accomplish this without undermining the strengths of liberal arts education will require more than just tinkering at the margins. It will require some reconceptualization of liberal arts education and of its relationship to society, some restructuring of the academic program, and some consideration of career preparation as one of several major outcomes of the liberal arts experience.

### The Professions as a Model

In addressing these themes, liberal arts educators may benefit from an analysis of how the professions and professional education address similar issues. My purpose in making such an analysis is not to advocate the professional model of expertise as a replacement for liberal arts education, but to suggest that one form of education may reasonably draw on the strengths of another. An appraisal of the professions, especially the undergraduate professions, may also remove vocationalism as the strawman opponent and recast the need for specialized expertise as the real dilemma for liberal arts education.

The professions are typically defined in terms of characteristics made famous by Abraham Flexner in his studies of several professions and updated by a number of analysts.[7] These characteristics include, a service orientation which does not advance the self-interest of the professional at the expense of the client; an association with the client based on a dispassionate assessment of the client's needs; a specialized and largely theoretical body of knowledge acquired during an extended period of formal education; standards for entry, for professional practice, and for ethical conduct; and a strong professional association or other mechanism for maintaining professional standards.

Another characteristic, and one which underlies most of the others, is autonomy both for the individual practitioner in his/her relationship with the client and for the profession collectively in its relationship with society.[8] 'Only professionals are competent to judge other professionals' is the claim by which professionals govern their own standards of admission and practice.

For our purposes, the significant shortcoming in this list is that it is designed to differentiate the professions from other forms of work and does not adequately reflect the fact that the professions do share certain characteristics with those other forms of work, even though the emphasis placed on theoretical knowledge as the basis for professional practice makes the professions appear to be more like the liberal arts.

Work is a form of action intended to bring about or control change. A profession is a highly advanced form of work involving expertise in complex tasks engaged in on behalf of others. Unlike the liberal arts, which are concerned with explanation, or more broadly with meaning, the professions are concerned ultimately with outcomes, with what 'works.' Because the professions draw heavily upon the liberal arts and in turn relate to the world of practical affairs, the professional model can help the liberal arts establish a stronger link between systematic theoretical knowledge and the world of practice.

Two additional characteristics of the professions, often overlooked, define elements of the professional model that may be helpful to liberal arts educators in addressing the issue of career preparation. The professions typically establish a formal, often legal, relationship with society based on the premise that the autonomy granted to the individual practitioner and to the profession collectively must be balanced by a commitment by professionals to serve individual clients in ways that ultimately benefit society as well. The expense of professional education and the autonomy granted to the profession collectively are borne by society because of the presumed public benefits generated by the professions. A similar presumption of social responsibility in liberal arts education and of the obligations of liberal arts graduates to society is currently lacking, and is the first of the major problems we shall address.

Secondly, the professions actively socialize their students to accept the norms of the profession and expect students to act as professionals while they are students. Professional education also provides opportunities for students to explore the conditions of practice before making a full commitment to the field. Professional education thus embodies not only preparation in knowledge and skills, but the development of professional attitudes and the exploration of individual interests as well. These latter dimensions of career preparation are especially important to liberal arts education if it is to offer career preparation while continuing to emphasize the personal growth and intellectual development of students. With these characteristics briefly described we can examine the professional model for insights regarding the problem of expertise in relation to liberal arts education.

### The Expert's Relation to Society

Currently, liberal arts education lacks an adequate rationale for its relationship to society. Because of this, liberal arts educators are unable to develop a reasonable set of expectations for their own graduates and a case for potential employers regarding the roles liberal arts graduates are prepared for in the work-place. Ironically, their relationship to society is a major problem for the professions as well, because our society is suspicious of expertise, cautious about power generally, and particularly distrusts forms of power, such as expertise, that are not easily understood. But for all the myths that professions have been prone to create about themselves regarding their responsibility to society, no one has come up with an alternative to the exercise of expertise based on an autonomy and trust granted in return for not placing personal interest above that of the client and society.

Although broad claims are made for the problem-solving abilities and concern for values of liberal arts graduates, these claims are not linked to a service orientation or to role expectations that would convince an employer to hire a liberal arts graduate because of his/her education. When a corporation hires an accountant or an engineer it has a reasonable expectation of what it is getting in competence and in commitment to the mission of the organization. When a corporation hires a liberal arts graduate, however, it does not know what level of competence or commitment to expect.

The late twentieth-century American concept of liberal arts education is dominated by the qualities of being liberated and of personal fulfillment. These qualities are to be attained through the study of the several disciplines comprising the liberal arts. Although being liberated has an obvious social dimension, it is seldom articulated as, for instance, in the claim that complex democratic society demands that persons in leadership roles address issues beyond the narrowness of particular perspectives. But having liberated their graduates, what would liberal arts educators have them contribute to society? The current focus on personal development and fulfillment without an accompanying concern for social responsibility makes liberal arts education appear to be a primary force behind me-ism and the new narcissism. In the current discussions over excellence in education, liberal arts educators have an opportunity to re-establish their claim that the development of individual talent is a major benefit to society. Whether they will press that claim, and whether they will convey their expectations for social responsibility to those of talent remains to be seen.

Liberal arts education has also lost for the most part two major links with society. The first, which had ceased to be of major importance by the mid-twentieth century, was a strong component of service and of social responsibility rooted, originally, in religious observance. Harvard was an institution of strong religious orientation founded to educate the leaders and servants of society be they ministers or others. As a religious orientation was replaced by a secular humanistic perspective, social responsibility and service lost status as major themes in liberal arts institutions.

The second and related link, now largely diminished, was that liberal arts education constituted a socialization for roles of leadership in a relatively stable society. The process of socialization was masked by an emphasis on maintaining the great traditions of Western civilization. But the outcome was graduates who understood, and stood to benefit from an acceptance of, the dominant values of society. That process and that outcome came unglued in the student revolts of the 1960s. The implication was not lost on those of economic and political influence as liberal arts students actively sought to alter the shape of society. For many, and on hindsight for even more, the student reaction to Vietnam represented several ideals of a liberal arts education. Nevertheless, the relationship between that education and the dominant economic and political elements of society was severely strained.

Liberal arts education may continue to function as a socialization process for a small number of institutions enrolling students from affluent families whose successful passage into the labor market is reasonably assured. For the vast majority of institutions and programs, however, some restructuring of mission is in order.

Restating the social and economic role of liberal arts education will require more systematic attention than is possible here. The service orientation of the professions offers one cornerstone for such an effort, coupled with a more explicit orientation towards preparing graduates capable of assuming an economic role in society. However, the critical and liberating qualities of the liberal arts should not be subordinated to the acquisition of technical skills in the quest for an economic role. Achieving a proper balance will be difficult. Until such a perspective or some alternative emerges, however, the relationship between liberal arts education and society will remain unclear and the roles of its graduates in that society uncertain.

## From Theory to Practice

The second dimension of the problem of expertise is how to prepare graduates more effectively to use their liberal arts competencies in occupational roles. In a broad sense this is part of the question of how to relate theory to practice, and here the professions have much to offer liberal arts education. Indeed, proponents of the liberal arts are often misinformed regarding the role of systematic knowledge in practical affairs and hence they misdirect their efforts to prepare liberal arts students for careers.

The liberal arts, in which are included the sciences, are the arts and sciences of explanation or more broadly of meaning. They explain how things are as they are. The professions, in contrast, are agents of intervention, of controlled change. Professional knowledge is necessarily prescriptive; it has to fashion interventions that are 'correct.' The basic question to be asked of planned intervention is not 'How does it work?' but 'Will it work?' That turns out to be a far more complicated question than simple verification of a routine procedure. Professionals deal with complex situations, which, although similar to those encountered in the past, inevitably involve problems of adaptation. The power of professionals' knowledge is demonstrated by their ability to fashion effective interventions in complex and ever changing situations. The power of scientists' knowledge is demonstrated by their ability to explain how things are as they are. Although their knowledge bases overlap, the intentions of professionals and scientists are different.

Professionals must cope with multiple, often conflicting objectives, and with uncertainty. Decision making involves trade-offs among competing claims rather than solutions that maximize the attainment of a single goal. Uncertainty forces professionals to be cautious in the use of rational techniques because the outcomes may be subject to considerable error.

Like scholars, professionals must also function within limits. Many of these define the systems within which action must take place. For example, engineers cannot defy the law of gravity, they must understand and function within it. The distinction between scholarship and professional practice here is that for the scholar, understanding the system is usually the object of scholarship, whereas for the professional it is the means (the definition of conditions and possibilities) to an end (action). Time, money, and social and individual values also define for the professional, as well as for the scholar, the limits of what is possible.

A further distinction is that unlike the sciences which deal with classes of things, professionals must cope with the specifics of particular situations. Much of the knowledge of particulars cannot be readily codified, let alone explained by theoretical concepts. Preparation for professional practice thus involves a good deal of practical knowledge acquired primarily in a work setting.

The final distinction between prescriptive and descriptive knowledge is that intervention often involves side effects or unanticipated consequences. An intervention may work but unanticipated consequences may cancel its benefits. Here, however, the link between the prescriptive knowledge of the professions and the descriptive knowledge of the liberal arts disciplines is strongest. Until we are sure how something works, we cannot be sure what the consequences of any intervention might be. Basic scientific knowledge is thus fundamental to effective professional practice and the advancement of practice is dependent upon the underlying disciplines. This fact is too seldom grasped by either liberal arts educators or professionals.

Professional competence thus involves three types of knowledge. The first is the knowledge of the basic disciplines that provides an explanation of the systems, for example the biological system, into which interventions are introduced, and explains how those interventions affect the system. The second type of knowledge is a knowledge of the technologies of the professions, the general principles and processes of intervention used to achieve the intended outcomes. Third, is the body of practice knowledge related to particular professional tasks and settings.

Liberal arts education of course is education in the basic disciplines. Grudgingly, liberal arts programs have begun to offer internships and other field experiences that at least expose students to some practice knowledge. What liberal arts education has failed to provide in most instances is initial preparation in one or more technologies appropriate to a range of career opportunities. These technologies include policy analysis, operations research, decision making, planning, and design.

Liberal arts education has also failed to provide students with a basic understanding of the fields of expertise and the organizations in which they will function as graduates. Liberal arts institutions have left the study of business and of business organizations to schools of business, of engineering to schools of engineering, and of public administration to schools of public administration. As a result, liberal arts graduates fail to link their understanding of the basic disciplines with either competence in technologies related to these disciplines or an awareness of the contexts in which these technologies will be used. As specialized expertise increases its role in society, liberal arts graduates are neither liberated from the narrowness of 'technique' nor competent to use it for public as well as for personal benefit.

## Career Development in Professional Education

A third area where liberal arts educators might profitably examine the approach of the professions is career development. Traditionally, liberal arts educators have resisted responding to the career interests of their students on the ground that premature choice and specialization would lock students into inappropriate careers before they had explored a range of possibilities. By catering to students' career interests, goes the argument, universities would also focus students' attention on the utility of particular liberal arts subjects and thus work against the liberating qualities of those fields. In reality, American liberal arts colleges *are* responding to the career interests of students. Their efforts are fragmentary, however, and are often motivated by problems of recruitment and retention rather than by the desire for effective education.

Professional education in contrast conceives of formal education within a broader pattern of career development. Activities such as career advising, opportunities for exploration of alternative specialties, and placement are thus integral elements of professional education. Professions such as engineering and medicine have begun to recognize the expense and loss of talent resulting from students deciding late in their program of study that they are not interested in the field or that they lack major skills. For this reason, early exposure to the actual practice of the field has become part of many professional programs. Career advising is also integrated into the educational program since the academic advisor is typically a practitioner in the field. Finally, since professional schools are judged heavily on the success of their graduates in the field, they consider placement as one of their major responsibilities.

These developmental aspects of the professions' approach to career preparation will prove more difficult for liberal arts educators to adopt. The process of education for a profession is more explicitly one of socialization to the profession in which the students acquire and adopt the norms and patterns of behavior associated with the profession. Professional schools are heavily staffed by members of the profession who provide role models that make explicit the expectations of the profession. The student is seldom far away from someone who is practicing and modeling the skills, values, and attitudes of the profession.

The attributes of a liberal arts education observed in faculty are filtered through advanced graduate degrees. Liberal arts faculty, like members of any other profession, practice their fields of specialization and their behavior reflects their professional expertise. Students who do not plan to become academics rarely glimpse ways to use their liberal arts education in their own lives. They are offered little assistance in relating what they are learning to the practice of careers and other life tasks.

Because the faculty in professional schools are typically drawn from the profession, their relationship with students is likely to be that of mentors who guide the students from the role of student to that of practitioner. Liberal arts faculty also act as mentors, but their education and their interests ill prepare them to work with the career development of students outside their own field of specialization. Ironically, career advising is typically far more structured in liberal arts institutions than it is in professional schools. In the latter, career advising and mentoring is an accepted responsibility of the professionals, rather than a marginal activity assigned to persons who are often not members of the faculty.

Although liberal arts education can be described as essentially a process of socialization, that process currently lacks a career dimension for many students. As indicated earlier, the expectations are vague regarding how graduates are expected to use their preparation in the life of society. Development of a coherent position on the issue, at least at the institutional if not at the national level, would be a major step. Liberal arts institutions could attempt to recruit a more diversified faculty and staff. The curriculum and the life of the institution could be organized to provide faculty and students more opportunity to model the competencies that liberal arts graduates would, in turn, exhibit in their chosen careers. Finally, faculty and staff could be given more information about career options for liberal arts graduates and could accept a commitment to the career development of students beyond formal advising. They could take on the more significant role of mentor.

### Elements of Career Preparation

In previous writing I have identified six essential elements of career preparation within a liberal arts framework:[9]

1   Liberal arts education has to emphasize the development of general intellectual competence, particularly of competencies required in logical and quantitative analysis and in written expression.
2   Liberal arts graduates have to be prepared in general technologies such as systems analysis or computer applications appropriate to a range of entry-level positions. To be most effective, this specialized expertise has to be built upon the foundation of general competencies just described.
3   Liberal arts students have to acquire an understanding of the context in which they will function in their chosen careers. For most students, this means they have to acquire some understanding of business organizations and of the American economic system.
4   Career related competencies as they are acquired have to be credentialed in ways that identify them as competencies related to occupational tasks. At some point, credentials should be established in a work related setting such as an internship or other field experience.
5   Students have to be given opportunity to gain awareness of and to explore career alternatives. Opportunities should also be given to

verify levels of ability and of interest through direct experience.

6  Institutions have to assist graduates in entering the job market by providing access to information and necessary job seeking skills and by making efforts to bring together qualified students and potential employers.

In addition, I now conclude that a priority has to be to establish a set of expectations regarding the outcomes and uses of a liberal arts education and the relationship to society of those who have acquired such an education. These expectations should clarify for society at large, for potential employers, and most importantly for liberal arts institutions and their graduates, the ways in which the 'expertise' of a liberal arts education may be used to benefit society. Liberal arts education is a form of expertise acquired to a considerable degree at public expense. The public has a right to know what benefits it can expect from liberal arts education and from placing liberal arts graduates in positions of responsibility.

Liberal arts education has to reach its own conclusions regarding how these goals are to be achieved. The issues are complex and resolving them without undermining the fundamental intentions of the liberal arts will not be easy. As a start, the issues have to be acknowledged as they exist, not as ideological constructions invented to protect institutions and their supporters. This examination of the nature of the professions and of professional preparation hopefully can assist in clarifying the issues and in providing some approaches to their resolution.

## Notes

1  'Vocationalism,' as I understand it, is the pursuit of education for strictly utilitarian purposes. Recent surveys have emphasized the fact that securing a job is the most important goal of college freshmen. My own research, (1980) *Student Perspectives of Career Preparation in Liberal Arts Education*, Chicago, Associated Colleges of the Midwest, p. 38, indicates, however, that among liberal arts college students at least, level of interest in career is independent of commitment to traditional liberal arts goals. Liberal arts students I contend deserve and desire both a meaningful career and a chance to fulfill traditional goals of a liberal arts education.

2  E. ASHBY (LORD ASHBY) (1963) *Technology and the Academics*, London, MacMillan.

3  S. HABER (1974) 'The professions and higher education in America: an historical view,' in *Higher Education and the Labor Market*, M.S. GORDON (Ed.), New York, McGraw-Hill, pp. 256–80.

4  The most comprehensive study bearing upon the problem was conducted by the CARNEGIE COMMISSION ON HIGHER EDUCATION (1973) *College Graduates and Jobs: Adjusting to the New Labor Market Situation*, New York, McGraw-Hill. This study, and most others on the same topic, rely heavily on data from the Bureau of Labor Statistics. The BLS data are updated periodically and nothing in more recent figures suggests changes in the original Carnegie Commission conclusions.

5  Data about liberal arts graduates are difficult to acquire. Annual reports by the

College Placement Council and Northwestern University on positions available and hiring nationally indicate that opportunities for liberal arts graduates lag far behind those for professional graduates. My estimate of a forty per cent oversupply is made on the basis of these reports, plus interviews with placement directors at a number of institutions. The oversupply is even greater in the humanities and most of the social sciences, and less so in several of the natural science areas.

6   At least among Black students, the proportion of graduate enrollments declined between 1972 and 1980, while the proportion of undergraduate enrollments increased markedly. Enrollment of Blacks in undergraduate liberal arts areas generally followed the pattern of other students. See, (1983) 'Participation of black students in higher education: A statistical profile from 1970–71 to 1980–81', *National Center for Educational Statistics Special Report*, Washington, DC, US Department of Education, pp. 83–327.

7   These studies are cited and summarized in somewhat different form by E.H. SCHEIN (1972) *Professional Education*, New York, McGraw-Hill, pp. 8–9.

8   *Ibid.*, p. 9.

9   H.B. SAGEN (1979) 'Careers, competencies, and liberal education,' *Liberal Education*, 65, Summer, pp. 150–66. Also, H.B. SAGEN (Ed.), (1978) 'Issues and alternatives in career preparation and the liberal arts: an initial appraisal,' in *Career Preparation in the Independent Liberal Arts College*, Chicago, Associated Colleges of the Midwest, pp. 19–66.

# Community Colleges and the Liberal Arts: Tried Concepts, New Contexts

*Alfred Kolb*

In 1967 I recall seeing Dustin Hoffman in a film with the catchy title of 'The Graduate.' One scene particularly comes to mind — the one in which the neophyte, fittingly toasted and celebrated in the suburban rite of passage known as the Graduation Party, about to enter the wide, wide world of work, is summoned to the side of one of his many doting relatives. This kindly relative, with a leer, wink, an elbow–nudge, leans over and whispers the 'secret word' into the graduate's ear. It's *plastics*! The formula, even in 1967, was both painful and funny.

Were this affecting scene recast for the realities of the mid-eighties — 1984 being a watershed year — the whispered slogan should doubtless be *computers*! In 1967 I could manage a grimace at these sweetly–gone–sour juxtapositions. Even now I recall the nervous titters, the suppressed laughter that rippled through the audience at this formulaic disclosure. But in 1984 I am no longer amused; I am, in fact, mightily perturbed that such 'well-meant' advice continues to be 'passed along' by educators, guidance counselors, and clergy, who seem consistently to have guessed wrong about where the jobs are or where they might be. Mr. Hoffman has, in the interim, gone on to more challenging roles. Educators have marked time.

Painful as it is, we do know that there is an over–supply of PhDs in certain fields, that the PhD is not always the most appropriate degree, that the world of work does not rotate around plastics, and that work with computers, as a potential job for large numbers of college graduates, is spurious. How sweet it is to be deaf to the lessons of history! How painful it is to acknowledge that the fast-food industry and the human service fields, especially their low-paying, low prestige components, now employ more people, and will in the future require many more than the technologies.

Those desiring data need only refer to the Rumberger report.[1] That report also sounds the old saw regarding whether it is better to train or to educate, for there is still fundamental disagreement whether or not entry-level high technology jobs will require more or less specialized training. Once again, *mirabile dictu*, the merit of general education, the type of learning that does not lend itself to the quick fix or the band-aid approach to study, that develops critical thinking, effective communication, inductive and deductive reasoning, that relies on extrapolative logic — this kind of education is being revived.

With such 'discoveries' being touted in the trade journals, educators need hardly be reminded that the 1980s remain a 'down decade' for the Liberal Arts,[2] nor do they require the Presidential Commission's report on Excellence in Education[3] to remind them of how sorry a state education is in. In their collective hearts and minds they have long known that much of the quality, many of the standards, have, since the silent fifties and the screaming sixties, been leeched from the profession. The Commission's report should hardly come as a surprise. Nonetheless, in response to criticism, there has been a heartening closing of ranks, and a rapid-tattoo return to basics, to the serious teaching of reading, communication, and computation skills.

Nowhere is this return more marked than in the community colleges, where non-traditional, underprepared students must be economically and efficiently readied either for job-entry or for further college-level learning. This 'mission' comes to community colleges both as a blessing and a curse; in effect, it is a 'mission impossible.' These institutions are expected to educate more reluctant and poorly prepared students, in more diverse ways, in less time, for less money, with less staff, in more crowded facilities than four-year post-secondary institutions have to expend on their lower division students.

Indeed, funding formulas persist in mirroring the time-honored academic pecking order of universities at the top of the money heap, and community colleges at the bottom. That community colleges *do* produce a valid, market-able product is commendable, that student success, either in the marketplace or in further education is disproportionately high, is miraculous. Little thanks are due the upper division post-secondary institutions for this achievement, yet community college personnel continue to listen attentively to caveats from the colleges and universities on how to provide these institutions with 'more qualified, more mature, more academically skilled' students. Indeed, Gleazer put the issue rather neatly more than a decade ago:

> The community college cannot do everything. Its role needs defini-
> tion and delimitation in relation to the services of other agencies and
> institutions .... If comprehensiveness, low cost to the student, local
> responsiveness, continuing education are desired characteristics of
> community college programs, what kind of financial 'reward' system
> should be developed? Not many support patterns at either state or
> federal levels are now deliberately designed to encourage institutions
> to move toward generally approved goals.[4]

In their monumental work on the community college in America, Cohen and Brawer observe that the 'reason for the growth of community colleges is that this century has seen a plethora of demands placed on the schools at every level.'[5] Historically, the growth and acceptance of two-year colleges can be traced in the names used to describe them. Changes in nomenclature and function also reflect shifts in the overall student and teacher profiles. Originally conceived as safety-valves, lower division 'feeder institutions' for four-year colleges and universities, they were called junior colleges. Subsequently, when their purview extended to general education and vocational/technical training, these institutions became known as community colleges. At present, with many maintaining satellites at branch campuses and outreach centers, with curricula spanning the disciplinary gamut from developmental or compensatory education to lifelong learning these institutions have become known as comprehensive community colleges. Though this designation may contain the hope and/or the promise of cradle to grave, soup to nuts education, the name may entail more of a snare and may be of disservice to the colleges in the long run. For such titular aggrandizement, aside from being unrealistic, simply reinforces the perception that the community college can do it all, whatever 'it all' might be.

These changes are all noted and documented in Cohen and Brawer's study.[6] Indeed, this work provides keen insights on the past and present conditions that nurture and inhibit the community colleges. Living with educational ironies is a way of life at the community colleges, which have always had to shape curricula to reflect the exigencies of skewed funding patterns that over-emphasize the vocations and technologies while decrying the lack of interest in the 'humanistic disciplines.'

There is no diminution of interest in the humanities, however, simply a diminution of funds. Naturally, where there is no monetary support, there is a diminished incentive for intellectual endeavor. But the lament that community colleges have lost interest in defending the humanities is galling and insulting to those who still look to the liberal arts as a vehicle for personal growth. Cohen and Brawer portray faculty at community colleges as divided and demoralized:

> Lacking any consensus as to the content of liberal education, and lacking confidence in their prescriptive authority ... 'to impose their values upon others' — educators were in a weak position to mount a defense of anything other than an educational supermarket, where customer preferences, ... were clearly for the more immediately utilitarian and basic items on the shelf.[7]

Undercut by the competition and keen marketing tactics of business and industry, surprised and weakened by periodic internecine feuding which erupts ever more fiercely as the number of liberal arts students declines, faculty have either unwittingly or deliberately participated in a compromise of their academic mastery, their allegiance to pure scholarship and scholarly endeavor. Over the years this insidious erosion has resulted in faculty morale problems which leave the liberal arts to founder in a morass of petty squabbling. Little wonder, given this interpretation of events, that critics of the community college find it so easy a mark:

Whereas the university organizes the intellectual world in a division of *intellectual* labor and necessarily accomodates a plurality of diverse intellectual stances, the community college organizes its world in a division of *faculty* labor and necessarily accomodates a plurality of diverse instructor stances. The amorphous, sporadic monitoring of instructors by department chairpersons, deans of instruction, accreditation teams, and peers is of little consequence. Instructors' work is influenced by the writers of textbooks they use, the speakers at conferences they attend, the new information they learn in in-service programs or on their own. But the enterprise is chaotic, directionless.[8] (Author's Emphasis.)

It is debatable whether community colleges are the *only* post-secondary institutions which 'necessarily accommodate . . . diverse instructor stances,' or whether it is *only* in the four-year colleges and the universities that 'division of intellectual labor and . . . plurality of diverse intellectual stances' occur. Professing this does not necessarily make it true, and an *ad hominem* approach to such matters can hardly be considered creditable.

If indeed evaluation of faculty and curricula seems futile because of perceived shortcomings which are ostensibly beyond the purview of any individual college, what entity has foisted these specious measurements of teaching effectiveness on the community colleges? The answer is the Graduate Schools of Education, just the institution that Cohen and Brawer call 'home.' To be sure, all this measured research, this busy scurrying about, does provide research material for enrollees of Graduate Schools of Education.

However, what is most maddening about such Pharisaic pronouncements, what is particularly unfair, is that virtually all community college faculty have experienced graduate school, though virtually none of the graduate faculty has experienced the community college. Furthermore, the experiences of community college instructors in graduate school have surely influenced (albeit not necessarily positively) their educational and intellectual choices. To fault faculty, who have been apt learners from scholars such as Cohen and Brawer, for instructional incompetence is tantamount to blaming the victim!

Still, Cohen and Brawer's findings should not be entirely disregarded; theirs, however, is an ancillary point of view, ancillary for precisely the reasons that legislators, trustees, community action groups, local industries, and citizens' advisory boards also represent ancillary attitudes and opinions. These groups have certainly had a strong history of influencing community colleges, have tried to influence the teaching and teachers in community colleges, have tried to indicate the type and degree of education that community colleges should or should not undertake.

However, these often well-meaning interest groups, in their individual and collective exertion of power — whether fiscal, political, social, or academic — are part of the problem; pressure from these groups accounts for community colleges defining their mission as 'meeting the needs of the community's citizens.' It apparently escapes general notice that those citizens whose needs require the services of the community college are rarely sophisticated, articulate, or organized enough to have their diverse needs recognized, let alone met. These hapless citizens, like the hapless community college faculty ostensibly there to address their needs, are, in fact, not the prime movers but the moved.

What ultimately emerges when community colleges are evaluated depends not so much upon the college but upon the particular bias of the evaluator. More than the other branches of higher education, community colleges have grown accustomed to the architectonics of the evaluation process. Because so much evaluation occurs as a matter of course, community college personnel have adapted to the periodic intrusions that accompany such investigations. The process can best be characterized as academic Darwinism. Given the diverse, even disparate aspirations of its multiple constituencies, assessed through the eyes of the various interest groups, community colleges frequently hit upon knee jerk responses, quick fixes or interim measures that are basically palliatives. They are attempts at defining essential contours without a reliable lexicon of true measures. The process is akin to seeking a true image by gazing into a series of fun-house mirrors. The way out does not lie in such contemplation. It is difficult to gain definition if there is scant opportunity for self-examination in a reliable looking glass.

The preceding is prolegomenon for what must occur if the liberal arts are to survive and revive in community colleges. That these concerns are genuine can be gleaned not only from forecast studies, education source books, and professional journals, but in the realities of the market place and in the preparation, or lack thereof, which students bring to the college of their choice.

Government alarms and warnings to improve the sorry state of general higher education are not only tardy and inadequate,[9] they are trivial side issues which miss the point. One need only review higher education funding patterns for colleges and universities in order to ascertain that substantial sums are spent for the high-power end of the scholarly continuum — specifically, the colleges and universities — and lip service is given to the rest.

To ensure viable community college programs in the next decade, the lesson of 'The Graduate' must not be lost. Computers are *not* the solution, but are the most recent emanation of an old and troubling problem — how to confront and assimilate change, how to deal with complexity and uncertainty. These are the areas which the liberal arts and sciences have delineated as their metier: to clarify values, interpret events, analyze and assess options, and predicate outcomes — these have traditionally been the preoccupation of liberal studies. Machines whose memories outstrip people's capacity to assess merits and/or to determine the limitations of these wonderful aides, become inoperable. New linkages must be established to demonstrate that computers are only as effective as are the abilities and aptitudes of those who design or operate them.

Having been for too long buffeted by vested interests, community colleges must be given opportunity to discover themselves. Cohen and Brawer assert:

> The demise of the academic disciplines as the organizing principle of collegiate courses has both reflected and served to limit faculty members' awareness of recent trends in their academic fields, an awareness important even for such a seemingly simple task as evaluating the new textbooks that appear. But it is important for more than that; the academic disciplines need reconceptualizing to fit compensatory, career, and community education, the institution's dominant functions. This reconceptualization cannot be made outside the colleges themselves. For the sake of the collegiate function, community college instructors must reify their own disciplines. It is difficult for a group that has severed connection with its disciplinary roots to accomplish that.[10]

In response, it could be noted that it would be difficult for community college faculty to seek aid in reconceptualizing the academic disciplines from the four-year and/or graduate institutions, inasmuch as these have never construed compensatory, career, or community education as their cup of tea.

Where, then, should community college faculty turn to find expertise? The answer is that those who deal with the material — in this instance, the community college student — themselves know what does and does not work. The product is, after all, continually being 'field tested.' There are follow-up questionnaires, feasibility studies, community resource centers, and citizens' advisory committees that pass judgment on the quality of the product. When these opinions and recommendations are taken into account, as they usually are, changes occur quite rapidly. The community college is one educational institution that operates according to the industrial model of 'product acceptance.'

Indeed, the strength of these institutions inheres in the basically sound impulses and reliable instincts of enlightened faculty and administration as to what must be done. They know it best, know the community, know its needs, and are sensitive to its students' aspirations. They also know what can and cannot be accomplished in a period, a semester, or a year. Through application of the self-actualizing *sui juris* principle, those in the community college must redefine its role, then reconstitute the curriculum, and, finally, set its institutional parameters. In the process it may well happen that old concepts (critical thinking, logic, communicatory skills) can be linked or applied to new or unusual job/work contexts; multiple disciplines might investigate and/or focus on medical ethics, environmental entropy, economic Darwinism, business ethics, personal morality, and community priorities. It is also possible that, in this process, the community college as an institution may finally be perceived as an entity, *sui generis*. Such a recognition could be accompanied by an institutional liberation, permitting exploration and development of multiple functions beyond the narrowly academic. Even Cohen and Brawer intimate that this might be a possibility.

> Currently the community colleges are suffering from a gap in perception .... Funding patterns are at variance if the community college is something other than a school ....
> Because so few scholars are concerned with community colleges, there is no true forum.[11]

Each community college, because of its uniqueness, its multiple functions and diverse constituencies, has the potential for reification built in. If these colleges can extricate themselves from the prevailing university bias, their personnel will discover and take pride in the refreshing fact that these places are colleges at last, serving the transfer function for a relatively small portion of their clientele. What makes community colleges truly comprehensive is that they are used as a focus field of other agencies and are a community-based agency as well. Considerable assessing, upgrading of skills, personal enhancement, self-paced improvement occurs. Much of this takes place in a non-structured perhaps in a seeming haphazard fashion. And there is heavy reliance upon the counseling function. Generally, clients are referred to other agencies or are guided through multiple referrals in order to achieve personal growth and some vocational or technological individuation. Occasionally some clients become students and are moved to the four-year colleges and universities for further education or additional training in the field.

Objective examination of the workings of comprehensive community colleges should bring these aspects to light; moreover, once realized and accepted, these data will clarify the primary mission of the full-service community college. This mission is assuredly not to polish each intellectual facet of the clients but to determine the essential nature of the article — to separate the magma, the dross, the chaff — to flush out the rubbish and then to transmit the purified article to the appropriate locale for further refinement and/or additional purification.

In order to be adept processors, to gain the desired end — a more viable, more marketable, more socially adept person than had been discernible initially, the comprehensive community college must become even more assay-oriented. From this perspective it would be reasonable to expect the community colleges to diversify and to experiment, to apply multiple strategies, various instructional modalities; numerous types of interactions ought to be attempted in order to induce the desired outcome efficiently, effectively, and humanely. That level of high quality, that sort of streamlined enterprise, has not yet been observed.

If these measures were implemented in the future, it seems plausible that selected teaching combinations, computer assistance in instruction, work-study or cooperative education opportunities, field-based practicums and apprenticeships, self-paced or tutorial study, and lifelong learning experience will become not only more pervasive, but more innovatively applied, especially in areas that have, up to this point, been slow to accredit such non-traditional avenues of acquired learning. It also appears likely that curricula will undergo significant changes, both in form and content.

For example, what the students need to acquire would be ascertained from careful testing, and appropriate courses would be developed to fit the desired outcomes. Such an approach could yoke faculty and bridge disciplines in a unique or even unorthodox manner. To this end, an entire term might be devoted to the shared discourse in computer programming, computer program analysis, mathematics, and logic. Composition could be taught and continually monitored and reinforced in such areas as literature, history, government, art history, music history, sociology, geography, psychology and the traditional sciences, especially in those courses requiring essay responses and attributive competencies. Where memorization and taxonomic capabilities are desired, in courses such as survey of science, biology, botany, foreign languages, allied health, and certain segments of psychology, a systems approach to rote learning could be attempted, to be followed by modular components that emphasize the particular field in which the individual student is interested.

Indeed, the very meaning of disciplinary area, or term or credit, or course would either be redefined or become extinct. Studies already show that, while requiring more knowledge, speedier absorption, quicker response, more work covered, we are at best standing still and in all probability going backwards, at least in terms of basic affective skills. More can be gained by requiring less, by making haste slowly. Philosophy, history, composition, sociology, government, psychology, and literature can be effectively and affectingly purveyed from a single text, provided that text is caringly selected and inventively organized and taught.

Faculty would be less concerned that students read widely, than that they understand whatever they read. Community college students are rarely bookish, and asking them to read widely leads to their reading superficially. More, in this case, is really less. Efforts would be made to see that students read deeply and well. What really matters, then, is not so much the uniqueness of each discipline or the diversity of approaches, but their shared focus, their basic common denominators.

For a different insight on what the future contour of the comprehensive community college might be we might well be guided by futurists such as Naisbitt, who observes,

> We are living in the *time of the parenthesis*, the time between eras . . . .
> The time of the parenthesis is a time of change and questioning . . . .
> As we take advantage of the opportunity for job growth and investment in all the sunrise industries, we must not lose sight of the

need to balance the human element in the face of all that technology .... The most formidable challenge will be to train people to work in the information society. Jobs will become available, but who will possess the high-tech skills to fill them? Not today's graduates who cannot manage simple arithmetic or write basic English .... The place to make a difference politically is at the local rather than the national level. Whether the issue is energy, politics, community self-help, entrepreneurship, the consumer movement, or wholistic health, the new creed is one of self-reliance and local initiative.[12] (Author's Emphasis.)

How very closely these concepts parallel the direction and thrust educationally, of the community college. And Naisbitt concludes,

Although the time between eras is uncertain, it is a great and yeasty time, filled with opportunity. If we can learn to make uncertainty our friend, we can achieve much more than in stable eras.

In stable eras, everything has a name and everything knows its place, and we can leverage very little.

But in the time of the parenthesis we have extraordinary leverage and influence — individually, professionally, and institutionally — if we can only get a clear sense, a clear conception, a clear vision, of the road ahead.

My God, what a fantastic time to be alive![13]

## Notes

1 See J. Magarrell (1983) 'Job market for college graduates called "bleak" for rest of 1980s, *Chronicle of Higher Education*, XXVI, No. 16, June 15, 1, cols. 2 and 3, 12, cols. 1–5. Hereafter cited as *Chronicle*.

2 See, for example, United States Department of Labor (1982) *News*, Bureau of Labor Statistics, Boston, MA May 15.

3 See (1983) 'Our nation is at risk,' in *Chronicle*, XXVI, No. 10, May 4, 1 and 11 ff.

4 E.J. Gleazer, Jr. (1973) *Project Focus: A Forecast Study of Community Colleges*, New York, pp. 237–8.

5 A.M. Cohen and F.B. Brawer (1982) *The American Community College*, San Francisco, Jossey-Bass, p. 2.

6 *Ibid.*, see 'Background: the expanding role of the community college,' pp. 1–28

7 *Ibid.*, pp. 295–6, *passim*.

8 *Ibid.*, pp. 297–8.

9 Refer to the report of the National Commission on Excellence in Education or the roster of grants given out periodically by the National Endowment for the Humanities.

10 Cohen and Brawer, *The American Community College*, p. 300.

11 Cohen and Brawer, p. 365, *passim*.

12 J. Naisbitt (1982) *Megatrends: Ten New Directions Transforming Our Lives*, New York, Warner Books, pp. 249–50, *passim*.

13 *Ibid.*, p. 252.

# Timing of the Educational Process

*Harold Goldstein*

Over fifteen years ago I attended a seminar on designing training programs for industry. The instructor began by asking us to take out a sheet of blank paper and draw a telephone dial. He told us to include all the numbers and letters in their proper places and sequences.

After a couple of minutes he asked that any of us (twenty five participants) certain we had drawn it accurately please show it on the board at the front of the room. No one stirred. 'I realize lots of people are shy to volunteer, so instead of coming up front,' he chuckled, 'just raise your hands if you're positive you've gotten it absolutely correct.' No hands shot up. A couple of half-raised arms went back down with the words 'absolutely correct.' He waited a few seconds and then told us: ' Start the letters at number two. There are no Q and Z.' About six of us had drawn it correctly; I was not one of them.

We went on to discuss the need for motivation to learn before any true learning takes place. How many times had we looked at, touched, played games with and used a telephone dial without having learned its configuration? Some of us guessed into the thousands. Obviously, we had never felt a need to learn it, so we never had.

The educational paradox, then, is not so much whether we should teach more liberal arts or professional courses, but when we should teach what to whom. Timing is a key issue. What we teach needs to be determined by what people need to be learning, and 'when' is at the time they need and are ready to learn. Piaget's work suggested that much of what and when to teach children is dependent upon their innate abilities to learn at different stages of their lives.[1] Other studies have shown that not only are we more capable of learning at certain stages of our lives than others, but we are also more able to apply that learning at certain times. A study by Harvey C. Lehman indicated the ages at which people would be most creatively productive, by subject matter:

| *Before 30* | *30 to 34* | *35 to 39* | *40 and above* |
|---|---|---|---|
| Chemistry | Mathematics | Astronomy | Novels |
| Poetry | Physics | Physiology | Architecture |
| | Botany | Opera | |
| | Symphonies | Philosophy | |

One might infer from this study that companies and other organizations, if they wish to maximize the creativity of their workers, would do well to include age range as a criterion for selection. It follows that people should be educated in a particular field at, or close to the age when they will best apply their knowledge.

In the United States, in 1980, according to the Department of Health, Education, and Welfare, we spent about $142 billion on public and private education from kindergarten through graduate school — about 7.7 per cent of the gross national product. That is three times as much money spent on his or her education as for the average student in France, Britain, or Japan. Additionally, about 30 per cent of all Americans are involved in educational institutions as students or employees. That amounts to 64 million Americans in all; 60 million students and 4 million employees. Yet, in American society, education is accepted as an activity for people under thirty. Hardly one per cent of people over the age of thirty are attending a college or university. Despite studies indicating their heightened abilities to learn and use certain subjects and their desire to do so, most people over thirty find themselves either unable or unwilling to 'go to school' as we think of the school process.

On the other hand, studies show that most American students are far younger than thirty. In the fall of 1978, the American Council of Education surveyed 187,603 students entering 383 colleges and universities. Over 90 per cent were younger than twenty. The studies further showed that the motivation for their pursuing education had little to do with their desire to learn a specific subject. Sixty per cent decided to go to college to make more money, 75 per cent to get a better job, 58 per cent to get a general education, and 57 per cent to meet new and interesting people.[2] In 1972, the United States Government surveyed 18,000 high school seniors, and 68 per cent wanted more emphasis on practical work experience. Obviously our students are motivated to get credentials and useful 'experience' so that they can begin to earn money. They learn only in order to obtain their credentials. Hence, it is common for the most frequently asked question in class to be, 'Will this be on the test'?

Some people do go back to school when they are older. I have been teaching evenings at the University of San Francisco for five years and find that all the older students I teach are more motivated to learn than are the usual day students or than I remember my fellow students having been when I attended College.

The motivations towards learning of older students are far stronger than those of younger students and their ability to learn is not hampered. As David Wechsler in *Measurements and Appraisal of Adult Intelligence* points out, a person's IQ is fairly constant from age six or seven on.[3] Therefore, change in a person's willingness to learn is more likely to be caused by change in motivation than by change in ability.

We are supposed never to stop learning. Yet, for most, the end of their school career marks the end of their pursuing education, whether liberal arts, science, or professional. Management employees occasionally attend company-sponsored seminars in general or specific managerial topics, and other employees may attend specific programs their employers sponsor. But most of these are quite short and rarely at the participant's option. Again, the question of motivation to learn.

When running seminars for company clients I try to assure that the participants view the seminars as elective, or to assure that the 'required' seminar be linked directly to a specifically identified and communicated need of each participant. It makes an enormous difference in their willingness and ability to learn as well as the likelihood that they will use their learning in their work environment.

We are supposed never to stop learning, yet the reality of responsibilities generally militates against the lifelong learning concept. When we finish our formal schooling we get a full-time job or take on full-time home duties. This leaves little time to pursue further education. We strive to 'get good' at our jobs and often stay at them for protracted periods. I have worked with many executives in a position to promote from within their organizations who pass over an internal candidate because he or she is so good at his or her present position that the company does not want to lose that asset. This policy works in the short-term for the company, but in the long-term the employee can get restless, resentful for having been passed over for promotions, and seek employment elsewhere. The need for allowing the employee educational growth is not acceptable to many companies which see such growth as threatening.

I do not wish to suggest that people are never stretched at work. New jobs do provide challenges. But far too often those who get promoted are the ones who have already demonstrated their capabilities to do the new job, so that its educational challenge to them is minimal.

Once we have proven ourselves, we can proceed to a job we know we can do. And then, years later, when technology is creeping up on us and we feel it is about to pass us by, we are too tied to our life-style and our responsibilities to re-enter the educational world. We hire more recent graduates and step aside. As the discipline of formal learning has fallen farther behind us, and as we have come to accept the idea that education is for the young, the option of new educational experiences for ourselves becomes less plausible and often seems ludicrous. Ogden Nash had a wonderful way of summarizing this sentiment: 'Progress might have been all right once, but it's gone on far too long.'[4]

We need to rethink the timing of our educational process. The pressures generated by schools and businesses to get as many credentials as quickly as possible force students to go for the 'right' or easiest degrees, rather than what they need and want at the appropriate time.

A former employee and friend, now successfully heading a consulting firm, went through undergraduate school (majoring in management) on a work-study program. Every four months he would switch between a job and school. Not only did he attribute much of his outstanding grades to the mixed environments, he felt particularly well prepared to begin full-time work upon graduation. However, based on counseling he received, he chose to get a 'quick' MBA from a good school before he accepted a job. He graduated in one-and-a-half years but was bored. The schooling was far less exciting than the work world would have been, and based on his undergraduate schooling and his work experiences, he breezed through to the MBA, relatively unchallenged. But he had achieved the credential. A few years later, having settled into the life-style of full-time work, he regretted not having studied psychology, literature, and history in graduate school, rather than having gone to the right school for the right degree.

He was fortunate, however, in that his work-study experience taught him that he could do both and be better off for the mixture. He re-entered the formal education setting, took classes in the humanities area he felt he needed and wanted to have, and maintained a job in a consulting firm during his non-scholastic time. The company for which he had been working would not keep him part-time and so lost him — a valuable asset to their operation with a record of more than five years' successful work. Within three years of having re-entered school he was ready to found his now successful consulting business.

But he is clearly the exception. Most go on in their positions until hitting their mid-career or mid-life crises, then look at renewed formal education as an option for the young not for themselves. Again, another evidence of poor timing of the education process.

Few companies make any allowances for the idea of lifelong learning. Rarely do they recognize the advantages of including education in a career. I have already cited two examples where companies could lose valuable human assets because of a reluctance to provide their employees the opportunity for additional educational experiences. A company loses when an employee does not see any chance for advancement or growth even though he or she has demonstrated the ability to learn or to do new activities.

Companies assume that the realities of business make it too expensive for them to permit employees to take off the time needed for education. That is a superficial analysis. The demands placed on businesses, particularly in the rapidly changing market place, are to stay at least current with society's needs and directions, as well as to be flexible enough to change. Therefore, businesses need workers who can learn quickly, foresee trends, accept new goals and prepare themselves for them, quickly and willingly. Those organizations that encourage and build opportunities into employees' career or tenure are those that will have employees more able to meet the changing needs of their market places. These needs are not limited to technological changes. Creativity in general is a key to success, as is the ability to analyze, broadly and thoroughly, to express ideas clearly and acceptably, to incorporate lessons from the past, and to chart futures. Companies are myopic if they believe the education needed for all these skills stops upon graduation from an MBA or any other program. Lifelong learning is needed and is becoming indispensible from a productivity, competition, and human asset perspective. The time provided to individuals for this educational process must be looked at as a necessary investment, not as a frivolous expense.

The Johnson and Johnson Corporation makes some exceptions. About ten years ago I implemented a program for them in which they brought promising junior executives from various companies they owned throughout the world to the United States for one to two years. Their entire families joined them in the United States for total immersion into a new life-style. Formal courses were included for the employees along with real work responsibilities so that they could learn new technologies, practices and philosophies and try applying them immediately. They were selected not on their scholastic record but on their record of accomplishments and their desire to enter the program.

Another program we established was a work-study program in Asia for Asian managers. The participants worked six months and then attended formal school for six months during a two year period. IBM and Xerox grant sabbaticals to their executives to pursue constructive interests. Although these programs are work-oriented, at least they take into account the advantage to companies and their workers of altering the concept that education ends once a career begins.

Nevertheless, those same corporations, like almost every other business, set great stock in the credentials already accumulated by students before they have had work experiences — again, providing stress on young people to attend classes when they are not motivated to learn, and cutting off our opportunities to re-enter the education process later in life when our motivation to learn is higher.

New technologies for teaching are being introduced in American classrooms at every level of education. Many are introduced because it is claimed that we cannot motivate students to learn, otherwise. Yet, we rarely look at the timing of what we teach to whom. R. Buckminster Fuller said, 'Humanity is acquiring the right technology for all the wrong reasons.'[5] We need to figure out the best ways to teach those people already motivated to learn.

We need to embark on a radical change in the relationship between business and education. Although staggered educational experiences might be precisely what is needed, I cannot believe that the business and education communities could quickly institute a successful change of that magnitude. However, a plan to do so eventually, or to move in that direction, would be helpful.

First, businesses need to recognize the value of allowing employees time for educational pursuits. The investment made will pay off in a far longer term than a quarterly or even annual financial statement. The Chairman of the Board of Johnson and Johnson told me, in answer to a question as to what traits he looked for in senior management, that he wanted people with a 'garbage-can mind.' He went on to explain that he meant people with almost limitless curiosity about the world, who could pursue that curiosity through increased learning. Further, they would be able to apply their learning to the business they were in or to new ventures.

Of course, I agree completely with that philosophy, and I have seen it work in numerous organizations when given the chance. But there are so many obstacles in terms of environmental cues telling businesses to act according to short-term returns on investment that even the most meaningful philosophies are rarely put into practice.

Perhaps if more work-study programs were used in businesses early on in careers it could become an acceptable practice for people to interrupt working time for educational time and vice versa. Universities need to make such programs more readily available and reach out to the business community to become partners in the effort to design new timing for education. Again, in the long-term a change of timing would greatly benefit the entire education process; more people would study for more of their lives and would be more motivated to do so. Teaching would be a more rewarding activity and the new technologies could be applied for the 'right' reasons.

Radical changes, though, are not likely no matter how badly needed they may be. Changing the curriculum of schools seems an impossible task despite the non-learning taking place in our school systems. To alter the view that one must get all one's education while young would require cooperation from schools, parents, and businesses, cooperation that just does not exist.

So perhaps high school age could be the starting point, or as early as fourteen which is a legal work age in some jurisdictions. We could begin interspersing education with life experience allowing more options as to what is to be learned so that individuals can concentrate their energies on subjects they are motivated to learn and apply. Maybe the first step is to encourage colleges and universities to push for more work-study programs and for businesses to encourage them, as well.

Altering both the concepts and the practice of education from 'get it while you're young' will take a long while, but the first step is the hardest and most critical. That is the recognition of the need to alter the timing of our education-al process.

We need to be more clear about the priorities and goals of education in general. Then we can determine how best to accomplish them. We will need to determine when in a person's life he or she is most likely to learn, remember and apply important subjects and concepts. *The separation of liberal arts from professional education is an outgrowth of our trying to cram all of our learning into too small a period.* There is no answer as to which we need to stress more or spend more time, energy, and money on. We need all of it and at the right time. Creating a demarkation in subjects certainly does not help the process and probably furthers the argument of taking the 'right' degree as soon as you can.

Obviously the issue needs more in-depth research. This thesis is simply to state a concept: We learn best when we are motivated to learn. What we need to do is create an environment that will allow us to implement that concept within our society.

### Notes

1   J. PIAGET (1977) *The Development of Thought: Equilibration of Cognitive Structure*, New York, Viking Press, p. 1.
2   AMERICAN COUNCIL OF EDUCATION (1978) *Fact Book for Academic Administration*, Washington, DC, American Council of Education.
3   D. WECHSLER (1972) *Measurement and Appraisal of Adult Intelligence*, Baltimore, Williams and Wilkins, p. 3.
4   O. NASH (1975) *I Wouldn't Have Missed It*, Boston, Little Brown and Co., p. 4.
5   R. BUCKMINSTER FULLER (1976) *And It Came to Pass — Not to Stay*, New York, MacMillan Company.

# The Modern American College: Integrating Liberal Education, Work, and Human Development*

*Arthur Chickering*

Many of us have been asking, 'Can colleges and universities provide both liberal education and preparation for work?' In my judgment we have been asking ourselves the wrong question. The proper question is, 'Can liberal education and preparation for work be separated?' Higher education has traditionally answered, 'No.' C.P. Snow, in the appendix to *The Masters*, tells how 600 years ago Cambridge University was born. The first students who came to meet with tutors in Cambridge village were poor, slept where they could and often went hungry. Like many students since then, they endured those hardships because that education could lead to jobs in teaching, in the church, in the courts, in the royal administration.[1] The first college in this country, Harvard, was established principally to prepare men for teaching, medicine, law and the ministry. Since those early beginnings each college, student and parent has assumed that a college education would lead to a better job as well as a better life. So the traditional assumption of colleges and universities has been that liberal education and preparation for work, should and can, go hand in hand.

But does that traditional answer make sense today? Do changes in human needs and purposes or changes in social conditions and the world of work call for new responses? Must liberal education and preparation for work necessarily be integrated if the ends of both are to be soundly achieved, or can one area be dealt with while the other is set aside? To answer these questions we have to examine what we mean by liberal education and preparation for work.

## Liberal Education

One of the first, and in my judgment, one of the best definitions of a liberal education is from Cardinal Newman's *The Idea of a University*, published originally in 1852:

* This chapter has been developed from a paper prepared for the Memphis State University Professional Development Program, Spring, 1981.

A University training ... aims at raising the intellectual tone of
society, at cultivating the public mind at purifying the national taste,
at supplying true principles to popular enthusiasm and fixed aims to
popular aspiration ... at facilitating the exercise of political power,
and refining the intercourse of private life. It gives a man a clear
conscious view of his own opinions and judgments, a truth in
developing them, an eloquence in expressing them, and a force in
urging them. It teaches him to see things as they are, to go right to the
point, to disentangle a skein of thought, to detect what is sophisticated, and to discard what is irrelevant. It prepares him to fill any post
with credit, and to master any subject with facility. It shows him how
to accommodate himself to others, how to influence them, how to
come to an understanding with them, how to bear with them. He is at
home in any society, he has common ground with every class; he
knows when to speak and when to be silent; he is able to converse, he
is able to listen; he can ask a question pertinently and gain a lesson
seasonably when he has nothing to impart himself ... he is a pleasant
companion and a comrade you can depend upon .... He has a repose
of a mind which lives in the world, and which has resources for its
happiness at home when it cannot go abroad.[2]

That paragraph is hard to match for eloquence. Take it apart and you have
the key objectives of liberal education. Let me make some connections
between Newman's words and the jargon of our bulletins and mission
statements. Read 'a clear conscious view of his own opinions and judgments, a
truth in developing them,' and we have clarity of values and integrity. 'An
eloquence in expressing them, and a force in urging them,' gives us communication skills. Read, 'to see things as they are, to go right to the point, to
disentangle a skein of thought, to detect what is sophisticated, and to discard
what is irrelevant,' and we have critical thinking skills — analysis, synthesis,
and evaluation — those higher levels of Bloom's *Taxonomy of Educational
Objectives in the Cognitive Domain*.[3] 'To fill any post with credit and to master
any subject with facility,' speaks to preparation for work and learning how to
learn. 'He is at home in any society, he has a common ground with every
class,' calls for cultural sophistication and cross-cultural understanding. 'How
to accommodate himself to others, how to influence them, how to come to an
understanding with them, how to bear with them,' gives us empathy,
understanding, and respect for others. 'A pleasant companion and comrade
you can depend on,' proposes a loyalty and intimacy which goes beyond mere
understanding and tolerance. And, finally, 'a repose of mind which lives in the
world, and ... has resources for its happiness at home when it cannot go
abroad' refers to our basic sense of self in a social and historical context.

Communication skills, critical thinking, preparation for work, learning
how to learn, cultural sophistication and cross cultural understanding,
empathy, understanding and respect for others, loyalty and intimacy, sense of

self in a social-historical content — not a bad list. Each of us undoubtedly would add or amend, computational skills, for example, are absent. But this list will serve for now as we turn to preparation for work.

## Preparation for Work

Today it is hard to know what we mean by 'work.' *The Oxford English Dictionary* gives us nine pages of small type. Even *Webster's New Collegiate* has so many definitions, some of which could apply equally well to vigorous recreation or leisure, that clear distinctions between work and other activities are difficult to make.

Primitive societies probably had no concept of 'work.' Those that still exist frequently have no vocabulary that distinguishes between 'work' and 'free time.' In such societies, a person does what is expected, which includes domestic duties, gathering and raising food, performing various rituals and ceremonies, occupying time with conversation, singing, dancing, sleeping, eating and sex. People feel as constrained to do one as they are to do another. 'Work' becomes a category only when we try to classify these various activities. And if we limit the definition of work to those activities involved with gaining sustenance and producing goods, then people in primitive cultures spend much less time in work than we do.

Greek and Christian thought set work clearly apart. For the Socrates of Xenophon, work was an expedient, and in Hesiod's *Works and Days* it is a necessity and a curse. *The Bible* indicates that work became necessary because of a divine curse. When Adam ate that apple, he turned the world into a workhouse and threw away Paradise without toil; the Lord said to him 'Cursed is the ground because of you; in toil you shall eat of it all the days of your life; thorns and thistles it shall bring forth to you; and you shall eat the plants of the field.'[4] The Protestant ethic turned work and play into opposites and in some of its more extreme manifestations equated play with sin. Thus the idea became embedded in Western culture that if an activity is to be called work, it must be something painful, and unpleasant.

Now we are moving toward a view that work is not a curse but a blessing. Useful occupations are an antidote to stagnation. Achievement, contribution, and productivity are the cornerstones for self-respect. Our changing orientation is consistent with the changing nature of the activities called *work*, as we have moved from an agrarian, through an industrial, to a 'post-industrial' society.

Today the center of the work force is the 'service worker' and the 'knowledge worker.'[5] Expansion of the services sector has led to increased demand for professionals in education, health, management, science, and engineering. An advanced service economy depends upon well-educated people, because the key to effective service is quality. However, achieving high-quality service is more complicated than producing high-quality goods.

It is easier to produce high quality television sets than high-quality programming for television, just as it is easier to design high-powered automobiles, and supersonic airplanes than to design environments and transportation systems that serve human needs effectively.

With the expansion of services in the economy and the changing nature of the activities called work, we need to make a distinction between *work* and *job*. As Green observed: 'There is an enormous difference between the person who understands his career as a succession of jobs and a person who understands the succession of jobs he has held as all contributing to the accomplishment of some work.'[6]

Bearing in mind the distinction between work and jobs, we can address the kinds of competence required in preparation for work. For answers we draw from research that has identified the skills and abilities required for effective work. George Klemp and his associates identified successful individuals working in a variety of settings: military services, counseling, small businesses, police, sales, consulting, civil service, and industrial management. They discovered what these people were doing that made them successful, and examined why they were doing it. The authors reported:

> Our most consistent — though unexpected — finding is that the amount of knowledge one acquires of a content area is generally unrelated to superior performance in an occupation and is often unrelated even to marginally acceptable performance. . . . In fact, it is neither the acquisition of knowledge nor the use of knowledge that distinguishes the outstanding performer, but rather the *cognitive skills* that are developed and exercised in the process of acquiring and using knowledge. These cognitive skills constitute the first factor of occupational success.[7]

What were the cognitive skills most important to success at work? Information processing and conceptualizing skills which bring order to informational chaos were critical. These skills require the ability to synthesize information from prior analyses and from diverse sources. 'The ability to understand many sides of a controversial issue' was also critical. Persons with this skill resolve informational conflicts better than those without it. Without such skill conflicts tend to be resolved by denying other points of view. Disputes, therefore, are not well handled. The final cognitive skill important for success was 'the ability to learn from experience . . . to translate observations from work experience into a theory that can be used to generate behavorial alternatives.'

Interpersonal skills were the second factor contributing to success at work. They were defined as, 'Communication skills . . . fluency and precision in speaking and writing is important, of course, but often it is the nonverbal component of communication, both in sending and receiving information, that has the greater impact;' and 'accurate empathy . . . defined as both the diagnosis of a human concern (based on what a person says, how he or she behaves) and as an appropriate *response* to the needs of the person . . . Accurate empathy helps clients and co-workers understand what is being said or done in a way that makes them feel they are themselves understood.'

However, these cognitive and interpersonal skills do not by themselves guarantee effectiveness. The third critical factor found was *motivation*. According to Klemp motivation depends upon 'the way one defines oneself as an actor in the motive-action sequence.' Those who are proactive, who take action to overcome barriers to their progress have an advantage over those who are reactive, who fail to seek for new opportunities.[8] To sum up then, effective performance in the world of work involves clearly identifiable cognitive skills, interpersonal skills, and motivational characteristics.

To what extent are these kinds of competence and personal characteristics consistent with those typically taken as the aims of liberal education? Figure 1 compares Newman and Klemp. There seems to be striking agreement, which supports higher education's traditional response concerning liberal education and preparation for work. Can liberal education and preparation for work be separated? The answer is 'No.' Must liberal education and preparation for work necessarily be integrated if the ends of both are to be achieved? The answer is 'Yes.'

*Figure 1:   Liberal education and preparation for work*

| Newman | Klemp |
|---|---|
| Liberal education objectives | Competence and characteristics for work |
| communication skills | communication skills |
| critical thinking | information processing skills<br>conceptualizing skills |
| preparation for work | |
| learning how to learn | ability to learn from experience |
| cross cultural understanding | ability to understand many sides of a<br>    complex issue |
| empathy, understanding and respect<br>    for others | accurate empathy<br>positive regard for others |
| loyalty and intimacy | giving assistance<br>controlling impulsive feelings |
| sense of self in social and<br>    historical context | define oneself as actor, cognitive<br>initiative, proactive stance |
| clarity of values, integrity | |

Note that in this discussion we are focusing on some key, perhaps generic, areas of competence and personal characteristics which characterize both the goals of liberal education and the qualities required for success in work. This focus has major implications for curricular and course content, distribution requirements and core curricula, and the place of liberal education in two and four year colleges, universities, and in technical and professional institutions. Learning and personal development can be fostered through a wide range of 'content' areas. Cognitive skills, interpersonal competence, and motivational characteristics described by Klemp and his colleagues can be fostered through the full range of our courses in humanities, natural sciences and social sciences which characterize the arts and science curricula. They also can be fostered through courses devoted to professional preparation in business administration, engineering, health sciences, social services, and law. They can be addressed in many complex areas for technical training. Unfortunately, we seem locked into the notion that liberal education objectives should be relegated to courses within the arts and science curriculum, usually offered at introductory level to beginning students. However, these basic kinds of competence and personal characteristics can be learned through most academic activities.

They also can be systematically addressed through many 'extra-curricular' activities. The most forward looking student personnel services administrators, in their writing and programmatic activities, are already being quite intentional about this. They make use of 'development contracts' and 'developmental transcripts' in their work with students in residence halls, club activities, and student government.[9]

This means that there is much more concern about educational processes and teaching practices than is typically the case. We don't get much mileage from basic cognitive skills if students simply read a single text, listen to lectures, and complete multiple choice exams. What we need instead are educational resources, teaching practices and homework assignments which ask students themselves to draw inferences from readings and films, to synthesize materials from diverse sources, to evaluate the validity and reliability of different kinds of evidence and argument. We don't get much leverage on interpersonal competence if students work in isolation, in competition with each other, without any opportunity or need to work with others or to broaden their understandings by using human resources as well as print and pictures. What we need instead are collaborative projects where students have to work together to create a joint product or performance. And we need methods for evaluation and grading which do not pit one student against another, which recognize the value of effective collaboration and respect for diverse points of view and varied talents. Most performance in the world of work requires these skills yet there is little in our teaching practices which encourage them. And we don't contribute to social awareness when our academic studies make no connection with real life situations. We need a much heavier dose of 'experiential learning' throughout our curriculum so that the links between theory and practice may become more apparent.[10]

*Figure 2: Some milestones of ego development\**

| Stage | Code | Impulse control, Character development | Interpersonal style | Conscious preoccupations | Cognitive style |
|-------|------|----------------------------------------|---------------------|--------------------------|-----------------|
| Presocial | | | Autistic | | |
| Symbiotic | 1–1 | | Symbiotic | Self vs. non-self | |
| Impulsive | 1–2 | Impulsive, fear of retaliation | Receiving, dependent, exploitative | Bodily feelings, especially sexual and aggressive | Stereotyping, conceptual confusion |
| Self-protective | | Fear of being caught, externalizing blame, opportunistic | Wary, manipulative, exploitative | Self-protection, trouble, wishes, things, advantage, control | |
| Conformist | 1–3 | Conformity to external rules, shame, guilt for breaking rules | Belonging, superficial niceness | Appearance, social acceptability, banal feelings, behavior | Conceptual simplicity, stereotypes, cliches |
| Conscious-conformist | 1–3/4 | Differentiation of norms, goals | Aware of self in relation to group, helping | Adjustment, problems, reasons, opportunities (vague) | Multiplicity |

| | | | | | |
|---|---|---|---|---|---|
| Conscientious | 1–4 | Self-evaluated standards, self-criticism, guilt for consequences, long-term goals and ideals | Intensive, responsible, mutual, concern for communication | Differentiated feelings, motives for behavior, self-respect, achievements, traits, expression | Conceptual complexity, idea of patterning |
| Individualistic | 1–4/5 | Add: respect for individuality | Add: dependence as an emotional problem | Add: development, social problems, differentiation of inner life from outer | Add: distinction of process and outcome |
| Autonomous | 1–5 | Add: coping with conflicting inner needs, toleration | Add: respect for autonomy, interdependence | Vividly conveyed feelings, integration of physiological and psychologic causation of behavior role conception, self-fulfillment, self in social context | Increased conceptual complexity, complex patterns, toleration for ambiguity broad scope, objectivity |
| Integrated | 1–6 | Add: Reconciling inner conflicts, renunciation of unattainable | Add: cherishing of individuality | Add: identity | |

Note: 'Add' means in addition to the description applying to the previous level.
* Loevinger, Jane (1976) *Ego Development*, San Francisco, Jossey-Bass Publishers, pp. 24–25.

## Conceptual Frameworks from Human Development

Having established the correspondence between desired outcomes for liberal education and the competence and personal characteristics required for effective work, we are ready to ask, 'Are there conceptual frameworks which can provide guides for today's students and institutions?' I believe there are. I find them in the research and theory concerning human development and learning.

Figure 2 presents Jane Loevinger's sequence of developmental structures, each of which comprises an interwoven fabric of impulse control and character development, interpersonal relations, conscious preoccupations, and cognitive complexity. Loevinger describes the later stages thus:

> More people have recognized this (conformity) stage than any other .... This is the period of greatest cognitive simplicity. There is a right and a wrong way, and it is the same for everyone all the time, or for broad classes of people .... Rules are accepted because they are socially accepted .... Disapproval becomes a potent sanction. There is high value for friendliness and social niceness .... Individual differences are scarcely perceived. The way things or people are and the way they ought to be are not sharply separated .... People in the conformist state constitute either a majority or a large minority in almost any social group ....
>
> The transition between the conformist and the conscientious stage is marked by heightened consciousness of self and inner feelings. The transition appears to be modal for students during the first two years of college. A related aspect of the transition is perception of multiple possibilities in situations. Rules are seen to have exceptions or to hold only in certain contingencies. Inner states and individual differences are described in vivid and differentiated terms .... Motives and consequences are more important than rules *per se*. Long term goals and ideals are characteristic: ought is clearly different from is .... The moral imperative remains, but it is no longer just a matter of doing right and avoiding wrong. There are questions of priorities and appropriateness ....
>
> The transition from the conscientious to the autonomous stage is marked by heightened sense of individuality and a concern for emotional independence .... What characterizes this transitional stage is the awareness that even when one is no longer physically and financially dependent on others, one remains emotionally dependent .... The autonomous stage is so named partly because one recognizes other people's need for autonomy, partly because it is marked by some freeing of the person from the often excessive striving and sense of responsibility during the conscientious stage. Moral dichotomies are no longer characteristic. They are replaced by a feeling of the complexity and multifaceted character of real people and real situa-

tions. There is a deepened respect for other people and their need to find their way and even make their own mistakes .... The autonomous person has the courage to acknowledge and to cope with conflict rather than blotting it out or projecting it onto the environment.

In most social groups one will find no more than 1 per cent, and usually fewer, at the highest or integrated level .... Only a few individuals reach the stage of transcending conflict and reconciling polarities that we call the integrated stage.[11]

These Loevinger quotations give a general sense of the major stages of human development. While there are differences in terminology and in significant details, the level of agreement among theorists is sufficiently strong and broadly based to provide one set of solid information.

Loevinger's schema posits relationships between cognitive style, or intellectual development, and 'character development'. The necessary relationship between intellectual and ethical development is recognized explicitly by both Kohlberg and Perry. Figure 3 juxtaposes stages of ego development and intellectual development with the stages of moral and ethical development set forth by Kohlberg and by Perry. Kohlberg emphasizes shifting orientations toward authority, other, and self, such that self-chosen principles eventually replace those given by authority, or defined by peers or the general culture. Perry describes increasingly complex intellectual processes by which moral issues are analyzed, and values and commitments are defined while recognizing contrasting values and commitments of others. Although their emphases differ, both formulations integrate cognitive/intellectual development with moral/ethical development. They demonstrate the necessary interdependence of these two major dimensions of human development.

## Liberal Education, Work, and Human Development

Figure 4 shows some relationships among all these conceptual frameworks. These areas of development, and the progression they describe are congruent with those in Figure 1 which were articulated by Cardinal Newman and identified in the research of Klemp and his colleagues. These theories of human development, from different areas of behavioral science research, provide more detailed ways to conceptualize the paths to be traveled if the desired qualities for liberal education and work are to be achieved.

Examine Loevinger's stages of ego development in Figure 2 for example. There she describes developmental sequences that relate to the competence and personal characteristics associated with liberal education and effective work. The sequences labeled *Conscious Preoccupations* and *Cognitive Style* describe the changes necessary for a person to achieve high level communication skills, critical thinking ability, conceptualizing skills, and the ability to understand

Figure 3: *Stages of ego development associated with moral and ethical development**

*Ego Development*

| Author | | | | | |
|---|---|---|---|---|---|
| Loevinger (1970) | Presocial | Impulse-ridden, fearful | Self-protective | Conformist | Conscientious | Autonomous |

| Author | | | | | |
|---|---|---|---|---|---|
| Loevinger (1970) | Presocial | Impulse-ridden, fearful | Self-protective | Conformist | Conscientious | Autonomous |
| Kohlberg (1968) | Egocentric | Obedience-and punishment-oriented | Instrumental egoism and exchange | Good-boy-approval-oriented | Authority-, rule-, and social-order oriented | Social contract legalistic orientation / Moral principle orientation |
| Perry (1970) | | Basic duality | Multiplicity prelegitimate | Multiplicity subordinate multiplicity correlated or relativism subordinate | Relativism correlate, competing, or diffuse | Commitment forseen / Initial commitment, implications of commitments, developing commitments |

*Moral and Ethical Development*

* Adapted from Kohlberg, 1973, p. 46.

| Ego development | Moral and ethical development | | | Intellectual development | |
|---|---|---|---|---|---|
| | (Kohlberg) | (Perry) | (Loevinger) | (Piaget) | (Bloom) |
| Amoral | Egocentric | Basic duality | Stereotyping, conceptual confusion | Symbolic, intuitive thought | Memorization |
| Fearful-dependent | Obedience-punishment oriented | | | Concrete operations, 1. Categorical classification | Application |
| Opportunistic | Instrumental egoism and exchange | Multiplicity prelegitimate | Conceptual simplicity, stereotypes, cliches | Concrete operations, 2. Reversible concrete thought | |
| Conforming to persons | Good-boy, approval oriented | Multiplicity subordinate multiplicity correlate or relativism subordinate | | | |
| Conforming to rule | Authority, rule, and social order oriented | Relativism competing, or diffuse | Conceptual complexity, idea of patterning | Formal operations, 1. Relations involving the inverse of the reciprocal | Analysis |
| Principled autonomous | Social contracts legalistic orientation | Commitment-foreseen | Increased conceptual complexity, complex patterns, toleration for ambiguity, broad scope, objectivity | Formal operations, 2. Relations or propositions involving triads | Synthesis |
| | Moral principle orientation | Initial commitment, implications of commitment, developing commitments | | Formal operations, 3. Construction of all possible relations; Systematic isolation of variables; Deductive hypothesis testing | Evaluation |

165

many sides of a complex issue. The sequences labeled *Impulse Control*, *Character Development* and *Interpersonal Style* describe the changes necessary for cross cultural understanding, empathy, respect for and readiness to assist others, and the control of impulsive feelings. A sense of self in a social and historical context, clarity of values and integrity, the capacity to define oneself as an actor, to exercise cognitive initiative and to be proactive all depend upon a person reaching at least the Conscientious stage of development. These qualities gain increased strength at the Autonomous and Integrated stages.

Secondly, each stage is additive; what occurs is a structural transformation of the ingredients of earlier stages.

Thirdly, 'ego development is at once a developmental sequence and a dimension of individual differences in any age cohort.'[12] Age and stage are not highly correlated. These conceptions are descriptors of individual differences among typical college age students as well as among diverse adults throughout the life cycle. Therefore, the implications are as pertinent for those of us who teach only traditional students as for those concerned with older professionals in degree programs or continuing education courses.

Finally, Loevinger is explicit that developmental stage is not necessarily associated with increased happiness, adjustment or mental health. She says,

> There is a temptation . . . to assume that the best adjusted people are those at the highest stages. This is a distortion. There are probably well adjusted people at all stages . . . . Probably those who remain below the conformist level beyond childhood can be called malad-justed . . . . Some self-protective, opportunistic persons, on the other hand, become very successful . . . . Certainly it is a conformist's world, and many conformists are very happy with it though they are not all immune to mental illness. Probably to be faithful to the realities of the case one should see the sequence as one of coping with increasingly deeper problems rather than as the successful negotiation of solutions.'[13]

These principles have powerful implications for education. They make explicit several things that many good teachers have long recognized. First, development in the 'cognitive' and 'affective' domains is inextricably linked; full development in one area is difficult to achieve without concomitant development in the other major areas. Secondly, learning and human development is 'additive.' It always occurs out of the context of our past history, personal characteristics and current motives; it is always based on what we already know and can do. This makes information about the knowledge and competence a person has gained from work and life experiences especially critical in designing effective education for older students. That is why educational planning based on the assessment of experiential learning has become a major issue with increased concern for lifelong learning. Lastly, in any group of persons, of similar or different ages, there will be a range of individual differences in developmental stage and in the inter-relationships among cognitive style and competence, motivation, interpersonal styles and competence, impulse control and character development. Realization of this fact has led to an increase in individualized education, and self-paced instruction during the last decade. If Loevinger's developmental principles are sound, and all the evidence concerning human development and learning indicates that they are, the close relationships between the outcomes desired for liberal education and the competence and characteristics required for effective work become less surprising.

When we talk about achieving the ends of liberal education and about effective preparation for work, we are tackling the bedrock task of human development. Once we recognize that and become more knowledgeable about concepts for measuring human development, we will be able to achieve these aims of higher education more effectively with each of the students we serve.

The pedagogical value of the concepts for measuring human development is brought home when their relationships to differences among students in motivation, orientation toward knowledge and learning processes is examined. Figures 5 and 6 posit such relationships for four levels of ego development, moral development, and intellectual development. I present these figures with some trepidation, since they represent an oversimplification. Loevinger warns explicitly against this when she says, 'Though stage names suggest characteristics which are usually at a maximum for each stage, nothing less than the total pattern defines a stage.'[14] My object, however, is to oversimplify in order to provide a starting point for more complex thinking about application, experimentation, and research. The suggested relationships are consistent with research and theory, but they certainly need more detailed scrutiny and testing before they can stand as demonstrated propositions.

The point made by Figures 5 and 6 is that people at different levels of ego development have different motives for learning, and orientation toward knowledge, and that they prefer different educational practices, student-faculty relationships, and methods for evaluating their work. Many institutions are structured to serve those at one or two developmental levels although their students span the full range of levels. The educational practices and resources at most institutions are oriented almost exclusively toward people at the opportunistic, conforming to persons and conforming to rule levels of ego development.

The lecture-examination method, for instance, is responsive to these levels of ego development. The key dynamic here is the comfortable fit between the student's disposition to identify with persons in authority, to accept their definitions of right and wrong, to avoid punishment by deferring to their power and the teacher's assertion of authority, emphasis on dispensing information for students to memorize, and use of exams to punish wrong answers and reward right ones. When responsibility for lectures and examinations goes beyond the personal authority of the teacher, as often is the case, the method moves to an authority, rule, and social-order-oriented level. Here it is the system that defines right and wrong. The same authoritarian or authorita-

Figure 5: *Adult development and motives for education, orientations toward knowledge, and learning processes\**

| Ego development | Moral development | Intellectual development | Motive for education | What is knowledge? | What use is knowledge? | Where does knowledge come from? | Learning processes |
|---|---|---|---|---|---|---|---|
| Self-protective Opportunistic | Obedience-punishment oriented | Knowledge (simple recall) | Instrumental; satisfy immediate needs | *A possession* that helps one get desired ends; ritualistic actions that yield solutions | *Education to get:* means to concrete ends; used by self to obtains effects in world | From external authority; from asking how to get things | *Imitation;* acquire information, competence, as given by authority |
| Conformist | Instrument egoism and exchange Good-boy approval-oriented | Comprehension Application | Impress significant others; gain social acceptance; obtain credentials and recognition | *General Information* required for social roles; objective truth given by authority | *Education to be:* social approval, appearance, status; used by self to achieve according to expectations and standards of significant others | From external authority; from asking what others expect and how to do it | |

| | | | | | | | |
|---|---|---|---|---|---|---|---|
| Conscientious | Authority-, rule, and social-order-oriented | Analysis Synthesis | Achieve competence re competitive or normative standards; increase capacity to meet social responsibilities | *Know how:* personal skills in problem-solving; divergent views resolved by rational processes | *Education to do:* competence in work and social roles; used to achieve internalized standards of excellence and to serve society | Personal integration of information based rational inquiry; from setting goals; from asking what is needed, how things work, and why | *Discover* correct answers through scientific method and logical analyses; multiple views are recognized but congruence and simplicity are sought |
| Autonomous | Social contact, legalistic-orientation; Moral/principle orientation | Evaluation | Deepen understanding of self, world, and life cycle; develop increasing capacity to manage own destiny | Personally generated *insight* about self and nature of life; subjective and dialectical; paradox appreciated | *Education to become:* self-knowledge; self development; used to transform self and the world | Personal experience and reflection; personally generated paradigms, insights, judgments | *Seek new experiences;* reorganize past concepts on the basis of new experiences; develop new paradigms; create new dialects |

* Note that just as each developmental stage incorporates and transforms earlier stages, so also does each subsequent level of motivation, orientation toward knowledge, and learning. Adapted from materials developed by Dr. Harry M. Lasker and Cynthia DeWindt, Harvard Graduate School of Education.

Figure 6: Individual differences and educational practice

| Ego development | Intellectual development | Motive for education | Where does knowledge come from? | Institutional function | Teaching practice | Student-teacher relationships | Evaluation |
|---|---|---|---|---|---|---|---|
| Self-protective Opportunistic | Knowledge (simple recall) | Instrumental; satisfy immediate needs | From external authority; from asking how to get things | Arouse attention and maintain interest; to show how things should be done | Lecture-exam | Teacher is authority, transmitter, judge; student is receiver, judged | By teacher only |
| Conformist | Comprehension Application | Impress significant others; gain social acceptance; obtain credentials and recognition | From external authority; from asking what others expect and how to do it | Provide predetermined information and training programs, certify skills and knowledge | Teacher-led, dialogue or discussion / Open 'leaderless', 'learner centered' discussion | Teacher is a 'model' for student identification | By teacher only / By teacher and peers |
| Conscientious | Analysis Synthesis | Achieve competence re competitive or normative standards; increase capacity to meet social responsibilities | Personal integration of information based on rational inquiry; from setting goals; from asking what is | Provide structured programs that offer concrete skills and information; opportunities for rational analysis and | Programmed learning, correspondence study, televised instruction | 'Teacher' is an abstraction behind system; student a recipient | By system |

| | | | | | | |
|---|---|---|---|---|---|---|
| Autonomous | | Deepen understanding of self, world, and life cycle; develop increasing capacity to manage own destiny | needed, how things work, and why — Personal experience and reflection; personally generated paradigms, insights, judgments | practice, which can be evaluated and certified — Ask key questions; pose key dilemmas; confront significant discontinuities and paradoxes; foster personal experience and personally generated insights | Contract learning, 1: time, objectives, activities, evaluation negotiated between student and teacher at the outset and held throughout | Student defines purposes in collegial relationship with teacher | By teacher, peers, system, self; teacher final judgment |
| | Evaluation | | | | Contract learning, 2: time, objectives, activities, evaluation defined generally by student, modifiable with experience | Teacher is resource, contibutes to planning and evaluation | By teacher, peers, system, self; self final judge |

tive dynamic occurs except that it is more generalized. Of course lectures do also provide opportunities for the teachers to model skills for analysis, synthesis, and evaluation, and to ask students to go through similar exercises. There also are many 'right answers' useful for many students. So we need to recognize the potential values of typical practices as well as the limitations of them.

Socratic dialogue, or teacher-led discussions, respond also to the opportunistic and conformist levels. They provide rich information about the teacher's views and permit students to shape their own responses accordingly, receiving immediate rewards through the satisfying exchanges that result. 'Open,' 'leader-less,' 'learner-centered' discussions often suit the conformist level where sensitivity, pleasing and helping others, acceptance of group decisions are called for. Programmed learning, correspondence study, and most other forms of 'mediated instruction' currently used fit well the authority, rule, and social-order orientation.

Contract learning can take two forms. In one form the objectives are set by the student; the time, activities, and criteria for evaluation result from negotiations between the student and teacher. The contract is a commitment to the plan developed and the plan is to be held to throughout unless major events call for renegotiation. This approach to contract learning best fits the individualistic and autonomous stages of ego development. In the second form of contract learning the student, with or without help from the teacher and others, defines the objectives, time, activities, and criteria for evaluation. It will be held to flexibly and modified in the light of experience as it is pursued. This approach to contract learning best fits the integrated stages.

These different teaching practices also are expressions of different approaches to student-teacher relationships and to evaluation. The teacher as an authority, transmitter, socializer, judge, who carries sole responsibility for evaluation, best fits the self-protective and opportunistic stages. Where the teacher is a model, known well enough to permit student identification, and where evaluation is performed by fellow students as well as the teacher, the fit is with the conformist and conscientious-conformist stages. In programmed learning and other forms of mediated instruction the teacher is an abstraction behind the system. Criteria for evaluation are specified by the system and responses are usually mechanically scored. In contract learning the teacher is a resource person who contributes to planning and evaluation. The relationship may be more or less collegial, and the student may carry more or less responsibility for defining the program and for evaluation, depending on the approach used. Student-faculty relationships and approaches to evaluation in contract learning best fit the autonomous and integrated stages of ego development.

Any boxing of persons and educational practices, as in Figures 5 and 6 and in the paragraphs above, surely compromises the complexity of both. Such oversimplifications need to be met with questions, exceptions, counterarguments, and clarifications. In particular, we should recognize two points:

Autonomous students who are intellectually competent and skilled in interpersonal relationships can turn most teachers and learning environments to good use. Their behavior during lectures, preparation for exams, use of mediated instruction, conversations with fellow students — all will differ from that of their conformist or self-protective peers. So they will not necessarily experience those teaching practices in the same ways or be similarly influenced by them. Secondly, congruence between the student's ego development and the educational setting or practice which works well for acquiring certain kinds of knowledge may not help a student change from one level of ego development to the next. The limited research available to date suggests that change from one developmental level to another occurs most readily when a student encounters intellectual challenges, moral dilemmas, and interpersonal environments one stage above that at which she or he normally functions. When the gap is greater than one level, change seems less likely to occur.

These hypothetical relationships suggest ways to plan higher education in order to enhance adult development intentionally throughout the life span. We can modify our teaching practices, student-faculty relationships and approaches to evaluation in ways which recognize developmental diversity and help students at each stage move toward higher levels. Lectures, examinations, seminars, and group discussions can all be used to foster principled autonomy, and responsible, executive and reintegrative levels of intellectual development. Faculty members *can* enter collegial relationships with students as resource persons and at the same time be a source of critical appraisal and thoughtful evaluation.

Any institution, discipline, or professional school, will have students at all developmental levels. Because of this diversity we cannot simply pitch our teaching practices at a particular stage. Many opportunistic and conformist students come to higher education with important immediate and instrumental purposes that deserve to be met. Yet their needs will be fully served only if they are helped to see more clearly the developmental dynamics by which they are governed. Alternatives also need to be created that serve students at more complex levels of development. However, an institution cannot limit itself to those students. It has to be responsive to the full range of stages brought to it by the students it serves.

The need for more alternatives is especially important for the increasing numbers of middle age and older students entering our colleges and universities. As Aslanian and Brickell demonstrate, pursuit of higher education is primarily 'triggered' by some life transition, at work, at home, or in community responsibilities.[15] 'Returning students' span the full range of those developmental sequences described above. To serve them effectively we need orientation and advising programs, educational alternatives, flexible student-faculty relationships and opportunities for collaborative work which respond to their diversity. When the research on conceptual frameworks has been shared with students, as ways to think more deeply about themselves, their purposes and their education, they have responded positively, testifying to the connections between these theories and their own conditions. They have been encouraged to consider both career preparation and liberal education in planning their programs. These activities have been effective in community colleges and in four-year colleges and universities. They will need continued experimentation, development and evaluation if we are to respond effectively to the needs of those increasing numbers of middle age and older students pursuing lifelong learning.

## Conclusions

To recapitulate briefly, I have argued that the aims of liberal education and the kinds of competence and personal characteristics required for effective work are highly congruent. I have further argued that research and theory concerning human development, taking Loevinger's conceptions of ego development as a case in point, suggest the developmental sequences underlying the kinds of liberal learning and preparation for work required. If we can become more knowledgeable about the processes that encourage or stifle human development, we will increase our capacity to realize those objectives concerning liberal education and work which are central to our university mission and critical for society.

Before closing I want to address the issue of human engineering and social control. I am proposing that colleges and universities become more intentional in encouraging adult development. Indeed, in other writing I have proposed that colleges and universities take the major dimensions of adult development as organizing frameworks for their orientation and advising programs, their general education programs and core requirements, and their majors, and areas of professional specialization.[16] I suggest that teaching practices and activities, residential arrangements, and other institutional environments be organized in ways which encourage adult development.

Am I proposing a system that will serve the current establishment, cool out hot sources of social transformation, subtly develop more refined procedures for grading, classifying, and reinforcing class and ethnic categories? I have no clear cut answer, but I can share my perspectives concerning them and the reasons I urge we push ahead in spite of these real dangers.

The basic reason to push ahead is that there really is no choice. It is not a question of whether or not higher education should be in the business of human engineering and social control. It already is in that business. John Wilson, lecturer at Oxford, addresses the issue this way with reference to moral and ethical development:

> Performance in the moral area is surely not wholly *arbitrary* .... Such principles as 'facing facts,' 'not contradicting oneself,' gaining understanding and so forth ... are part of what it means to be a thinking human being, as opposed to an animal or a psychopath. Understand-

ing and following such principles is part of what we *mean* ... by 'being educated' in morality and other areas of life. They are an expansion of the concept of education itself, not a set of particular moral values. I repeat this because it is just as important that students ... grasp this as educators should. They, and we, would rightly resent any attempt to foist a particular morality or faith on them, but no one can sensibly object to clarification of what it means to be educated in the moral area.'[17]

Laurence Veysey addresses the issue more broadly in his detailed study, *The Emergence of the American University*.[18] He asserts that by the early twentieth century the university had become largely an agency for social control, with its primary responsibility being that of custodian for popular values. Its mission became to teach its students to think constructively rather than with an imprudent and disintegrative independence. Its degrees became emblems of social and economic arrival. The research and development activities of its faculty were to further the common welfare. Its own affairs were to be organized in a businesslike fashion which would reassure any stray industrialist or legislator who chanced onto its campus. The university became a place devoted to good fun: to football and basketball, and to club life and parties. To be sure Veysey goes on to recognize that this is not the whole picture. The university consistently tolerated its minority of malcontents, as long as they did not flagrantly threaten its public name. The faculty 'idealist' was permitted to survive. Strenuous dedication to goals that were absurdly unpopular, persisted in odd places within the institution.[19] But the dominant function was induction — carrying out the *rites de passage* — into the middle and upper-middle class and social control in the service of those values.

There is not much question as to whether our two and four-year colleges and universities, public or private, church-related or not, are in the business of social control and shaping human lives. They are. This work is the basis for state support, federal incentives and tax exempt status. Nor is there much question that we faculty members, in our teaching practices, course content and professional behavior do likewise.

Given this fact where am I left with my recommendation for intentional devotion to adult development? I am brought directly to questions like these: What consequences, for individuality or for society, will follow students' greater awareness of interactions between self and system? If increasing numbers of persons become aware and take part in creating their own futures, what then? If men and women throughout the life span become more conscious of the dimensions of ego development and of the dominant structures organizing their existence, how will their frameworks for judgment and action change? If they understand better the experiences which work for and against their own humanitarian concern, what conditions will they establish for themselves in the future and to what ends? If they see more clearly the forces steering their own professional or vocational development, recognize more fully the path on which they are set, contemplate the pros and cons of alternative directions, what will result? If they develop increased interpersonal competence and capacity for intimacy will that development be turned toward manipulation and exploitation or will it not? If they acquire more clear purposes, through better grasping the complex interactions among individuals' goals, institutional objectives and social values, what form will those purposes take?

My answers to those questions come down on the positive side, both for individuals and for society. Although I make no claim for definitive evidence, what evidence there is supports my optimism. The evidence to date does indicate that the direction of change in ego development is toward integrity, not toward opportunism, that moral and ethical development is toward commitment in relativism which places human welfare as the highest value. It indicates change toward increased intellectual competence and complexity, toward increased concern for collaborative modes of inquiry and for intimate relationships which involve the expansion of caring. Individual purposes and identities do become more clear and strong; with age they are put in larger perspectives of institutional objectives and social values. Persons do learn how to learn and how to take charge of their own development. We seldom reach those developmental goals we value. Our becoming typically falls short of that which we would become. But the striving is there in most of us. Thus it is that I argue for increased attention to those strivings, increased opportunities for each person to define more clearly those developmental issues significant for him or her, and increased devotion of institutional resources and expertise in the service of those purposes.

## Notes

1   C.P. SNOW (1976) *The Masters*, Middlesex, England, Penguin, pp. 300–12.
2   J.H. NEWMAN, CARDINAL (1973) *The Idea of a University,* Westminster, Md., Christian Classics Inc., pp. 177–8.
3   B.J. BLOOM *et al.* (1956) *Taxonomy of Educational Objectives*, New York, David Kay Co. Inc.
4   *Genesis* 3:17–18.
5   E. GINSBERG (1976) 'The pluralistic economy of the US,' *Scientific American*, 235, no. 6, pp. 25–9
6   T.F. GREEN (1977) 'Ironies and paradoxes,' in *Relating Work and Education*, D.W. VERMILYE (Ed.), San Francisco, Jossey Bass Inc., pp. 42–4.
7   G.O. KLEMP JR. (1977) 'Three factors of success,' in *Relating Work and Education*, p. 103.
8   KLEMP (1977) 'Three factors of success,' in *Relating Work and Education*, pp. 107–8.
9   See, for example, L.K. MILLER and J.S. PRINCE (1976) *The Future of Student Affairs: A Guide to Student Development for Tomorrow's Higher Education*, San Francisco, Jossey–Bass Inc.
10  See, for example, A.W. CHICKERING (1981) *The Modern American College, Part*

*Two: Implications for Curriculum*, San Francisco, Jossey–Bass Inc.

11  J. LOEVINGER (1970) *Measuring Ego Development*, San Francisco, Jossey–Bass Inc., pp. 4–6.

12  J. LOEVINGER (1976) *Ego Development*, San Francisco, Jossey–Bass, Inc., p. 13.

13  LOEVINGER, *Measuring Ego Development*, p. 7.

14  LOEVINGER, *Ego Development*, p. 15.

15  C.B. ASLANIAN, and H.M. BRICKELL (1980) *Americans in Transition: Life Changes as Reasons for Adult Learning*, New York, College Entrance Examination Board.

16  A.W. CHICKERING, (ed.) (1981) *The Modern American College*, San Francisco, Jossey Bass Inc.

17  G. COLLIER, J. WILSON, and P. TOMLINSON (1978) *Values and Moral Development in Higher Education*, New York, John Wiley and Sons, pp. 7–8.

18  L. VEYSEY (1965) *The Emergence of the American University*, Chicago, University of Chicago Press.

19  VEYSEY (1965) *The Emergence of the American University*, pp. 440–2.

# The Challenge to Education from New Technology

*Joan N. Burstyn*

The authors of this book have discussed liberal arts and professional and vocational education from both an historical and a contemporary perspective. This chapter will examine some issues discussed earlier in the book in light of our experience of the technologies through which people now acquire knowledge. I will argue that technology has influenced our beliefs concerning the nature of adulthood, and that new technologies will make obsolete many institutions people have taken for granted.

Today, a revolution in communications technology rocks the equilibrium of our culture. John Naisbitt has referred to this as 'the megashift from an industrial to an information society.'[1] The way individuals communicate with one another is changing dramatically. This change entails the development of new institutions, and the destruction of old ones. Because of this, our children's lives will differ radically from ours, and therefore we have to reconsider the value of what we teach and of the schools, colleges, and universities in which we teach it.[2]

We have to reconsider these, also, because we know that flexibility is the key to survival when technology changes. We have to educate people, therefore, to remain flexible in their ideas and habits even as they grow into adulthood. To do this, we have already made it a virtue for adults to maintain their childhood curiosity.

## New Characteristics of Adulthood

Adults need constantly to learn how to cope with new technologies. The skills they use to do so are different from the skills used by adults in pre-technological societies to cope with their lives. Those chosen to govern Plato's ideal state needed to learn wisdom; the education proposed for them, in the liberal arts, grammar, rhetoric, and logic, has been acclaimed as an ideal in western society for centuries. That ideal is an anachronism today. Though such an education may have been sufficient for those who were to become governors of an ideal state where technology was comparatively stable, and where other less privileged men and women were the practitioners who used what technology there was, it is not sufficient for men and women in an industrial democracy. Adults, today, need wisdom, but they need also to maintain the childhood ability to learn new motor skills and languages, in this case machine languages, to work with new technology, in new environments, and to live with new modes of communication.

Although we take for granted the virtue of maintaining a childlike curiosity, it became a virtue only with the development of industrialism. Prior to that time, the Greek idea that wisdom might be learned only by adults, together with the need for children to be productive as soon as possible, led people to 'hurry along' the process of maturation. For many centuries in Europe, and later in North America, the child was assisted in becoming adult as rapidly as possible.

Today, we not only perceive childhood to be a special category in its own right, we want adults to be children grown large. We have come to this belief because it is essential, in a society where technology changes every few years, for adult human beings to remain as adaptive as the young of the species. Where, once, adults considered themselves fully formed, we, of the twentieth century, find that idea non–adaptive. Adults who are rigid and unable to cope with new marketing systems, communication networks, or ways of travel are not able to flourish; if they survive, they do so in discomfort. Hence, the imperative of technological change has driven us to claim that maintaining the curiosity of childhood is a virtue. We encourage people to believe that they are able to change even as adults; if they do so they will be admired. We nurture the same curiosity and learning in adults as we do in children.

Until the nineteenth, and even until the early part of the twentieth century most people felt that a person was fully formed when he or she reached adulthood. Most religious conversions, for instance, took place among youths; and educators assumed that learning ended well before a man and a woman began their own childrearing. As recently as 1933 Dorothy Canfield Fisher wrote:

> Incredible as it may seem now, most of us remember the period when the belief that a grown person can learn nothing was accepted, without question, as an axiom. And when, under Professor Thorndike's guidance, we went through the terrific intellectual effort of really looking at that hitherto unquestioned belief to see what grounds there were for considering it true, and when we saw that it was patently absurd, we experienced the sort of excitement that Columbus must have felt at the dramatic end of his first transatlantic voyage.[3]

When the idea was introduced that adults, as they grow older, may continue to develop intellectually and emotionally, most people did not jettison the belief that adulthood was an unchanging state. In Piagetian terms, they merely assimilated the concept of adult development to their existing belief by saying that adulthood, or the state of being fully developed, was reached far later in life than they had been brought up to believe. Such assimilation proved unsatisfactory, however, once people accepted the idea that development is a process that never ends so long as a person lives.[4]

By accepting the idea that change continues throughout the lifespan we have abandoned people's historical definition of what it means to be adult. Adults in pre-industrial society had characteristics very different from adults of today. They knew their world, its customs and expectations. The experiences of most men and women were limited in time and space, so that, early in life, they could comprehend the demands that would be put upon them without fearing that their knowledge would become obsolete. A greater proportion of men worked for themselves, without anyone evaluating what they did. Those who worked for others might experience harsh treatment for errors they made, but rarely received constant monitoring of their work. People did not expect to live very long, so they did not consider preparing themselves for the process of aging.

All this has changed. Today, adults live in a society radically different from the one they knew as children. Drastic technological changes may take place even within the span of their adult years. Their experiences are broad, spanning not only the world as shown on television or in tours of foreign countries, but the solar system and the universe beyond it. The demands of society change constantly so that adults can never rest assured that their skills will remain marketable. Many people work for large organizations where their activities are regularly evaluated by their superiors. These evaluations are followed by interviews during which plans for improved performance are discussed; all workers, from entry-level packer to chief executive officer, are expected to 'grow on the job.' People's life expectancy is much longer (if we examine only medical expectations and not the danger of nuclear holocaust), so that they have to plan for adult life lasting fifty to sixty years.

### Education and Changing Concepts of Adulthood

When public schooling was first introduced the changes described above were all in the future. The people who designed the first schools to educate all the population did not envision education as a lifelong process. Education was an activity that applied to the very young. As people began to consider childhood a time for learning not work, the years devoted to formal education increased. Some few people, not even a substantial minority let alone a majority, extended their education into adolescence and early youth. For them, there were secondary schools and colleges or universities.

Thus, the definitions of education that we accept today were all formulated at a time when educational institutions served a different purpose from what they serve today. We have not asked ourselves whether the conceptual framework for education that we have inherited makes sense in today's world, or whether we should restructure the whole educational enterprise.

During the last two hundred years, the trajectory of education has lengthened steadily, with universities formalizing work at the post-baccalaureate level into masters and doctoral degree programs. New refinements have been introduced into the educational hierarchy, with first junior high schools and now middle schools dividing the elementary and secondary sequence, and with first junior colleges and now comprehensive community colleges established in the higher education sequence. However, the overall structure, with its emphasis on education for children, adolescents, and youth, remains intact.

Philosophers of education have struggled to define the purpose of education in terms relevant to their own times. Most often, they have justified the structure of education as it exists, rationalizing it in new ways. The cost of challenging established schools and universities becomes greater with each generation's investment in maintaining and upgrading them.

However, we are witness to a challenge to these institutions from new technologies which, whether we wish them to do so or not, will change existing structures. Therefore, now is a most appropriate time to raise issues of philosophic understanding so that any changes in structure that we make in the future may be guided by concepts other than those derived merely from the technologies available to us.

## Structure and Purpose in Education

Structures are always designed with a particular purpose in mind. Some purposes are straightforward so that any controversy that arises about structure will be narrowly defined; people may disagree, for instance, about the optimal physical structure or organizational design for a factory to manufacture leather handbags, but these are issues that will be decided rapidly, bearing in mind the overall purpose of the company to make a profit by producing leather handbags. Educational institutions, however, have purposes that are far more complex, so that controversy arises not only over the structures to be designed to carry out those purposes, but over the very purposes themselves.

Recently, there has been renewed discussion on what are the purposes of undergraduate college education. According to an essay in *The Washington Post* (July 16, 1984)

> The overwhelming majority of colleges and universities seem still to be adhering to the conviction, made fashionable during the student revolt (of the 1960s), that the purpose of the curriculum is to satisfy the desires of the students rather than their academic needs.[5]

The author does not provide the reader with his definition of students' academic needs. Nor are they spelled out in an article in *The Chronicle of Higher Education* (January 11, 1984) which claims that 'the chaotic contemporary liberal-arts curriculum addresses everything except the students' real and enduring needs.'[6] However, the latter article does outline the results of the chaotic curriculum, and from them one may deduce what students 'enduring needs' might be: graduates are unable to write or think analytically, they lack knowledge even of western history and literature, and they have been 'victimized by illusory promises,' of jobs after graduation. If they find jobs they often become 'stuck in entry-level positions because they lack basic expressive and analytical skills.' The author argues that:

> True education is not in the first instance a socially useful commodity; as academics — teachers, scholars, and intellectuals — we are here not to produce undergraduate trainees as replacement cogs for govern- ment and industry, but to encourage our students to become in- formed, thinking, and sensitive human beings.

The notion that the primary purpose of education is to 'encourage our students to become informed, thinking, and sensitive human beings' echoes the writings of Paul Hirst, who defined liberal education so as to differentiate it from education that encouraged students to *act*, as practical education which we refer to as professional or vocational education. According to Hirst, there are *forms of knowledge*, which he subdivides into mathematics, physical sciences, human sciences, history, religion, literature and the fine arts, and philosophy, and there are *fields of knowledge*, which he divides into theoretical and practical.[7] A liberal education aims to develop people's knowlege of the concepts, logic, and criteria of a discipline so they will understand how it 'works'. However, such knowlege does not necessarily lead people to *act* according to the criteria they have learned, and it is this lack of articulation between knowledge and action that has attracted the attention of some critics.[8]

Kenneth Charlton's chapter suggests that, historically, there is little support for a defense of liberal arts based upon their lack of relevance for action. The definitions accepted today, such as those formulated by Hirst, are different from those used in earlier times when the liberal arts were perceived as the vocational training needed by those who governed society. Although Hirst describes the liberal arts as theoretical and acknowledges that people need also to learn how to act, other scholars claim that the liberal arts provide a person with the best preparation for life. According to this definition, however, if students learn nothing else but the liberal arts they will know about the reason for and results of action, but not about how to act.

While Hirst remains flexible about the content of liberal education, others seem to have in mind a fixed curriculum similar to that which existed, they claim, when the educated were a community with a common intellectual heritage. Scholars such as the author of the *Chronicle* article cited above seem to have in their minds a mixture of arguments to support their idea of a unified curriculum of the liberal arts. As well as claiming that students should learn about a common cultural heritage, they argue for a unified theory of knowledge, providing skills in analytic thinking and a way to view knowledge that would link all college educated people with a common bond. In an earlier chapter, David Riesman has alluded to this view in his critique of the curriculum at the University of Chicago and at St. John's. Immanuel Kant searched for such a unifying principle of knowledge; for him, according to Ernst Cassirer, 'the theory of knowledge in all its ramifications remains a closely organized whole within which every part is assigned its own definite place.'[9] However, by the second half of the nineteenth century such a universalistic way of thinking had been abandoned. 'The mood for an *a priori* metaphysic' had gone, and several forms, similar to those proposed in 1940 by Cassirer, and others proposed later by Hirst, were accepted as the bases of knowledge.[10]

It was the burgeoning of experimental research in the nineteenth century, accompanied by increased specialization within the sciences, that led philosophers of education to abandon the search for a unified theory of knowledge. What we have witnessed in the twentieth century is increased complexity and specialization not only in the sciences but in the social sciences and humanities as well. Some voices, today, calling for a common curriculum in the liberal arts are those of people who deplore new specialties which, to their mind, have no claim to be considered part of the accepted forms of knowledge.

In the eighteenth and early nineteenth centuries students attending college had a set curriculum, but for over a hundred years students have taken a greater diversity of courses than critics of modern universities would have us believe. We can no longer return to a former conformity. We believe now that educational institutions should be open to all members of our society, whatever their race, religion, gender, or ethnic heritage. Similarly we believe that the curricula we teach should incorporate our knowledge of men and women of all races, religions, and ethnic heritage. The storehouse of knowledge is so vast, and the needs and desires of students so diverse that specialization has become a necessity. Diversity in the curriculum is an outgrowth of social and intellectual freedom.

Another reason that we cannot return to the conformity of the past is because academics have changed the definition of their work over the last century. Though they may be loathe to admit it, academics have a large responsibility for the complexity of the undergraduate curriculum. This century has witnessed the triumph of the research university over the liberal arts college. Where many academics in the nineteenth century spent their lives teaching an extant body of knowledge and counseling students, most academics in the twentieth century define their most important work as breaking new ground in scholarly research. As a result, there has been a tremendous increase in the knowledge of previously unexplored areas. Scholars have expanded the canons of their disciplines, in order to provide enough material for themselves and their graduate students to produce significant original research. In their enthusiasm for learning, they have collected and analyzed new forms of data, discovered new texts, reinterpreted existing ones, and enriched scholarly discourse with new conceptualizations. While one writer may claim that it is faculty pandering to student demand that has led English departments to teach science fiction and detective novels, and American Studies departments to teach the history and sociology of sports,[11] we can as readily claim that these topics are now taught because scholars have undertaken original research on them, and that it is faculty interest rather than, or as much as, student demand that has led to their inclusion in the curriculum.

### Knowledge and schooling

Mortimer Adler has suggested that most people have a false idea about schooling. They believe that the process of schooling from kindergarten to university will turn out educated men and women. This notion is wrong, Adler claims, because 'the young cannot be educated.'[12] Only mature people can be educated (although the immature can be trained,) and 'we cannot be mature without being aged through pain and suffering and grief. This kind of suffering children are spared, but they pay a price for being spared it. They remain immature, irresponsible, and unserious, in the basic sense of that word.'[13]

Adler's belief that children are uneducable, as he defines education, because they are spared pain, suffering, and grief would be challenged by many parents, psychologists, and teachers, who deal with children experiencing death, divorce, the break-up of their home, rejection by peers, and the violence of incest and rape. Despite Adler's opinions, people have changed their concept of childhood to include some attributes previously associated with adulthood, such as sensitivity to pain, suffering, and grief, at the same time as they have changed their concept of adulthood to include some attributes previously associated with childhood.

Although Adler seems to embrace certain definitions of adulthood and childhood that many have now abandoned, some of his ideas mesh with those expressed by Arthur Chickering in his discussion of adult education. Adler believes that education, which he defines as appropriate only for adults, has the following characteristics: first, it is voluntary, because the nature of adulthood is that one takes responsibility for one's own actions; secondly, those who participate in it consider themselves as equals, hence student–teacher relationships are inappropriate because they are by their nature unequal; and thirdly, education is '"interminable" — without end, without limit.'[14] According to Adler, the ultimate goal of education is wisdom. 'We would all like to be a little wiser than we are — to have a little more understanding, a little more insight, a little more comprehension of the human situation, of the conditions of our lives, of the world in which we live; to know better the difference between good and evil.'[15]

Many people now expect to continue educating themselves throughout their lives. We encourage people to return to school, either to upgrade their work skills, learn a new language, manage their money in the stock market or improve their cooking. Such learning, however, has few of the characteristics that Mortimer Adler defined as education. Few people, as adults, shape their education into a pattern encompassing their whole lives. Few concern themselves with getting 'wisdom;' most seek to learn new skills to keep up with technological changes, and obtain credentials for a better job. That education is all these processes, that indeed it should be all of them, is the contention of this book. In various ways, each author has shown that no one group of subjects, no one field of education has a monopoly on teaching 'wisdom' to the learner. Certainly, the traditional claim that the liberal arts have such a monopoly has been challenged by several authors. And the authors have discussed the lack of concern that colleges and universities have for the long term development of individuals. Harold Goldstein referred to the need for people to learn particular things when they are ready and not before, but such a mode of learning can be achieved only if someone assists each person to develop a lifetime plan for learning, something that is hinted at also by Chickering.

At the moment, our institutions cater for adult learning in a piecemeal fashion. Adults shop for courses as they shop for clothes; they look for something new to add to their wardrobe. Some people are taught at work, in universities, in adult education centers attached to high schools, or in YM/YWCAs and YM/YWHAs where courses have to be profitable or at least attract enough students to cover costs. Those courses that attract few students may be dropped in favor of extra sections of courses that attract many. Adult education is not considered 'serious', and its links to earlier learning are often unclear.

Although universities have, during the last one hundred years, developed sequential work at graduate level, with well-defined programs leading to masters and doctoral degrees, few institutions have begun to differentiate the stages of adult learning. The elder hostel movement is a beginning. International in scope, it focuses on the interests and needs of people fifty-five and older, who wish to acquire professional skills less often than young adults; instead, they are interested in broadening their theoretical and cultural knowledge. Older adults understand the significance of time in their own lives, hence they are often particularly interested in history and the other disciplines we call liberal arts.

The issue of sequential learning is linked to that of articulation among various educational institutions. Educators have not devized ways to articulate what is learned by adults, or by young adults, with what is learned by children, and adolescents. School districts arrange for teachers in elementary and secondary schools to articulate their programs, but articulation does not exist between schools and universities.

The greatest stumbling blocks to articulation are not physical, but intellectual and social. Articulation entails negotiation among equals. The details have to be worked out through a process of give and take, in which both sides share their perceptions of what students are able to learn at given times, and what they should be encouraged to learn. University professors, however, do not perceive schoolteachers to be their equals; professors feel they have a higher social status; intellectually they are closer to the frontiers of knowledge than are schoolteachers. Hence, they feel that professors, not schoolteachers, should define what students need to know by the time they become college freshmen.

University and college teachers' sense of social and intellectual superiority over schoolteachers has disastrous effects on education. First, it insures that the activities of professors will be differentiated from those of schoolteachers in order to maintain the distinction between the two. Since schoolteachers teach, professors tend to despise teaching. This attitude (fostered also by the university's emphasis on, if not obsession with, research activities,) affects the quality of university teaching, since few professors learn any teaching skills before they begin their jobs. A sense of superiority over schoolteachers leads professors, also, to despise themselves for the teaching they do. There is a deep-rooted ambivalence among college and university faculty, especially those at research universities, who find teaching to be personally rewarding. This ambivalence, towards teaching and towards themselves for being teachers, rubs off on those students who have arrived at college or university admiring their schoolteachers and intending to teach school as a career. They, like their professors, learn to despise the social status and intellectual capacity of schoolteachers.

Secondly, the university professors' sense of superiority over school-teachers prevents discussion among educators in schools and universities on ways to articulate individuals' learning experiences, thereby insuring that curricula and structures will not be optimized.

## The Content of Education and Lifelong Learning

The distinction that we have accepted between liberal arts and professional/vocational education, and our insistence that the two be considered as distinct ways of learning, make little sense when we view education as a process continuing throughout life. If we were to re-examine the content and the structure of education with the intention that each person would continue some kind of education throughout his or her life, we could restructure the sequence of learning.

Learning might be visualized not as a straight line, a hierarchy of development, but as continuous loops, each dealing with the same issues but in different ways. For instance, each person would need, in youth, to acquire a minimum of job skills, skills of communicating with and relating to others, coping skills for the technologies existing in society. However, all people would expect to upgrade these skills later in their careers.

Similarly, each person in their youth would learn the skills of observation, analysis and synthesis, using materials similar to those now taught in science, social studies, and literature courses, and language skills such as those learned through courses in mathematics, computer science, and the natural languages. These also would be taught in greater detail later in life, when people would be more eager to broaden their understanding of theory, and more willing to immerse themselves in history and philosophy because the chronicle of their own lives would be partially written already and they would wish to understand its significance.

Lastly, each person in their youth would learn to function as a participant in groups, both those that are task-oriented and those organized to provide on-going social interactions. This learning would be accompanied by examination of the role of the individual in a participatory democracy. As with the topics described earlier, this knowledge would be reconsidered, and these skills would be honed later in life.

If they were to view learning as a lifelong enterprise, to be experienced afresh by each person at different stages of life, educators could work with children, adolescents, youths, and middle aged and older adults to devize learning experiences that were sequentially and intellectually more meaningful than those we offer currently.

## Technology and the Acquisition of Knowledge

Schools and universities have made learning into a group activity. The invention of the book made lectures and their accompaniment of note-taking an anachronism, yet the lecture has persisted for centuries since the invention of printing. Although there have been attempts to provide individualized instruction, the preferred method of teaching is to groups. Most teachers would agree that group interaction is essential for learning, that discussion — the sharing of ideas — is crucial to the learning process. Yet there are many things that are best learned alone, and modern technology has provided new means for individuals to do this.

The computer, as it is now used but not necessarily as it will be used in the future, is a more conservative invention than television, since the user relies on the words and numbers that are traditional tools of learning.[16] Thus the computer is more acceptable to the academic community than either television or film. Scholars have pointed out that the invention of print imposed on learning an artificial, linear, sequential mode.[17] In life, we experience a multitude of sensations all at once. Print reifies the written word and narrows experience to sensations transmitted in sequence from the eye to the brain. The popularity of oral learning, through group interaction, may have been maintained in unconscious rebellion against the constrictions of the printed word.

While film and television have restored some aspects of experience that print lacks, they have changed people's touchstones for evaluating reality. What is real and what is imagined are both presented to the viewer through the same medium; what is seen as a natural shape, rather than as a symbol to be read, appears to be real. One's grounds for evaluating 'reality' are thereby lost. When a photographer can use the camera to show a monarch butterfly bursting from its cocoon, with far more detail than any eye could see; when TV reporters can photograph the homes, the workplaces, and the public gatherings of people in distant lands that the viewer may never visit; and when script writers can create characters whose thoughts and actions viewers share, day in day out for years, watching their expressions of fear and pleasure, learning more about these characters than they learn about their own best friends, yet never meeting them in person, the meaning of reality has changed.

For centuries, since the invention of the telescope and the microscope, scientists have acknowledged this other form of reality, the one that can be known only through the use of machines whose veracity one takes on faith. With the spread of television, the number of people experiencing this other reality has mushroomed, and so have the uses to which it has been put.

Why should it be more 'real' to travel in a bus through Colorado, viewing the scenery through the rectangle of a window, than to stay at home and view the scenery of Colorado through the rectangle of the TV screen? Why should it be more 'real' to experience the loss of an acquaintance whom one met regularly in the flesh, than the loss of an acquaintance whom one met every day on the screen? Meeting someone in the flesh would surely provide opportunity for experiencing the other person by touch and smell as well as by sight, and through conversational interaction that a meeting on the TV screen denied, yet if much of the satisfying conversation of friends takes place as reveries that each party indulges in while alone, then the difference between the two situations may not be enough to make one real and the other unreal.

From the perspective of education, just as books provide an opportunity for people to rehearse situations and experience emotions that are not feasible in their own lives, so TV and film provide similar learning opportunities. Yet educators have been slow to accept knowledge obtained from TV or film as genuine, in part because the volume of material is enormous and cannot be controlled easily by teachers.

Control has recently become less possible with the marketing of video cassettes, personal computers, printers, and copiers for the home market. In the past, the production of cheap books made it possible for individuals to learn on their own, to make their own interpretations of the *Bible*, to read criticisms of their governments, and to circulate their own comments on events. The results of that revolution, brought about by the printing press, took centuries to spread. Now, video cassettes and personal computers provide new forms of empowerment to those who can afford to purchase them.

As with the printed word, the danger is that those who dominate in society will gain advantage first, and that this will mean the exclusion of certain groups from the benefits of new technology. For instance, when literacy first spread among the community in the north east United States, it was chiefly men, not women, who gained access to such learning, just as in the southern states it was whites, not blacks, who were taught to read. The women and black men living then who remained illiterate found the disparity between them and white men had increased. In an earlier day, there had been a rough equality between the races and sexes with relation to reading, since most people were illiterate.[18] Today, not only are computers relatively expensive but the data-bases available for them are held by private profit-making companies. Thus, there is a danger that material previously in the public domain and stored, for instance, in public libraries will, in future, be available only to those who can afford to subscribe to data-base services.[19] These are issues that need to be discussed not only among educators, but among the public at large.

As well as causing inequalities of access, the current revolution in technology may eliminate some jobs, and de-skill others. This possibility has serious educational implications. Educators have to reconsider the skills people will need for the future. We do not know whether there will be jobs for everyone, as we have been accustomed to define the word 'job', hence we have either to restructure jobs so that paid work is spread among as many people as possible or we have to de-emphasize the work ethic we have fostered assiduously in our population. In his book *Electronic Illusions*, Ian Reinecke suggests that the projected number of new jobs in computer programming has been grossly overestimated. Program 'packages' have undercut the need for individualized programs. Even though the percentage of computer specialists in the United States grew by 41 per cent between 1970 and 1976, their numbers rose only to 394,000. 'That amounts to a rise from one third of 1 per cent to one half of 1 per cent of the total workers employed in the United States in that period.'[20] Many other jobs in computer manufacturing are located in Asia where labor is cheaper than in the United States, and even those jobs are being eliminated by new technology. At the same time, new technology is eliminating jobs in other areas through the introduction of robots. Although we may rejoice that people will no longer have to perform certain dull, repetitive jobs, or some that threaten life, such as working in mines, we have no guarantee that sufficient new jobs will be generated to replace those that will be eliminated.

If, for a moment, we accept the possibility that as many as one million people in the next two decades will leave school and not be able to find a job, then we have to consider what skills they will need in order to live comfortably and happily. Can we, as a society, differentiate at an early age between those who will be paid workers and those who will not? Is that a fair way to proceed? If it is, then we should prepare those students who will not find jobs for a different life from paid workers. We cannot treat them as though they have failed, since we, as a society, will have decided in their youth that they shall be non-workers, or at least non-paid workers.

Societies have experience of both non-workers and non-paid workers. Non-workers have often been the most wealthy in a society, not the poorest. Aristocracies have had at their disposal the service of others; according to their choice, aristocrats have lived a life of indolence or of intellectual or philanthropic activity. Others in society have been non-paid workers, on whose work the well-being of paid workers has depended. Women, as homemakers in industrial society, have been non-paid workers. Their financial support has been supplied by paid workers in their families.

In order to achieve equality, people in industrial societies abandoned their acceptance of leisured aristocracies. They accepted, however, the inequality resulting from women being 'employed' as unpaid workers in the household and family. Nearly two hundred years ago, shortly after the industrial revolution had begun to solidify women's role in a cash economy as unpaid household workers, some women in Europe and the United States began to challenge that assignment. Women could not rely on the men in their households to support them; illness, death, economic recessions, and the vagaries of human nature intervened to make such reliance uncertain. Women had to learn how to earn money for themselves in order to survive. Thus, women's education was designed to meet both the ideal and the real: to prepare women first for paid work while they were single (and, if need be, for paid work later in their lives,) and then for unpaid work in the home as married women. As an historian of education, I perceive that the self-designed education that some women in the early nineteenth century organized for themselves, and later deplored as unsystematic, was in fact functional for the lifestyle of women in the home. There, life was not structured with regularity as in the factory or business office; duties were not assigned by others, they had to be defined and carried out by oneself. Hence, an education one designed for oneself, relying on others for guidance but not for definition, gave practice in the skills of self-motivation for a productive, self-directed life.[21]

In our own day, in the United States, more than 50 per cent of all married women work for pay. It seems likely that the trend towards more married women taking paid work will continue. As a result, will people need to choose another group to work unpaid? Or, is society moving towards a time when many people will not have paid work because machines will accomplish so much for them? If that is the case, will people be paid *not* to work in the same way that farmers are paid *not* to plant crops?

Though the source of income may prove to be different for the non-employed men and women of the future than it has been for non-employed women in the past, the pattern of such people's lives may be more similar to that of married women of the nineteenth and early twentieth centuries than to that of men in the same period. Women in the home had to structure time for themselves, and initiate activities on their own. The regularity of school bells, and instructional activities designed by teachers, may have served to prepare boys and girls for office and factory, but they did not provide women with either skills for or practice in organizing time for themselves. Nor do they provide these today for those students who cannot and will not in the future get paid work.

## Education for Living Not Merely for Working

If, as a democratic society, we decide that we cannot prepare people for different types of lives from childhood, and therefore that we have to prepare everyone for some periods of paid work and some periods of unemployment, we shall have to provide each person with both skills for work, and skills to withstand unemployment. These issues were discussed during the 1930s when unemployment seemed the permanent lot of many men and women. Since the second world war, expansion of the United States' economy has changed the focus of discussions on education. Only recently, with the economic crisis of the early 1980s, and the rapid changes brought about by the introduction of computers and robotics in industry, has the discussion of the 1930s seemed relevant again. At that time, for instance, William F. Russell suggested that 'perhaps every American citizen should have an alternative vocation. Developed as recreation in the beginning, these avocations might serve as a refuge in times of illness and mental distress, and in times of unemployment might become a foundation from which to make a new start.'[22] Even this suggestion, however, perceives the need to provide people with education that is vocational in the narrow sense of providing them with the means to make a living.

Because we make a distinction between education for action, which we call technical or professional education, and education for understanding, which we call liberal education, we may find people resist education they perceive to be 'irrelevant' because it does not provide them with skills for action. Kenneth Charlton, elsewhere in this volume, contends that such a distinction as we make was not accepted by people of the sixteenth and seventeenth centuries. At that time, what we call a liberal education was a practical education for certain people in society.

Since we are moving into a new phase of industrial society, sometimes called post-industrialism, we shall have to consider what kind of education is practical. While all people will need both technical skills, and the flexibility to learn new ones periodically throughout their lives, they will need also the ability to take learning into their own hands, which McClintock has called the hallmark of 'studying' as it was conceived in an earlier time.[23]

At the same time, all people in the society may find themselves needing to upgrade their skills at some moments in their lives. This kind of upgrading may take the form of improving skills one already has or of changing one's skills completely. Many people now learn on the job, pick up what they need as they go, but we know that this is a 'hit or miss' procedure, and that some people are given more assistance by their peers in learning new skills than others. Once people's desire to upgrade their skills is recognized as a legitimate aspiration, then the processes for upgrading them can be opened to those people who have previously been unsuccessful in doing so.

As well as learning skills, people also wish to enhance their role in society, and add to their understanding of life. Democracy is changing under the impact of new technology. Each person's ability to participate in and to influence events has grown. Yet we pay little attention to the need for adults, through informal and formal education, to learn more sophisticated ways to evaluate issues, acquire greater understanding of the origins of problems and of the difference of cultures and thus improve their ability to function as citizens of their own country and of the world. Thomas F.Green has recently discussed the forms that conscience takes in technical society. He speaks of conscience as craft, as membership, as sacrifice, as memory, and as imagination.[24] All these are areas for exploration and growth through education.

### Hierarchy and Equality in Education

As Ivan Illich has pointed out, once learning becomes formalized into courses, it becomes the province of those who can pay to take the courses. A hierarchy is established, and those who have learned the facts or methods for themselves, without benefit of a course, are perceived by others, and by themselves, as being uncredentialed.[25]

Thus, there is a continual tension in education, between the pull towards hierarchy and differentiation, and the desire for equality. A balance between the two has to be found. However, the balance is always temporary. Every few years existing structures have to be reordered in order to maintain or re-establish the balance that people at that time find desirable, or at least tolerable.

In our society, today, we are designing new credentials, and thus creating new hierarchies, for people in the communications industry. We have entered into the process without planning. Colleges have not discussed the implications of their new programs for the institution as a whole. They have given little attention to the best form of education for computer and communications graduates, how large programs should be, or how to establish and maintain both a racial and a gender balance among those gaining credentials. We have initiated no public debate on these issues, only on the need for computer literacy in society.

We rarely discuss the issues raised above because we are loathe to admit that our society has structural problems that go beyond education. It is far easier for us to excoriate the schools than face the broader social issues that may be causing a breakdown in the process of education.

The paradox of our time is that we have to respond to technologies we do not yet fully understand, whose implications we only faintly grasp, whose long term effects we can only surmise, and to do this, we have to use a vocabulary and an institutional structure fashioned, in its turn, as a response to a technological revolution that took place nearly two hundred years ago. We are like nineteenth-century women playing tennis in ankle length skirts; our movement is constrained and our potential for success is limited.

While several authors in this book challenge the relevance of dividing the liberal arts from professional and vocational education, others challenge the definition of liberal arts education as it is currently understood. Most of the authors expect the educational institutions that exist to continue in a similar form into the forseeable future. For them, the task is to reshape educational institutions in order to meet the needs of a changing society. In support of their position, there is evidence that the educational system responds to change in predictable, and therefore reassuring, fashion.[26]

However, new educational tools are at hand that could undermine our process of credentialing and make schools, colleges, and universities obsolete. Each person who can afford to buy the machines and subscribe to the organizations that supply the materials, may soon have access to enough materials to create their own education. (Already some parents, unhappy with the public school system, teach their children at home using education programs designed by private companies.)

Television and film have provided new ways of obtaining knowledge. Those who have been videotaped may acquire a new awareness of themselves in relation to others. Videotapes are already used extensively in training such practitioners as teachers, physicians, and lawyers. Those who watch television and film may become expert at watching and interpreting facial expressions; their understanding of non-verbal communication is sharpened. They may acquire a different perception of reality from those who do not watch television and film. This new perception may, in the future, become the dominant perception in society, and it may affect every aspect of life. The ability to hold conferences by telephone, to transmit printed materials across hundreds of miles in minutes, and to relay to earth the results of experiments in space, all these things have revolutionary implications for education.

When change comes suddenly, as happens often in societies dedicated to technological innovation, people tend to deny that the change is significant; they call an automobile a horseless carriage, drive it at a slow pace along roads designed for horses, and house it in a stable. Only years later do they admit that automobiles have different characteristics from horses. In education, the temptation to act in this way is very strong, because educational institutions provide credentials that determine, or at least influence strongly, people's working lives. This book is written in the belief that the current revolution in communications technology calls for radical change in the content and structure of education, and that such a change can take place only by examining existing educational practices and questioning their relevance.

## Notes

1  J. NAISBITT (1984) *Megatrends: Ten New Directions Transforming Our Lives*, New York, Warner Books, p. 1.
2  This sense of being at the vortex of technological change is not new. In 1931, W.F. RUSSELL wrote: 'The industrial revolution is not a movement that is spent. Its full effects have not yet been reached. A society different from anything that man has ever seen is developing. There is certain to be an educational lag, but we must reduce it as much as possible. It is our duty to study the social changes round about us, carefully to estimate the trends, and then to derive the educational implications.' (June 1931) in M. ELY, (Ed.), (1936) 'To open a new frontier,' *Adult Education in Action*, New York, American Association for Adult Education, pp. 39–40.
3  D. CANFIELD FISHER (1933) 'To meet the challenge of free choice,' in M. ELY, (Ed.), *Adult Education in Action*, June, p. 13.
4  For a discussion of the difficulties we encounter when we 'wed the imperfect notion of "adulthood" to the complex idea of "development"' (p. 226), see O.H. SMYTHE (1978) 'Practical experience and liberal education: a philosophical analysis,' Ed. D. thesis, Graduate School of Education, Harvard University, pp. 226–30.
5  J. YARDLEY (1984) 'The great student revolt: twenty years after Berkeley and still giving in,' *The Washington Post*, Monday, 16 July, B1, B8.
6  F.KRANTZ (1984) 'The liberal arts' "noble vision," employment-related education, and the free-market curriculum,' *The Chronicle of Higher Education*, 11 January.
7  P. HIRST (1974) *Knowledge and the Curriculum: A Collection of Philosophical Papers*, London and Boston, Routledge and Kegan Paul, p. 46.
8  J. ROLAND MARTIN (1981) discusses other critiques of Hirst and develops her own in 'Needed: a paradigm for liberal education,' *Philosophy and Education 1981*, Chicago, National Society for the Study of Education, pp. 36–59.
9  E. CASSIRER (1950) *The Problem of Knowledge: Philosophy, Science, and History Since Hegel*, New Haven, Yale University Press, p. 15.
10 *Ibid.*, pp. 14–19. The book as a whole lays out CASSIRER's views on the structure of knowledge.
11 YARDLEY, 'The great student revolt,' *The Washington Post*, B8.
12 M. ADLER (1982) 'Why only adults can be educated,' in *Invitation to Lifelong Learning*, R. GROSS, (Ed.), (Chicago, Follett Publishing Company, pp. 89–102. Originally published in 1956 as 'Adult Education,' in *Great Issues in Education*, The Great Books Foundation.)
13 *Ibid.*, p. 92.
14 *Ibid.*, pp. 98–9.
15 *Ibid.*, p. 99.
16 J. NAISBITT identifies three stages in the acceptance of a new technology: First, the new technology follows the line of least resistance, and gains acceptance in a non-significant area; secondly, it is used to improve existing technologies; and thirdly, it gives rise to the discovery of new activities based upon its own special characteristics. (*Megatrends*, pp. 19–25.)
17 See, for instance, M. McLUHAN (1962) *The Gutenbary Galaxy: The Making of Typographic Man*, Toronto, Toronto University Press.
18 K. KISH SKLAR has examined the differential spread of literacy among men and women in Massachusetts. The implications of technology and social change

causing increased disparities between the sexes and between majorities and minorities has been discussed by J. KELLY (1976) 'The social relation of the sexes: methodological implications of women's history,' *Signs: Journal of Women in Culture and Society*, 1, no. 4, Summer, pp. 810–12.

19 I. REINECKE (1982) *Electronic Illusions: A Skeptic's View of Our High-Tech Future*, Harmondsworth, Penguin Books, chapter 11 'Harvesting the information crop.'

20 *Ibid.*, p. 236.

21 This issue has still to be explored by historians of education. There are memoirs and diaries describing how women educated themselves outside the formal structure of schools, but these records have not been examined from the perspective of the value of self-directed study as a preparation for the life women led. Recent works that suggest this would be a useful field of research include H. HEINEMAN, (1983) *Restless Angels: The Friendship of Six Victorian Women*, Athens, Ohio University Press, D. GORHAM (1982) *The Victorian Girl and the Feminine Ideal*, Bloomington, Indiana University Press, and JOAN N. BURSTYN (1984) *Victorian Education and the Ideal of Womanhood*, New Brunswick, Rutgers University Press, 1984.

22 RUSSELL, 'To open a frontier,' in M. ELY, (Ed.) *Adult Education in Action*, pp. 40–1.

23 R. MCCLINTOCK, 'Reaffirming a great tradition,' in *Invitation to Lifelong Learning*, pp. 47–78. (Originally published as 'Toward a place for study in a world of instruction,' *Teachers College Record* 73, 2 (December 1971).)

24 See T.F. GREEN (1984) *The Formation of Conscience in An Age of Technology*, Syracuse, NY, Syracuse University and the John Dewey Society.

25 I. ILLICH (1971) *Deschooling Society*, New York, Harper and Row, Harrow Books, pp. 16–8, and 56–7.

26 See T.F. GREEN (1980) (with the assistance of D.P. ERICSON and R.H. SEIDMAN,) *Predicting the Behavior of the Educational System*, Syracuse, NY, Syracuse University Press.

# Note on the Authors

**Joan N. Burstyn** is Dean and Professor, School of Education, Syracuse University

**Kenneth Charlton** is Professor Emeritus of the Department of Education, King's College, London, England

**Arthur Chickering** is Distinguished Professor of Higher Education, Memphis State University

**Harold Goldstein**, an industrial consultant, is Director, Organization, Planning, Analysis and Development (OPAD), Oakland, California

**Alfred Kolb** is Chairperson, Division of Humanities, Quinsigamond Community College, Worcester, Massachusetts

**Gordon Law** is Professor of Vocational Education, Rutgers University

**Sheila M. Pfafflin** is a District Manager of American Telephone and Telegraph Company (AT&T), New York

**David Riesman** is Professor Emeritus, Department of Sociology, Harvard University

**H. Bradley Sagen** is Professor of Higher Education, University of Iowa

**Harold Silver** is Principal, Bulmershe College of Higher Education, Reading, England

**Mary Waldron**, an Educational Consultant, was formerly Head, English Department, Rainsford School, Chelmsford, England

**Henry R. Winkler** is President Emeritus, University of Cincinnati

# Index